VISUAL QUICKSTART GUIDE

QUICKEN 2001

for Macintosh

Tom Negrino

Peachpit Press

Visual QuickStart Guide
Quicken 2001 for Macintosh
Tom Negrino

Peachpit Press
1249 Eighth Street
Berkeley, CA 94710
(510) 524-2178
(800) 283-9444
(510) 524-2221 (fax)

Find us on the World Wide Web at:
http://www.peachpit.com

Peachpit Press is a division of Addison Wesley Longman
Copyright © 2001 by Tom Negrino

Editors: Becky Morgan, Cliff Colby
Production coordinator: Lisa Brazieal
Compositor: Christi Payne, Book Arts
Cover design: The Visual Group
Indexer: Rebecca Plunket

Notice of rights
All rights reserved. No part of this book may be reproduced or transmitted in any form by any means, electronic, mechanical, photocopying, recording, or otherwise, without the prior written permission of the publisher. For information on getting permission for reprints and excerpts, contact Gary-Paul Prince at Peachpit Press.

Trademarks
Quicken, QuickBooks, TurboTax, and MacInTax are registered trademarks of Intuit Inc. Quicken.com is a trademark of Intuit Inc. Visual QuickStart Guide is a trademark of Peachpit Press, a division of Addison Wesley Longman.

Throughout this book, trademarked names are used. Rather than put a trademark symbol in each occurrence of a trademarked name, we state we are using the names only in an editorial fashion and to the benefit of the trademark owner and with no intention of infringement on the trademark.

Notice of liability
The information in this book is distributed on an "As Is" basis, without warranty. While every precaution has been taken in the preparation of the book, neither the author nor Peachpit Press shall have any liability to any person or entity with respect to any loss or damage caused or alleged to be caused directly or indirectly by the instructions contained in this book or by the computer software and hardware products described in it.

ISBN 0-201-72226-7

9 8 7 6 5 4 3 2 1

Printed and bound in the United States of America.

Dedication

To my father, Joseph Negrino, who has touched so many people's lives, becoming more than their accountant; he's become their friend. Thanks for the inspiration, Dad.

Special thanks to:

The folks at Peachpit:

My editor, Becky Morgan, for her sharp eyes and incisive comments.

Lisa Brazieal, production goddess extraordinaire.

Nancy Ruenzel and Marjorie Baer, for continuing to believe in the project.

Everybody else:

Intuit's Adam Samuels, who cracked the whip and got the answers when I needed them.

Tom Baer, for his work on the last edition, much of which survives in this one.

My agent, David Rogelberg of StudioB.

Thanks always to Dori Smith. "Your love for me/must be/the speed of light."

TABLE OF CONTENTS

	Introduction	**ix**
Chapter 1	**Introducing Quicken 2001**	**1**
	Installing and Running Quicken 2	
	Activity Areas 5	
	Finding Your Way Around 6	
	The menu bar 6	
	The backdrop 6	
	The toolbar 7	
	Customizing Your Workspace 8	
	Securing Your Data 11	
	Getting On-Screen Help 14	
	Balloon Help 14	
	Quicken Help 14	
	User's Guide 15	
	What Other Programs and Services Come	
	with Quicken Deluxe? 16	
Chapter 2	**Setting Up Accounts**	**17**
	Creating a Data File 18	
	Using Accounts 20	
Chapter 3	**Tracking with Categories**	**23**
	Assigning Categories 24	
	Assigning Subcategories 26	
	Using Tax Links 28	
	Using Classes 29	
Chapter 4	**Using the Account Registers**	**33**
	Entering Checking Account Transactions 34	
	Sorting Registers 37	
	Splitting Transactions 38	
	Entering Paychecks 40	
	Entering Credit Card Charges 41	
	Transferring Money Between Accounts 42	
	Changing Transactions 45	
	Finding and Replacing Transactions 46	
	Using Data Entry Helpers 49	
	QuickMath 49	
	QuickEntry 50	

Table of Contents

Chapter 5   All About QuickFill — 51
How QuickFill Works 52
Memorizing Transactions 53
Using QuickFill Transactions 54
Editing QuickFill Transactions 55
Deleting QuickFill Transactions 56

Chapter 6   Writing and Printing Checks — 57
Writing and Editing Checks 58
Getting Ready to Print 63
Printing Checks 64

Chapter 7   Using the Calendar — 67
Working with the Calendar 68
Scheduling and Paying Your Bills 73
Adding Calendar Notes 76
Using Billminder 77

Chapter 8   Using Quicken Insights — 79
Using the Insights Page 80
Adding to Your Insights Page 83
Diving Beneath the Surface 85
On to the Internet 87

Chapter 9   Balancing Your Accounts — 89
Balancing Accounts 90
Correcting Differences 93
Letting Quicken Fix the Problem 94

Chapter 10   Dealing with Credit Cards — 95
Tracking Credit Card Transactions 96
Controlling Credit Card Debt 99
Controlling Debt by Budgeting 100
Using the Budget Monitor 102

Chapter 11   Online Banking and Bill Paying — 103
Applying for Online Banking 104
Going Online 106
Paying Bills Online 109

Chapter 12   Creating Reports — 113
Using Reports 114
Using EasyAnswer Reports 115
Using QuickReport 116
Zooming in on the Details 117
Using Standard Reports 118
Customizing Reports 119
Using Memorized Reports 122

Table of Contents

	Using Shortcut Reports	123
	Printing Reports	124
	Register and List Reports	125

Chapter 13 Creating Graphs **127**
- Using EasyAnswer Graphs 128
- Using a Standard Graph 130
- Creating a Net Worth Graph 131
- Customizing Graphs 132
- Using Memorized Graphs 133
- Printing Graphs 134

Chapter 14 Working with Loans and Mortgages **135**
- Creating Loans 136
- Making Loan Payments 140

Chapter 15 Setting up Investment Accounts **141**
- Using Investment Accounts 142
- Setting up Your Portfolio 144

Chapter 16 Managing Your Investments **149**
- Portfolio Maintenance 150
- Using Quicken.com's Investment Tools 153
- Buying and Selling Securities 154

Chapter 17 Planning for the Future **157**
- Using the Planning Tools 159
- Web-Based Planners 160
- The Retirement Planner 163
- Reducing Consumer Debt 167
- Getting Organized 171
- Using the Financial Calculators 174

Chapter 18 Quicken at Tax Time **175**
- Planning for Taxes 176
- Creating Tax Reports 180
- Exporting Quicken Data to TurboTax 182

Chapter 19 Using Quicken.com **183**
- Getting Around on Quicken.com 184
- Finding Investment Information 186
- Choosing a Mutual Fund 187
- Insights on Investing 189
- Getting Tax Information 190
  - Downloading tax forms 191
- Finding Low-Rate Credit Cards 192
- Other Areas of Interest 194

Index **195**

Introduction

Money pervades our lives, simultaneously desired and disdained. Most of us can't get along without it and would love to have more of it. Yet many of us don't do an especially good job of managing the money that we do have. How often have you heard people say things like "I don't know where all my money goes"? Many people live from paycheck to paycheck, just getting along with no financial plan for the future and hardly any control over their financial present. In the meantime, they're building up consumer debt and digging themselves a hole that will take a long time to get out of.

Sound familiar? It certainly does to me; I was one of those people for many years. I finally got fed up with feeling that my finances were out of my control, so one December evening I bought a copy of Quicken Deluxe and promised myself that I would start using it when the new year began. Unlike some of my other New Year's resolutions, I did start using Quicken, and melodramatic as it sounds, it changed my life. I used Quicken to take stock of my finances and identify where I was handling my money poorly. Then I came up with a plan to pay off my debts and start saving for the future. I then kept track of my plan using Quicken's reports and graphs. Today I'm happy to say that I no longer wonder what my financial picture is, because

Introduction

Quicken gives me all the information that I need. There were some ups and downs, but I made it to fiscal sanity. So can you.

If you want to get better control over your finances, this book is for you. I'll show you how to use Quicken to help you get out of debt, manage your present finances, and invest for the future.

Welcome, iMac owners!

I'd especially like to welcome aboard owners of Apple's cool iMac computer. In fact, you folks are one of the main reasons this book was written; when I found out in 1998 that every iMac would include a copy of Quicken Deluxe, I suggested to my editors at Peachpit Press that iMac owners deserved a book about Quicken that was as friendly as the iMac itself. I was sure that the iMac was going to be a hit. Luckily, they had the good sense to agree. With Quicken Deluxe 2001 shipping with iMacs beginning Fall 2000, it made sense to update the book this third time for the new version and for all those new iMac owners.

Just the facts, Ma'am

I have to admit that I don't have a lot of patience for computer books that are thick and heavy enough to cause injury if you accidentally drop them on your foot. I'd rather open a book, find out how to do a task, and toss the book back on the shelf without wading through endless blather and more details than I ever wanted to know.

In this book, I've organized different financial tasks into chapters, and within each chapter are step-by-step directions that tell you exactly how to accomplish various tasks.

My assumptions about you

In writing this book, I've made the following assumptions about you. First, you own Quicken Deluxe 2001 and a Macintosh powerful enough to run the program. That's not a difficult requirement, as Quicken 2001 will run on any machine using a PowerPC processor, with at least 32 of RAM and virtual memory turned on, running Mac OS 8.6 or higher. You'll also need a monitor with a video resolution of 800 x 600 or higher. That pretty much means that if your Macintosh was built anytime after about 1994, and you've been reasonably diligent in upgrading the Mac OS system software, chances are it will run Quicken just fine.

I've also made the assumption that you're familiar with the basics of using a Macintosh. You don't need be a Mac guru, although you shouldn't be stumped by concepts like selecting text, clicking and dragging, and using files and folders. If you need to brush up on the essentials, allow me to suggest that you pick up a copy of the excellent Mac OS 9: Visual QuickStart Guide, by Maria Langer, coincidentally also published by Peachpit Press.

Last, I've made the assumption that if you have bought this book, you're a person of uncommon discernment, style, and grace.

If you're just leafing through these pages in a bookstore, I'm trusting you not to let me down.

What's not in this book

Because I wanted to write a book that was genuinely useful, rather than one that slavishly touched every base and documented every Quicken feature, I had to decide what I didn't want to put in the book. So I looked through Quicken for features that were little used or that weren't that great. The first feature to get the heave-ho was Budgeting.

Introduction

Making budgets is one of those things that everyone says they want to do but hardly anyone really does. This isn't just my opinion; I've seen surveys of real Quicken users that bear me out. My apologies to you if you are one of the few, the proud, who really do budgets. A close relative to Budgeting is Forecasting, which also did not make the cut.

Although I've included two chapters on investments, those chapters are intended for the relatively light-duty investor. If you have a modest stock portfolio, some mutual funds, and some other savings plans, the investment chapters should work just fine for you. But it you're constantly churning your portfolio, buying and selling options, and otherwise serious about playing the markets, you might find my investment chapters to be a bit thin.

I've also skipped over some of the less interesting of Quicken's companion programs, such as the Quicken Home Inventory program, which is one of the few outright flops in the otherwise-excellent Quicken package.

Let's get started

A popular bit of pop philosophy states, "The journey is the reward." I'm afraid that my pragmatic side says that when it comes to money, I believe that "The reward is the reward." In this case, the reward of using Quicken can mean smarter control over your finances and in turn a better and richer life for yourself and for your family. That's a journey well worth taking. Thanks for joining me.

Tom Negrino

September 2000

INTRODUCING QUICKEN 2001

Welcome to Quicken Deluxe 2001! In this chapter, you'll learn how to install and start Quicken, convert old Quicken files (if you've been using a previous version of the program), use Quicken's interface, ask Quicken for help, and customize Quicken so that it works the way you do.

Chapter 1

Installing and Running Quicken

Like most programs these days, Quicken provides step-by-step instructions for installation as soon as you load the product's CD-ROM. In case you need a little extra information, here's a bit of guidance to help you get the application up and running on your computer.

Figure 1.1 The installation process begins when you click the Install Quicken icon.

To install Quicken 2001:

1. Insert the Quicken CD-ROM in your CD-ROM drive. Double-click the Quicken icon (**Figure 1.1**) in the Quicken 2001 Deluxe CD window that opens on your desktop.

2. The first screens that open deal with things like the license to use the software. Read them if you like; otherwise, keep clicking Agree, Continue, or Next until you get to the Install window.

3. Choose the Easy Install option (that's what most people do) (**Figure 1.2**). Click the Install button and Quicken will automatically finish installing the program. If you wish to, choose a location for the Quicken folder. By default, it will be put on the top level of your hard drive.

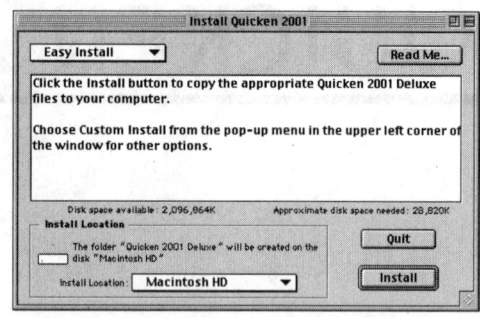

Figure 1.2 Most people choose the Easy Install option.

Introducing Quicken 2001

Quicken 2001 Deluxe

Figure 1.3 Double-clicking the program icon in the Quicken folder launches Quicken.

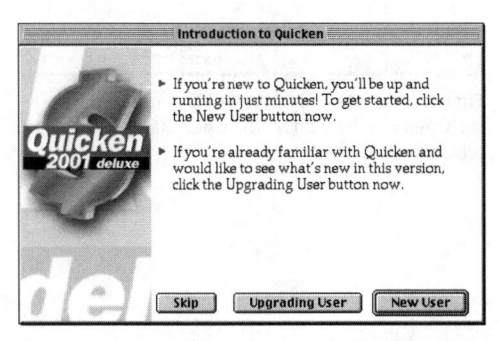

Figure 1.4 When you open Quicken the first time, you can use the tutorial to lead you through setting up a data file.

To launch Quicken 2001 the first time:

1. Double-click the Quicken folder on your hard disk to open it.

2. Double-click the Quicken Deluxe 2001 icon in the Quicken folder (**Figure 1.3**).

3. When Quicken asks you to personalize your copy, type in your name.

Quicken then offers a quick tutorial to help either new users or upgrading users (**Figure 1.4**). In the tutorial, users are guided step by step through the process of setting up a data file.

INSTALLING AND RUNNING QUICKEN

3

To convert old Quicken files:

1. Choose File > Open File. The Open file dialog box appears (**Figure 1.5**).

2. Navigate to the old Quicken file, select it, and then click the Open button.

   Quicken converts your old file into the current version's format.

After Quicken 2001 has successfully converted your previous version data file, it's important that you remove old versions of the Quicken application from your hard disk. You won't want to accidentally open your Quicken 2001 file with an older version because it's possible to corrupt your data.

When you convert Quicken 98 or Quicken 2000 files to the new Quicken 2001 format, you'll probably get a dialog box that asks if you want to turn some of your transactions into scheduled transactions. That's one of Quicken 2001's new features; see Chapter 7 for more on scheduling your bills.

✔ Tip

- The conversion process is irreversible, so be sure to save a backup copy of your older version Quicken file before you convert it to Quicken 2001. You might need to refer to it.

To quit Quicken:

◆ Choose File > Quit, or press ⌘Q.

   Quicken will close all open windows and return to the Finder. You don't have to worry about saving your work because Quicken automatically saves it for you.

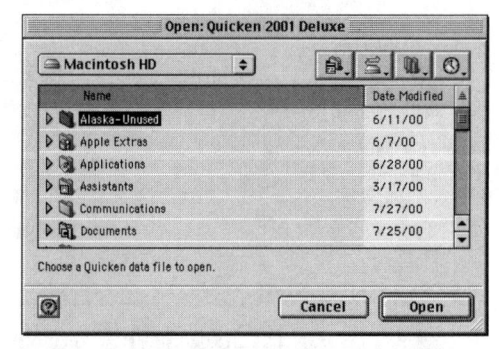

Figure 1.5 Locate and convert older Quicken files in the Open File dialog box. The Open dialog box may look different. That's OK.

Activity Areas

Intuit has divided Quicken 2001 into six activity areas, each representing a different set of financial tasks:

- The **Banking** area lets you work with different bank accounts, including checking, savings, and money-market accounts. You can also access your Financial Calendar, which shows you your financial transactions by date.

- In the **Investing** area, you'll track stocks, bonds, mutual funds, and other investments in your portfolio.

- **Planning** lets you budget and forecast your finances and figure out how to get out of debt, and its calculators can help you plan for your retirement.

- The **Reporting** area lets you create reports and graphs to show what's happening with your money.

- In the **Assets & Debt** section, you can deal with credit cards, loans, mortgages, and assets such as your home.

- The **Services** area gives you access to Quicken.com, Intuit's Web site with many financial planning tools. You can pay bills online, calculate your taxes, get advice on your 401(k), or get quotes on auto insurance and mortgages.

Finding Your Way Around

The Quicken 2001 program has a lot of features, and keeping track of them all can be a bit of a challenge. Let's start by taking a look at the Quicken window. At the top of the window is the standard Macintosh-style menu bar, where you'll find Quicken's commands. But to make it all a little more "Intuit-ive," the main user interface is a set of tabs and buttons in the tool bar to present the various features at your disposal.

The menu bar

There isn't much to say about the menu bar (**Figure 1.6**) except that you can make any of its commands keyboard shortcuts. As with any Mac program, the commands Quicken needs to do your bidding are located on the menus.

The backdrop

To reduce confusion between Quicken's windows and windows in the Finder, Quicken can hide the Finder and other applications behind a backdrop. If you want to get to the Finder, click in the dog-eared part of the backdrop at the lower-right corner of the screen.

Figure 1.6 The menu bar is compact but has everything you need to put Quicken to work.

The toolbar

The toolbar (**Figure 1.7**) provides another way for you to choose Quicken commands. You can select a tab and display a set of command and account buttons that pertain to each activity area.

Each tab has a customizable set of buttons that, when clicked, initiate actions by Quicken. Some of these actions involve going online; their buttons have cute little lightning bolts on them.

Below the command buttons are the account buttons that, when clicked, open the registers of your various accounts.

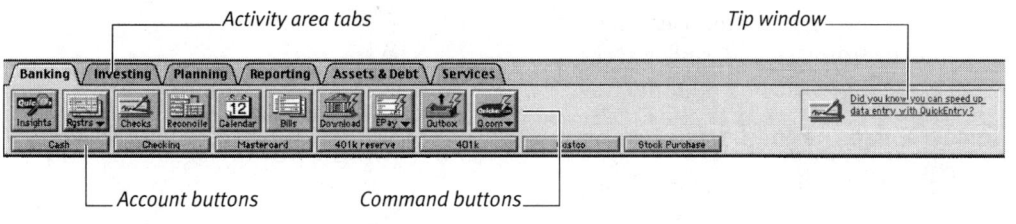

Figure 1.7 The toolbar is divided into four areas.

Customizing Your Workspace

Quicken gives you a variety of ways to customize the program to your personal style. For example, you can put the functions you use all the time at your fingertips and hide those you don't need.

To change or eliminate the backdrop:

1. Choose Edit > Preferences, and then click the General topic under the Customization category (**Figure 1.8**).

2. To change the color of the backdrop, scroll in the horizontal color area near the bottom of the window, select a color by clicking it, and then click the OK button.

3. To eliminate the backdrop, clear the "Show backdrop behind windows" check box and then click the OK button.

To customize the toolbar:

1. Choose Edit > Preferences, and then click the Toolbar topic under the Customization category.

2. Click the Configure Toolbar button to open the Configure Toolbar window that describes the buttons on the active tab (**Figure 1.9**). Note that the toolbar becomes outlined in red, signifying that it is ready for customization. Then you can do any or all of the following:
   - Drag command buttons from the Configure Toolbar window to the tool bar to install them, or drag buttons off the toolbar to remove them. Drag buttons around on the toolbar to rearrange them as you wish.

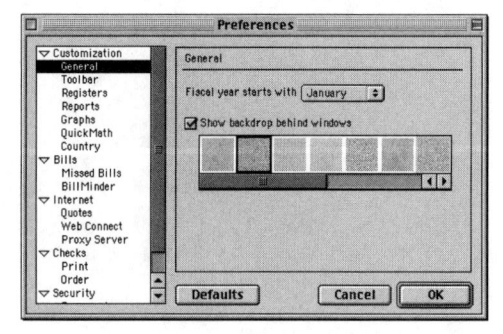

Figure 1.8 The backdrop can be changed or removed in the Preferences dialog box.

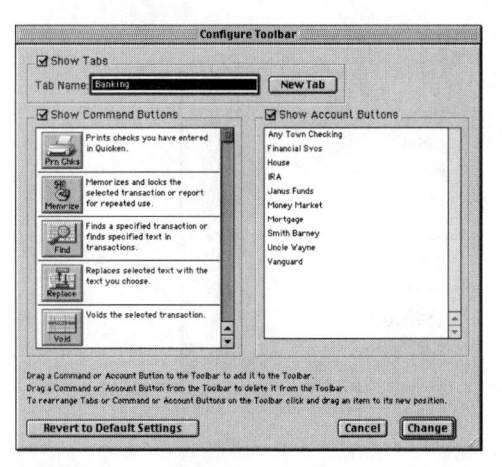

Figure 1.9 The Configure Toolbar window provides a high degree of customization of the interface.

- Drag the names of your accounts to a toolbar to install account buttons, or remove buttons by dragging them off the toolbar.
- Create additional tabs by clicking the New Tab button and typing a name in the field in place of Tab field. Tabs can be removed by dragging them down from the toolbar to the Configure Toolbar dialog box.
- Hide either or both sets of buttons or the tabs themselves by checking or unchecking their respective boxes.

3. Repeat this for each of the tabs whose toolbars you want to customize. You can add the same buttons to several toolbars.

4. When you're finished customizing, click the Change button at the bottom of the Configure Toolbar window. Or you can choose Cancel to leave the toolbar as it was or choose Revert to Default Settings to take it back to square one.

✔ Tip

- If you are using only a limited number of Quicken's functions, you may want to make more room on the desktop by unchecking the Show Tabs and Show Command Buttons boxes and leaving only a narrow bar with the account buttons at the top of the window (**Figure 1.10**).

Figure 1.10 A toolbar that includes only the names of your account registers doesn't use much of your valuable desktop real estate.

Chapter 1

To create your own Command-key shortcuts:

1. Hold down ⌘ and click the menu bar. The mouse cursor turns into the command symbol (**Figure 1.11**) and the menu appears.

2. Let go of ⌘ and select the menu command to which you want to assign the shortcut.

3. The Edit Command Key window appears (**Figure 1.12**) and shows you the name of the menu command and the existing shortcut (if one exists).

4. Type the letter or symbol of the key that will be combined with ⌘, and then click the OK button.

   If another menu command already uses the same shortcut key, Quicken will ask you to confirm your change. If you confirm, Quicken removes the shortcut from the other command and assigns the shortcut to the key you've selected.

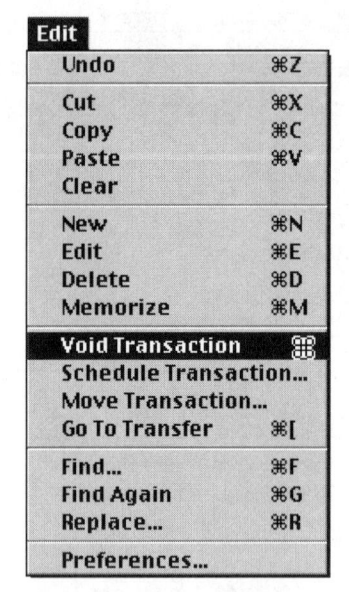

Figure 1.11 Hold down ⌘ while selecting a command from a menu to assign a keyboard shortcut.

Figure 1.12 Assigning a keyboard command to a function can make your work much more efficient.

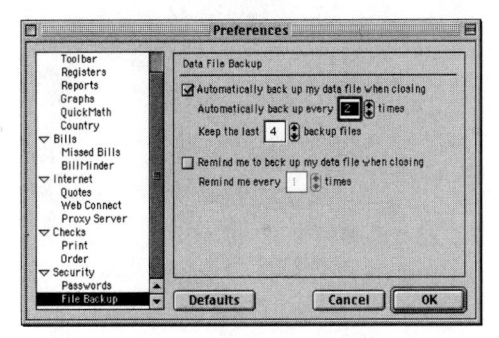

Figure 1.13 Quicken can—and should—be configured to automatically back up your data on a regular basis.

Securing Your Data

Protecting your financial information is important, whether from accidental data loss or prying eyes. You'll be spending countless hours working with Quicken in the next few years; spend a bit of extra time to make sure that investment isn't ruined.

To have Quicken automatically back up your data file:

1. Choose Edit > Preferences. The Preferences window appears.

2. In the scrolling list at the left edge of the Preferences window, scroll down and click File Backup (**Figure 1.13**).

3. Click the "Automatically back up my data file when closing" check box. Set how often you want the backup to occur by entering a number in the field next to "Automatically back up every X times."

4. Click the OK button.

✔ Tip

- The backup set with this feature should be made to a disk other than the same hard disk. There's isn't much use in backing up if your whole Mac melts down to slag or gets stolen. See the sidebar below on backup for more information.

Chapter 1

To protect your data file with a password:

1. Choose Edit > Preferences. The Preferences window appears.

2. In the scrolling area at the left edge of the window, scroll down and click Passwords (**Figure 1.14**).

3. To require use of a password when opening a file, click the Password button, and then enter a password in the Establish File Password dialog box (**Figure 1.15**).

4. To require use of a password when changing a transaction, click the Password button and then enter a password in the Enter Transaction Password dialog box.

5. Click the OK button.

✔ Tip

- **Warning!** If you later forget your password(s), the only way to get access to your data is to send your entire data file to Intuit. The company's crack team of code breakers will remove your passwords, but Intuit will also charge you a fee for the service.

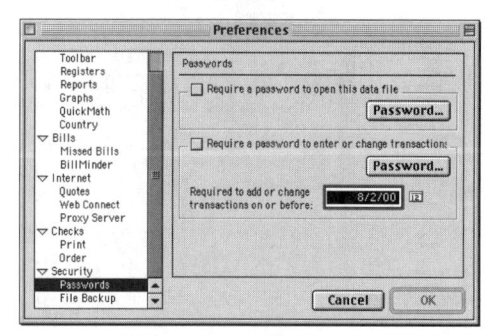

Figure 1.14 You can assign passwords to limit access to your files.

Figure 1.15 Enter your password twice to establish your file password.

Backing Up Isn't Hard to Do

Here's a hard fact of life: Computers crash. Although they don't crash that often, it happens. In fact, it always seems to happen at the worst possible times, such as when you need to pay your bills or do your taxes.

More often, your computer doesn't crash, but a document file does become corrupted and unreadable. This situation can occur for any number of reasons: a hardware failure, a problem with your system software, or other software incompatibilities.

Computer problems aren't the only reason you should be thinking about backups. Plenty of other things can go wrong, including fires, floods, theft, earthquakes, hurricanes, plagues of locusts—well, you get the idea.

One possible solution is to pray nightly to the Computer Gods, but this approach has a spotty success rate. A better idea is to keep backups of your files. A backup is a recent copy (or better yet, multiple copies) of your documents. You can copy the files to removable cartridge disks (such as the Iomega Zip or Jaz disks), or to a second hard disk, or you can buy a specialized backup device called a tape drive. You can even back up your files to remote storage facilities over the Internet, though you'll want to have a fast Net connection, such as a DSL line or a cable modem.

For many people, the Iomega Zip disk is the perfect balance between cost and convenience. The disk holds 100 or 250 MB (megabytes) of data and costs between $10 and $15, and the drive costs well under $200. Those prices are relatively economical, especially if you back up only your documents, which don't take up much space on your hard disk compared with your applications and the system software. Although having a full backup of your entire hard disk is nice, these days, when computers often come with 10 GB (gigabyte) hard disks, you would need dozens of Zip disks. You're better off backing up only your documents, which shouldn't take more than a few Zip disks, if that many.

Following a Backup Strategy

No matter which backup medium you choose, you should get into the habit of backing up regularly. Have a schedule. Get into the habit of backing up your files before you shut down your Mac, for example. If you keep all your documents in a single folder on your desktop, it's a simple matter to drag that folder to a Zip disk and copy the files.

Having multiple backup copies is the extra-safe way to go. You can easily rotate your backup copies so that you always have three good backups of your work. Many people use the idea of a "family" of backups. You start on Monday with a backup disk and copy your files to it. On Tuesday, you take a fresh, second disk and back up all your files again. On Wednesday, you repeat the process with a third new disk. Now you have three backup disks, each with a progressively older set of backed-up files. Wednesday's disk is the child disk. Tuesday's disk is the parent disk. Monday's backup—the oldest backup—is the grandparent disk. On Thursday, rotate the grandparent disk back to the front of the lineup (making it the new child disk), and use it to back up your files. Keep repeating the process, and you'll always have three days' worth of backups.

For even more protection, keep an extra backup off the premises in a safe place, such as a safe-deposit box. Bring in that backup and update it periodically—once a month, for example. Then take the backup off-site again. Having multiple backups does you no good if all your backup disks are destroyed along with your computer.

Chapter 1

Getting On-Screen Help

Quicken provides several options for on-screen help (although none are as wonderful as this book, naturally). Not surprisingly, you get to the program's help files via the Help menu (**Figure 1.16**).

Balloon Help

Choose Show Balloons from the Help menu to turn on Balloon Help, which shows you descriptions of items when you point at them (**Figure 1.17**). Balloon Help is useful to help you learn about unfamiliar features, but you'll probably grow tired of the balloons popping up everywhere you move the mouse. To turn off Balloon Help, choose Hide Balloons from the Help menu.

Quicken Help

Quicken Help is based on the new Macintosh Help system that was introduced with Mac OS 9. It is HTML based, so it can be read by any Web browser, or you can use the Mac OS Help Viewer to access it. Quicken Help gives you step-by-step instructions on how to accomplish tasks. The Quicken Help window is divided into topic areas (**Figure 1.18**). You are then guided step by step through the procedure associated with the topic you choose (**Figure 1.19**), with hypertext links to related tasks. This is the best help tool to use for learning new tasks.

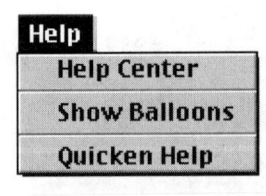

Figure 1.16 The Quicken Help menu displays a range of help options.

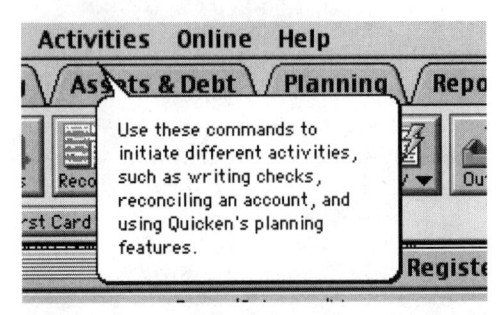

Figure 1.17 Balloon Help provides basic information in balloons that pop up on your screen.

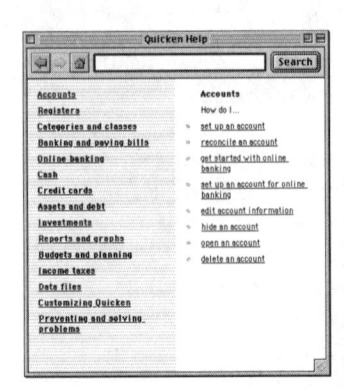

Figure 1.18 The Quicken help window offers categories, topics, and a Search capability.

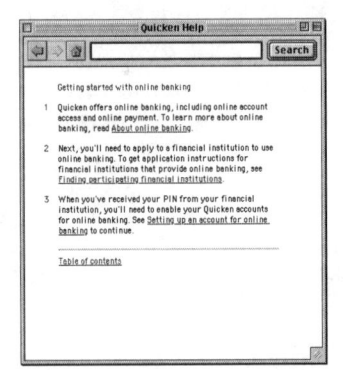

Figure 1.19 A topic provides step-by-step instructions, as well as hyperlinks to additional information.

User's Guide

Inside the Quicken folder on your hard drive, you'll find a file called User's Guide.pdf. This is the Quicken User's Guide in Adobe Acrobat format (**Figure 1.20**). The User's Guide is extensive and thoroughly indexed. If you don't already have Adobe Acrobat installed, you'll find the Acrobat Installer on the Quicken Deluxe 2001 CD-ROM.

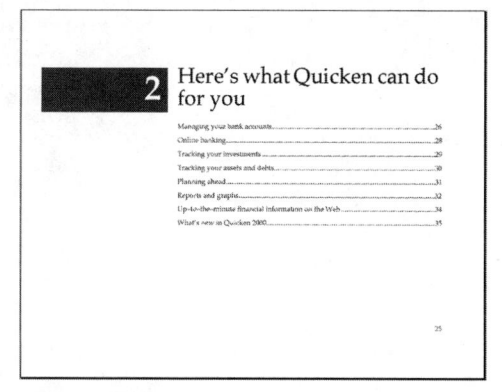

Figure 1.20 The User's Guide is an Adobe Acrobat document that provides a through explanation of how to use Quicken.

What Other Programs and Services Come with Quicken Deluxe?

Quicken Deluxe 2001, which is bundled with the Apple iMac computer and also sold separately, includes these useful additions:

- **QuickEntry** is a miniapplication that lets you enter transactions into any Quicken account without opening Quicken itself. For more on QuickEntry, see Chapter 4.

- The **Emergency Records Organizer** application saves your personal information in one place.

- The **Quicken Home Inventory** program helps you put together an inventory of your possessions.

The following services are available on Quicken.com (http://www.quicken.com).

- The **Tax Deduction Finder** steps you through a simple questionnaire that helps determine whether you might qualify for additional tax deductions.

- You can obtain a free copy of your **credit report.**

- The **Debt Reduction Planner** evaluates your debt level and steps you through creation of an action plan to get you out of debt faster.

- The **Retirement Planner** helps you create a plan to reach your retirement goals.

- In the **Net Worth Analysis,** you'll get a snapshot of your financial health.

Setting Up Accounts

Quicken stores all of your information on your hard disk in a data file that you create the first time you use the program. You generally need only one data file, but inside the data file you'll create a number of accounts. An account represents an asset (something that you own, such as the money in your checking account or some property) or a liability (a debt that you owe, such as the balance on your credit cards or a mortgage).

Quicken allows you to have as many or as few accounts as you wish (actually, the upper limit is 255 accounts, but most people won't use more than a couple dozen accounts). Some people prefer to use Quicken to track only their main checking account, and other people create many accounts to track every penny.

In this chapter, you'll set up your data file and learn about the different account types within Quicken.

Chapter 2

Creating a Data File

The first time you run Quicken, you'll need to create a data file to contain all your financial information. A data file must include at least one account, so you will create your checking account immediately after you create the data file.

To create a new data file and checking account:

1. Choose File > New File. The New File dialog box appears, asking if you're sure that you want to create a new data file (**Figure 2.1**). Click OK.

   The Save dialog box appears (**Figure 2.2**).

2. Navigate to where you want to save your data file, and enter a name for the file in the Name field.

   You can include Quicken's standard Home or Business categories in your data file. Categories are labels you assign to your transactions that help you track where your money comes from and goes to. If you plan to use Quicken strictly for home use, you'll probably be happy with just the Home categories. If you run a business with transactions that will affect this data file, you'll also want the Business categories. Either way, you can add or delete categories at any time, so the choices you make here are for your convenience, not a life or death decision.

3. Choose the Home or Business check box (or both), and then click the New button.

   The Set Up Account window appears (**Figure 2.3**).

4. Click the Bank radio button. You use this radio button to set up checking, savings, or money market accounts.

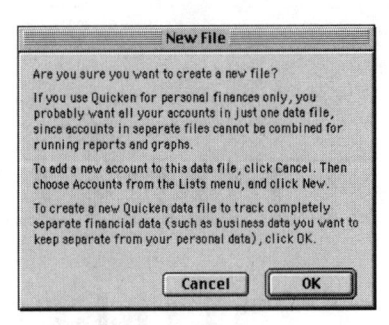

Figure 2.1 Reassure Quicken that you indeed want to create a new file by clicking the OK button.

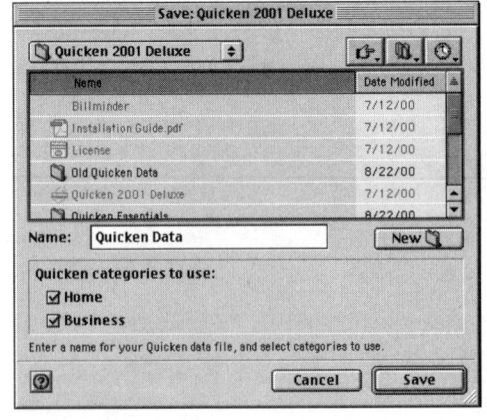

Figure 2.2 Choose where you want to save your data file and name it in the Save dialog box. You can also pick which set of categories to start out with.

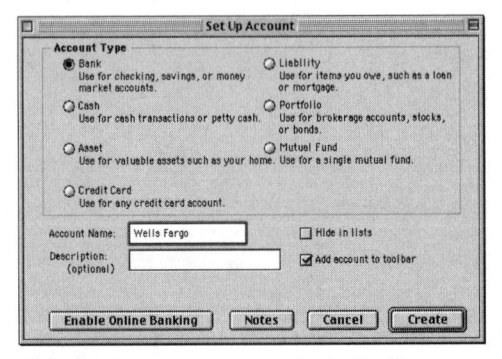

Figure 2.3 Create a new account in the Set Up Account window.

18

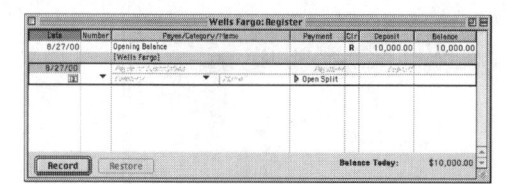

Figure 2.4 Quicken opens a register for the new account.

5. Enter a name for your checking account.

6. Enter a description for the checking account (optional).

   If this will be a often-used account, click the "Add account to toolbar" button (optional).

7. Click the Create button.

   Quicken creates the account and opens a register for the new checking account (**Figure 2.4**), ready for you to enter the opening balance in the Deposit field.

8. Type the ending balance from your last bank statement into the Deposit field, and then press [Tab] until the Date field is highlighted. Type in the last statement date, and then click the Record button (or press [Enter]).

✔ Tips

- Whenever you click the Record button, Quicken saves your work, so you don't need to worry about saving before you quit the program.

- You might at times want to have more than one Quicken data file. For example, if you and your domestic partner don't intermingle your funds, you'll each want to have your own set of financial records. If you have a business on the side, you might also prefer to keep your business accounts and records firmly separate from your personal information. Just switch between data files using File > Open File.

Using Accounts

Quicken has five kinds of accounts that you can use to track your assets:

- A **Bank** account tracks checking accounts, money market accounts, savings accounts, and debit cards. This is the only account type you can use to make electronic payments or to write checks.

- An **Asset** account tracks the value of an asset, such as real estate or your car.

- The **Portfolio** account type tracks brokerage accounts that contain financial instruments, such as stocks and bonds.

- A **Mutual Fund** account tracks a single mutual fund.

- A **Cash** account is unlike the rest of the accounts because no corresponding account exists in a financial institution. You use a Cash account to track out-of-pocket expenses. For example, let's say that you withdraw $100 from an ATM. In Quicken, that amount comes out of your checking account and goes into the Cash account. As you spend the money, you can make notations in the Cash account to track how that cash has been spent.

Quicken also has two account types to track your liabilities:

- **Credit Card** accounts can track your credit cards, equity lines, and other lines of credit.

- **Liability** accounts are usually loans, such as a mortgage or car loan.

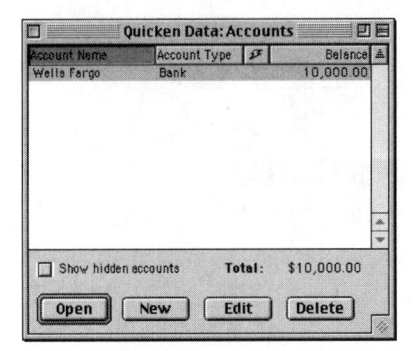

Figure 2.5 After you create a new account, it appears in the Accounts window.

To create a new account:

1. Choose Lists > Accounts to open the Accounts window (**Figure 2.5**).

Table 2.1

ACCOUNT TYPE	OPENING BALANCE	DATE
Bank	New balance from your last bank statement	Date of your last statement
Credit card	New balance from your last statement	Date of your last statement
Asset	The asset's current value	Today's date
Liability	The liability's current value	Today's date
Portfolio	See Chapter 15	
Mutual fund	See Chapter 15	
Cash	Current cash on hand	Today's date

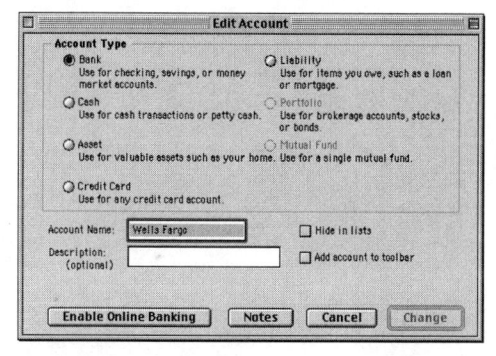

Figure 2.6 The Edit Account window allows you to change account information and hide an account.

2. Click New at the bottom of the Accounts window.

   The Set Up Account window appears (see **Figure 2.3**).

3. Select the radio button corresponding to the kind of account you wish to create, type in an account name, and enter a description (optional). If you want to add a button on the toolbar to open the account's register quickly, click the Add account to toolbar button (also optional). Click the Create button.

   Quicken creates the account, adds its name to the Account list in the Accounts window, and opens its register.

4. Enter an opening balance, and if necessary, change the date. See **Table 2.1** for guidance on which amounts and dates to use for opening balances.

To edit or hide an account:

1. If the Accounts window is not already open, choose Lists > Accounts or press ⌘A.

2. Select an account and click the Edit button.

   The Edit Account window (**Figure 2.6**), which looks just like the Set Up Account window, appears.

3. Change the account information. If you no longer use an account and you don't want it cluttering up your Accounts window, you can hide it by clicking the "Hide in lists" check box in the Edit Account window. Click the Change button.

To delete an account:

1. Choose Lists > Accounts, or press ⌘A. The Accounts window appears.

2. Select an account, and then click the Delete button. Click the Yes button when Quicken asks you to confirm the account deletion (**Figure 2.7**).

✔ Tips

- Although you'll hardly ever need to delete an account, if you do, you lose the record of all the transactions that ever occurred in that account. Because this can mess up your reports, you're usually better off hiding an account rather than deleting it.

- Wondering why you would want to hide an account? You probably won't want to do so until you've been using Quicken for a while and your financial circumstances change. For example, I used to own a particular set of mutual funds (part of my retirement portfolio). At a time when those funds stopped performing as well as I would have liked, I sold them and rolled the money over into a new set of funds. I created accounts for the new funds, and then hid the old ones. That way, I could still get all the performance and capital gains reports I needed about the old funds (that was useful at tax time the following year), but the old funds didn't clutter up my Accounts window and reports with zero balances.

- If you need to see accounts that you've hidden, click the "Show hidden accounts" check box at the bottom of the Accounts window (refer to **Figure 2.5**).

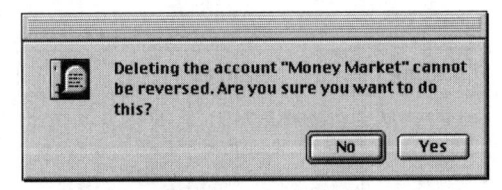

Figure 2.7 Quicken wants you to be sure that you really want to irreversibly delete an account.

Tracking with Categories

The point of using Quicken is to gain better control over your finances. And to achieve that control, you'll need to know where your money comes from and where your money goes. You use Quicken's *categories* to track the flow of money. A category is simply a label that you assign to a transaction. For example, when you buy food at the grocery store and record the transaction in a Quicken register, you can record it under the category "Groceries." Later, when you're curious about how much money you spend on groceries, you can create a report that adds up all of your transactions for groceries.

By categorizing all of your transactions in Quicken, you can generate reports about the details of your income and expenses; save time and money while preparing your tax returns; and if you're the truly disciplined type, even set up budgets and compare what you're actually spending to what you had planned to spend.

Assigning Categories

Because categories are used to track the flow of money, you are naturally concerned about whether the money is flowing in or out. Money that is flowing in, such as your paycheck and investment income, is tracked using *income* categories. Money that you spend on your mortgage, utilities, groceries, entertainment, and other bills is tracked using *expense* categories. A third type of category, the *transfer* category is used just to keep track of money that you move from one Quicken account into another. You don't have to create transfer categories; Quicken creates them automatically for you when you create an account.

You can—and should—assign a category to each transaction that you enter into Quicken. You should also use the same category names consistently throughout your Quicken accounts. For example, if you go to the doctor and pay with a check, you would enter that check under the "Medical" category in your checking account register. If on a subsequent visit you pay with a credit card, you would enter the transaction in your credit card account register using the category "Medical." This consistency is important: Consistent categorization leads to accurate reports, and correct reports give you a better picture of your finances.

✔ Tip

- When you created your data file (see Chapter 2), you probably included one of the preset categories lists, either the Home categories or the Business categories. You can use these category lists as is, but most people end up customizing their categories to better reflect their particular financial situations.

Tracking with Categories

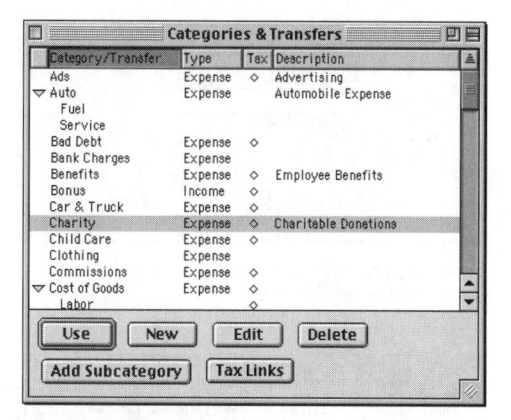

Figure 3.1 Click the New button in the Categories & Transfers window to create a new category.

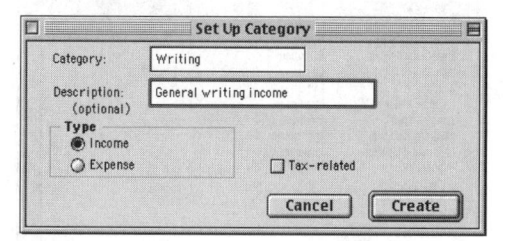

Figure 3.2 Enter a name and description in the Set Up Category dialog box.

To create a new category:

1. Choose Lists > Categories & Transfers, or press ⌘L.

    The Categories & Transfers window appears (**Figure 3.1**).

2. At the bottom of the Categories & Transfers window, click the New button.

    The Set Up Category dialog box appears (**Figure 3.2**).

3. Enter a name for the category in the Category box.

4. Enter a description for the category in the Description box (optional).

5. Select the appropriate radio button for the new category type (Income or Expense).

6. Click the "Tax-related" check box if you want to use the category to track tax-related income or expenses.

7. Click the Create button.

    Quicken creates the category and adds it to the list in the Categories & Transfers window.

ASSIGNING CATEGORIES

25

Chapter 3

Assigning Subcategories

You'll often want to track several types of income or expenses that are related to a single category. Quicken allows you to use subcategories to handle these relations. For example, under the Medical category, you might have separate subcategories for Doctors, Dentists, Prescriptions, and Insurance. Later, when you run an expense report, you'll be able to see just how much money you've spent on each of the Medical subcategories.

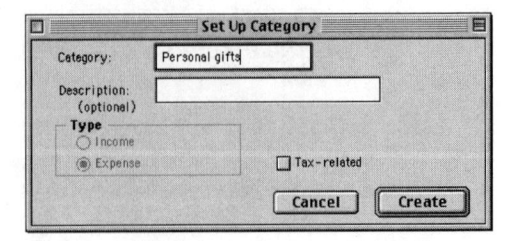

Figure 3.3 Enter the subcategory name and description in this window.

To create a subcategory:

1. In the Categories & Transfers window, select a category for which you would like to create a subcategory.

2. Click the Add Subcategory button.

   The Set Up Category window appears, but the Type radio buttons are dimmed (**Figure 3.3**). That's because a subcategory must always be of the same type as its parent category.

3. Enter the subcategory name in the Category box.

4. Enter the subcategory description in the Description box (optional).

5. If necessary, click the "Tax-related" check box.

6. Click the Create button.

   Quicken creates the subcategory, indenting it under the main category in the Categories & Transfers window (**Figure 3.4**).

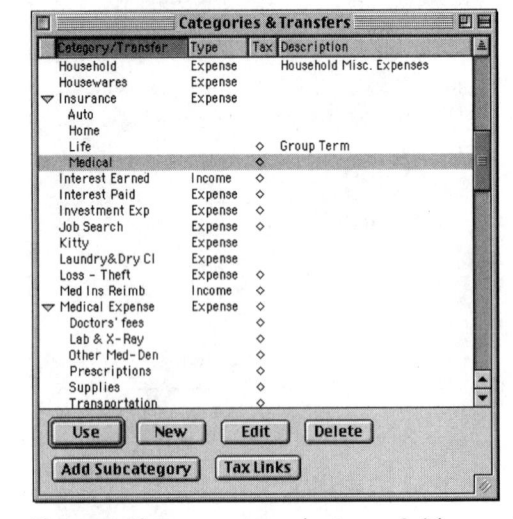

Figure 3.4 After you create a subcategory, Quicken adds its name to the Categories & Transfers window.

To edit a category or subcategory:

1. Select the category or subcategory in the Categories & Transfers window.

2. Click the Edit button.

   The Edit Category window appears. This window works in exactly the same way as the Set Up Category window, except that the button that accepts the changes you make is labeled Change, instead of Create.

3. Make your changes, and then click the Change button.

To delete a category or subcategory:

1. Select the category or subcategory in the Categories & Transfers window.

2. Click the Delete button. When Quicken asks you to confirm the deletion, click the Yes button.

✔ **Tip**

If you delete a category, the transactions in your data file that were assigned to that category end up with no category at all. As a result, those transactions won't show up where you expect them in reports that are sorted by category and could be hard to find. It's better to try to avoid deleting categories altogether or use the new Global Find and Replace feature in Quicken 2001 to change all the affected transactions to another category first and then delete the original category. For more about Global Find and Replace, see Chapter 4.

To sort the Categories & Transfers window:

◆ Click one of the column headings (Category/Transfer, Type, Tax, or Description).

   To reverse the sort direction, click the sort triangle to the right of the column headings.

Chapter 3

Using Tax Links

Quicken makes it easy for you to create tax reports at the end of the year (or at any time) by marking a selected category as tax-related and then linking that category to a line item from a particular U.S. federal tax form. Several of the preset categories are already assigned to tax forms; these are marked with a diamond character in the Categories & Transfers window.

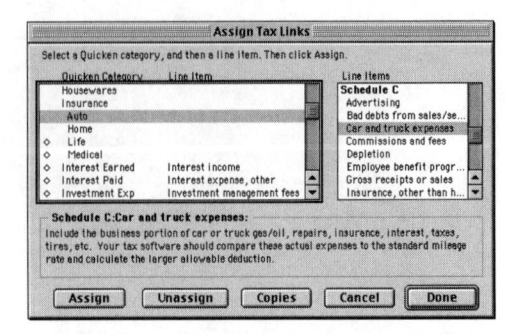

Figure 3.5 Select the appropriate federal tax form's line item from the list on the right to assign the item to a Quicken category.

To assign a tax link:

1. Select a category or subcategory in the Categories & Transfers window.

2. Click the Tax Links button.

   The Assign Tax Links window appears (**Figure 3.5**).

3. Scroll through the Line Item list, and select the appropriate line item. Then click the Assign button.

4. Click the Done button.

   Quicken links that line item to the category you selected in step 1.

✔ Tip

- Tax Links are linked to individual lines (by description, not by line number) on the various U.S. federal tax forms. These lines sometimes change from year to year as the tax laws (and therefore forms) change. Quicken 2001 is based on the 1999 tax year, so you should review your Tax Schedule report (see Chapter 16) to make sure that Quicken is categorizing Tax Links correctly for the 2000 and later tax years.

Using Classes

Classes are another way to group transactions. Classes do not replace categories; instead, a class adds an extra level to a transaction that has already been assigned to a category.

When you assign a category to a transaction, you can also assign a class to the transaction by adding a slash (/) and the class name to the end of the category name. For example, Bob's medical expenses could be categorized as Medical/Bob. This way, you can easily generate one report for the family's medical expenses (a category), another for Bob's expenses in general (a class), and another for Bob's medical expenses (sorting for both class and category).

Use classes to help you avoid unnecessary subcategories. In the example above, it's possible (although inefficient) to add a Bob subcategory, another for Lisa, and so on for the entire family, all under the Medical category. The trouble with this is that you would need to create such subcategories for every category that could be assigned to a different family member. Pretty soon, you'd have about a zillion categories and subcategories. Instead, it's better to create a class for each family member and then assign that class to transactions as necessary.

Unlike categories, preset classes don't come with Quicken; you'll have to create and define your own. Like subcategories, subclasses are easy to create and provide an extra level of classification.

Chapter 3

To create a class or subclass:

1. Choose Lists > Classes, or press ⌘K.
   The Classes window appears (**Figure 3.6**).

2. Click the New button.
   The Set Up Class window appears (**Figure 3.7**).

3. If you're creating a subclass, select the parent class, and then click the Add Subclass button.

4. Enter the name and (optionally) the description of the class, and then click the Create button.
   The name of the new class appears in the Classes window.

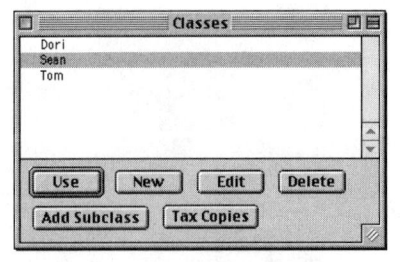

Figure 3.6 Click the New button in the Classes window to create a new class.

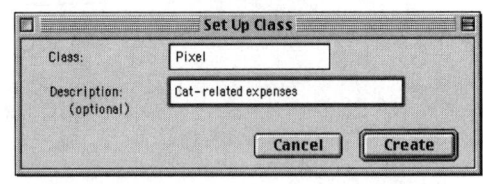

Figure 3.7 Enter the name and description of the new class here.

30

How Detailed Should I Get?

Quicken's preset categories are useful, but they're unlikely to completely satisfy your needs. No problem; just add more categories. But how much is enough?

The answer depends on the complexity of your financial picture and the level of detail to which you wish to track it. Here's an example. Robert is a salesman for a company and is constantly on the road. The company reimburses Robert for some, but not all, of his auto expenses, so he tracks those expenses in great detail. Under his main Auto category, he has included subcategories for Maintenance, Fuel, Insurance, and so on. Robert creates monthly Auto expense reports so that he can be reimbursed.

Susan works as an executive for the same corporation, and doesn't get reimbursed for auto expenses. She's curious to know how much she spends each year on her car. She doesn't care about the details; she just wants to know if her car expenses are growing or shrinking from year to year. So she uses one Auto category to track all expenses related to her car.

Your answer to the above question, then, depends on what kind of information is important to you. In general, you'll want to create subcategories for important elements so that you can track income or expenses in detail.

To edit or delete a class or subclass:

1. Select the class or subclass in the Classes window.

2. Click the Edit button.

   The Edit Class window appears, which works in the same way as the Set Up Class window.

3. Make your changes, and then click the Change button.

   or

   To delete, follow step 1 above, and then click the Delete button. When Quicken asks you to confirm the deletion, click the Yes button.

✔ Tips

- Classes are a great way to differentiate personal and business expenses. For example, you can create a class called Business and assign it to categories that you also use for personal expenses. (For example, you can classify some meals as Dining/Business.)

- If you have many clients, you can use classes to track income expenses for each client separately. In the same way, you can create classes for projects or particular jobs.

- You can't change a class into a category or vice versa.

- If you rename a class, category, subclass, or subcategory, Quicken replaces the old name with the new one in all transactions that contained the old name.

- The items in the Categories & Transfers window and Classes window can be moved in the list by dragging them up or down. In this way, it's easy to demote a category to a subcategory or a class to a subclass or to promote one to another.

USING THE ACCOUNT REGISTERS

4

A *transaction* can be anything that changes the balance of an account. For a checking account, it could be writing a check, making a deposit, or withdrawing cash from the ATM. For a credit card account, it could be making a payment or a purchase. And for a stock portfolio account, transactions include buying shares and reinvesting dividends.

Every account in Quicken has an account register in which you enter transactions. Quicken's registers look and act much like paper checkbook registers, which makes them familiar and easy to use. One nice difference from paper, however, is that a Quicken register does the math for you and keeps a running balance automatically.

In this chapter, you'll learn how to enter transactions in the account registers, how to enter your paycheck into Quicken, how to use Quicken to keep track of your credit cards, and how to use Quicken's data entry aids to save you typing and time.

Chapter 4

Entering Checking Account Transactions

Checks, deposits, and funds transfers from one account to another are all transactions that need to be entered in your account register. An *account register* (**Figure 4.1**) contains all the information (in boxes called *fields*) you need about a transaction, including date, check number, payee, payment or deposit amount, category, memo field, and a check box to indicate whether the transaction has cleared your bank.

Checks that you intend to print from within Quicken can be entered either in the register or in the Write Checks window. (See Chapter 6 for more about printing checks.)

You enter information in a register by typing in a field and then pressing Tab to move to the next field.

To enter a check or a deposit:

1. Select your account from the Account buttons in the toolbar (**Figure 4.2**), or click the Registers button and choose an account from the pop-up menu (**Figure 4.3**). You can also pull down the Lists > Registers menu (**Figure 4.4**) and pick an account from there.

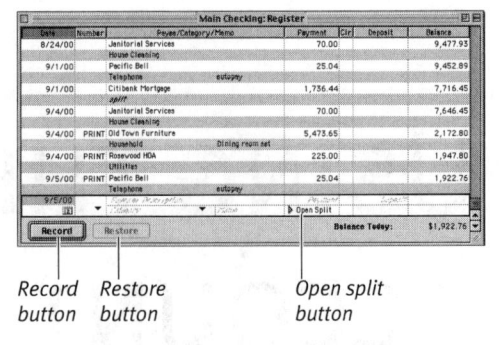

Record button   Restore button   Open split button

Figure 4.1 Enter transaction information in boxes called fields in the account register.

Figure 4.2 Clicking one of the Account buttons on the toolbar opens the account register.

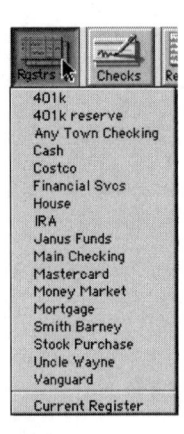

Figure 4.3 Choose a checking account from the pop-up menu.

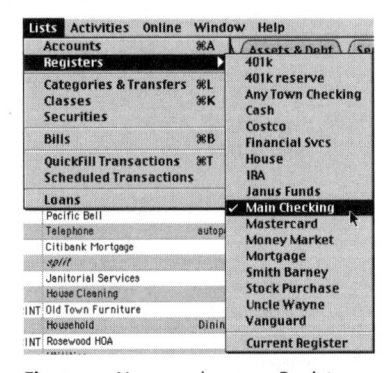

Figure 4.4 You can also open Registers from the menu bar.

34

Using the Account Registers

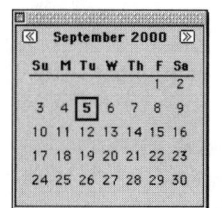

Figure 4.5 Click the calendar icon to change the date.

Table 4.1

Keyboard shortcuts for the Date field	
SHORTCUT	WHAT IT DOES
+	Next day
–	Previous day
t	Today
m	Beginning of the current month
h	End of the current month
y	Beginning of the current year
r	End of the current year
[	Same date last month
]	Same date next month
{	Same date last year
}	Same date next year

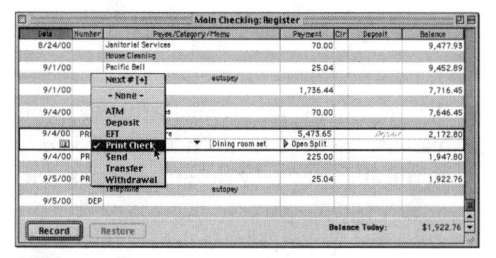

Figure 4.6 Choose a transaction type from the pop-up menu in the Number field.

2. The account register opens with the Date field highlighted and the current date filled in. If you want to change the date, type in a new date, or click the calendar icon underneath the date (**Figure 4.5**), or use the date keyboard shortcuts shown in **Table 4.1**.

3. Press Tab to move to the Number field.

4. If you're writing a check, enter the next check number in the Number field. To have Quicken automatically enter the next number in your check sequence, press the + key. If you're entering another kind of transaction, choose that transaction type from the pop-up menu in the Number field (**Figure 4.6**).

   See **Table 4.2** for the keyboard shortcuts you can use for transaction types.

5. Tab and enter the payee (for a check) or a description (for a deposit or transfer).

6. Tab across to the Payment or Deposit field and enter the amount.

7. Assign a category to the transaction by typing it into the Category field. The QuickFill feature fills in a category name from your list after you enter the first few letters. (See Chapter 5, and the tips below, for more information about QuickFill.) You can also use the pop-up menu in the Category field to select the category.

8. If you want to add a class to the category, type a slash (/) at the end of the category name, and then type the class name (optional).

9. Enter a memo about the transaction (optional, but often a good idea).

10. Click the Record button, or press Enter. Quicken saves the transaction and adds it to the register.

(continued)

ENTERING CHECKING ACCOUNT TRANSACTIONS

35

✔ Tips

- To use [Return] instead of [Tab] to move from field to field, choose Edit > Preferences and then click the Registers category in the left side of the window. Click the check box next to "Pressing Return tabs to the next field."

- If you need to write a post-dated check, simply enter a future date in the Date field. At the bottom of the register, Quicken will display the "Balance Today" and a future balance showing the balance as of the date of the post-dated check.

- To quickly enter a date in the current month, type the day in the Date field and press [Tab]. Quicken automatically enters the current month and year.

- You can't type a value in the Balance column because Quicken does the math for you.

- To prevent QuickFill from filling in information on a particular entry, hold down [Option] as you tab to the next field.

- You can turn off QuickFill entirely from the Edit > Preferences menu.

- You can enter ATM withdrawals quickly by using QuickFill and starting your description with a number. For example, if you regularly withdraw $80, use the description 80 *ATM*. The next time you record an ATM withdrawal, simply type 80 in to the Description field and Quicken will automatically fill in the rest of the information.

- In any field in which QuickFill works, you can use the up and down arrow keys to scroll alphabetically through the possible matches. For example, if you type "Ho" in the Description field, QuickFill might guess "Home Depot." Pressing the down arrow key would tell QuickFill to try the next possibility in the QuickFill list, "Home Savings." Pressing the up arrow key scrolls up alphabetically.

Table 4.2

Keyboard shortcuts for the Number field	
SHORTCUT	WHAT IT DOES
+	Enters the next check number
–	Subtracts a check number
a	ATM, an ATM transaction
d	DEP, a deposit
e	EFT, Electronic Funds Transfer
p	PRINT, a check to be printed
s	SEND, an electronic payment to be sent
t	TRANS, a transfer to another Quicken account
x	XFR, a transfer to another Quicken account (old, but still works)
w	WITHD, a cash withdrawal

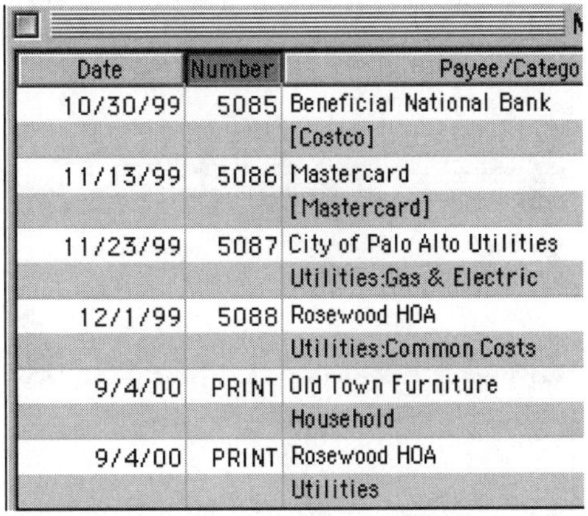

Using the Account Registers

Date	Number	Payee/Catego
10/30/99	5085	Beneficial National Bank
		[Costco]
11/13/99	5086	Mastercard
		[Mastercard]
11/23/99	5087	City of Palo Alto Utilities
		Utilities:Gas & Electric
12/1/99	5088	Rosewood HOA
		Utilities:Common Costs
9/4/00	PRINT	Old Town Furniture
		Household
9/4/00	PRINT	Rosewood HOA
		Utilities

Figure 4.7 Click the Date or Number column headers to sort a bank account register.

Sorting Registers

Most of the time you'll want to keep your bank registers sorted by date, but sometimes (like when you're trying to track down a particular check) you'll want to sort by the check number. Quicken lets you sort the registers for Bank accounts (but not any of the other account types).

To sort registers:

Open the register for the Bank account you want to sort.

To sort on Date, click the Date column header (**Figure 4.7**).

or

To sort on Number, click the Number column header.

✔ Tip

- It might look as though you could click the other column headings and sort by, say, Payee or Payment amount, but that's not the case. To get that kind of detailed information, you'll need to run a report (see Chapter 12 for the skinny on reports).

Splitting Transactions

Many transactions need to be divided among multiple categories. This is called *splitting the transaction*. For example, you might write a single check at a service station that covers both gasoline and auto repairs. When you enter that transaction, you will enter a category name and amount for each part of the split. You can split checks that you write or payments that you receive.

To split a transaction:

1. In the register, enter the date, check number, payee, and the payment or deposit amount.

2. Click the Open Split button (it doesn't look like a button, but it really is), choose Edit > Split Transaction from the menu, or press ⌘E. The split lines (where you enter additional categories and amounts) appear in the register (**Figure 4.8**).

3. Enter the category in the first Category field in the split, either by typing it in or by choosing it from the pop-up menu.

4. Type a memo in the first Memo field (optional).

5. Type the amount you want to allocate to the first category in the first Amount field.

    Quicken subtracts that amount from the total and puts the remainder in the next Amount field.

6. Enter the next category and amount on the next line. Repeat this until you have allocated the entire payment or deposit amount (**Figure 4.9**).

7. Click the Record button. The transaction is saved, properly allocated to multiple categories.

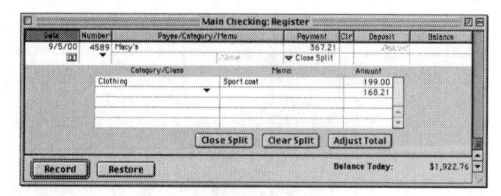

Figure 4.8 Use split lines to indicate separate payment categories in the register.

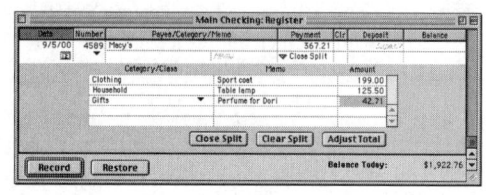

Figure 4.9 Enter category and amount information until you have allocated the entire payment or deposit amount.

✔ Tips

- If you want to split amounts but don't want to figure the total amount by adding yourself, Quicken adds up the total for you. For example, if you make one deposit that includes several checks from different categories, enter the amounts in all the split lines. As you add information, Quicken updates the total amount in the Deposit field.

- If you decide that you don't want to split the transaction after all, click the Clear Split button, which deletes all the information in the split lines.

- You can keep QuickFill from filling in splits by pressing [Option][Tab] to exit the Payee field. Quicken clears all of the QuickFill information except for the payee name.

- You can add as many lines of categories as you need to a split transaction.

- If you have a remainder on the last line of a split that you don't want to categorize, and you want to recalculate the transaction total, click the Adjust Total button. Quicken deletes the remainder and recalculates the total transaction amount.

Entering Paychecks

You enter paychecks as split transactions, but with a bit of a difference: Because paychecks are subject to payroll deductions, you need to show the net amount of your check as the deposit amount, and the gross amount and the payroll deductions in the split lines.

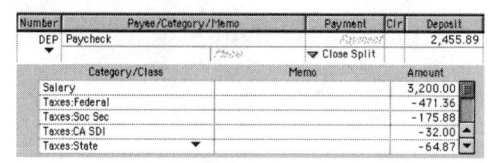

Figure 4.10 Enter your deductions as negative amounts so they will be subtracted from the gross amount.

To enter a paycheck:

1. Open a checking account register.

2. Enter the date, press the D key to add DEP to the Number field, enter a description, and then enter the net amount of your paycheck in the Deposit field. The net is your salary minus all the deductions: in other words, the amount of the check.

3. Click the Split button, opening the split lines.

4. In the first Category field, enter Salary.

5. Enter a memo in the Memo field (optional).

6. Enter the gross amount of your salary in the first Amount field. The gross amount is the amount you're paid before deductions.

7. In the next Category field, enter the first category for your deductions. For example, you might want to use Taxes:Federal as the category.

8. In this and all subsequent split lines, enter your deductions as *negative amounts* so they will be *subtracted* from the gross (**Figure 4.10**). Keep adding lines until all your deductions are allocated.

9. Click the Record button.

✔ Tip

- Most people's paychecks don't change very often. You can save a lot of repetitive data entry by selecting the transaction and choosing Edit > Memorize Transaction, or pressing ⌘M to memorize the amount.

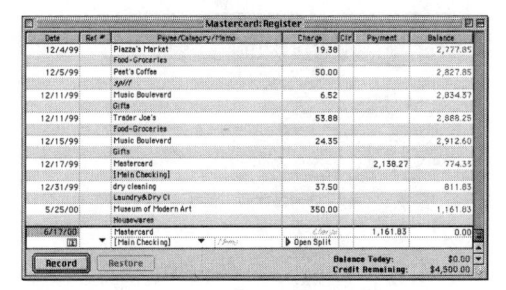

Figure 4.11 Enter information in the Charge and Payment fields in the credit card register.

Entering Credit Card Charges

Entering transactions in a credit card register is a lot like using a Bank account register except that the headings "Charge" and "Payment" appear rather than "Payment" and "Deposit" (**Figure 4.11**). Another difference is that in a credit card register, you prefer a zero balance—something most people wouldn't want to see in their checking account.

To enter credit card charges:

1. Select your credit card account from the Account buttons in the toolbar, or click the Registers button and choose an account from the pop-up menu.

    The account register opens with the current date filled in and the Date field highlighted.

2. If you want to change the date, you can type in a new date, or click the calendar icon underneath the date, or use the date keyboard shortcuts shown in **Table 4.1**.

    Notice that instead of the Check number field, an optional Reference number field appears. It's for the transaction reference number that your credit card company may list on your statement (some companies do, others don't bother). Don't feel compelled to use this field, but it's there if you want it.

3. Enter the payee and the amount of the charge.

4. Enter the category.

5. Enter a memo about the charge (optional).

6. Click the Record button, or press Enter.

✔ Tips

- You can dramatically reduce your data entry in credit card accounts by setting up the account for online banking, which lets you download all the transactions from the bank to the account register. See Chapter 11 for more information.

- Don't forget to enter finance charges when you get your credit card statement.

Transferring Money Between Accounts

Because you often need to transfer money between accounts, Quicken provides a way to perform this transaction. For example, when you write a check to make a payment to your credit card account, money flows out of the checking account and into the credit card account, decreasing the credit card's balance. Quicken makes it easy to update both accounts with one transaction so you don't have to enter the same transaction in both registers. To accomplish this, Quicken uses special categories called transfer categories, which refer to other Quicken accounts. You can view the transfer categories in your data file by choosing Lists > Categories & Transfers and scrolling to the bottom of the window (**Figure 4.12**). The transfer categories are the ones enclosed in the square brackets ([ ]).

In the first example below, you'll see how to use transfer categories to transfer money from your checking to your savings account. The next example shows you how to use the Transfer Money command to transfer money between accounts.

Figure 4.12 You can view the transfer categories in your data file by scrolling to the bottom of the Categories & Transfers window.

To transfer money from one account to another:

1. From the Account buttons in the toolbar, select the account from which you want to move money, or click the Registers button and choose it from the pop-up menu. You can also pull down the Lists > Registers menu and select an account from there.

   The account register opens with the Date field highlighted and the current date filled in.

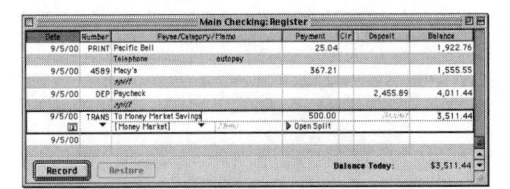

Figure 4.13 Click the Record button, and Quicken saves the transaction.

Figure 4.14 You can see a parallel transaction in the Money Market account register.

2. If you want to change the date, you can type in a new date, or click the calendar icon underneath the date, or use the date keyboard shortcuts shown in **Table 4.1**.

3. Press [Tab] and type *t* in the Number field. Quicken will enter TRANS to signify that this is a transfer.

4. Enter a description of the transfer in the Payee field.

5. Enter the amount in either the Payment or Deposit field, depending on whether you are moving money into or out of this account. (In this example, money is moving from this checking account to savings, so we enter the amount in the first amount field. If the money were flowing from savings to checking, you would put the amount in the second field.)

6. In the Category field, press the left bracket ([) key, and then type the name of the account to which you want to transfer money.

   or

   Choose the savings account from the pop-up menu in the Category field. Your register should now look something like **Figure 4.13**.

7. Click the Record button.

   Quicken saves the transaction in the checking account register and creates a parallel transaction in the savings account register (**Figure 4.14**).

To use the Transfer Money command:

1. Choose Activities > Transfer Money > Between Registers.

   The Transfer Money Between Quicken Registers window appears (**Figure 4.15**).

2. Enter the date, a description in the Payee field (Transfer appears here by default), the amount you want to transfer, and a memo (optional).

3. Using the "From" pop-up menu, choose the source account for the transfer.

4. Using the "To" pop-up menu, choose the destination account for the transfer.

5. Click the Transfer button.

   Quicken creates entries in both the source and destination accounts.

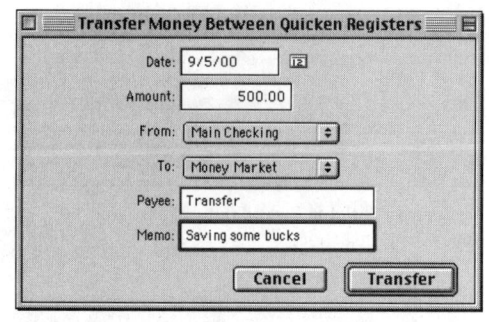

Figure 4.15 Enter transaction information in the Transfer Money Between Quicken Registers window.

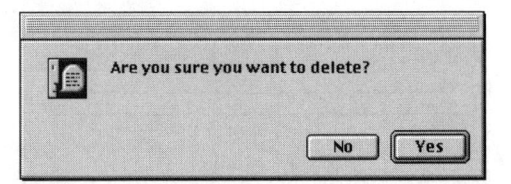

Figure 4.16 Click Yes to confirm the transaction deletion.

Changing Transactions

Unlike some other financial programs, Quicken allows you to make changes to transactions at any time. You can edit, delete, or void transactions whenever necessary.

To edit a transaction:

1. Open the account register that contains the transaction you want to edit.
2. Click a transaction to select it.
3. In any field of the transaction, select the incorrect information and type over it to replace it.
4. Click the Record button.

To delete a transaction:

1. Open the account register that contains the transaction you want to delete.
2. Click a transaction to select it.
3. Choose Edit > Delete Transaction, or press ⌘D.

   Quicken will ask you to confirm the deletion (**Figure 4.16**).
4. Click the Yes button.

   Quicken deletes the transaction.

To void a transaction:

1. Open the account register that contains the transaction you want to void.
2. Click a transaction to select it.
3. Choose Edit > Void Transaction.

   Quicken removes the amount in the Payment or Deposit field, recalculates the account balance (if necessary), and places the word VOID at the beginning of the Payee field.
4. Click the Record button.

Finding and Replacing Transactions

One of the new features in Quicken Deluxe 2001 is the ability to do a Global Find and Replace in your account registers. That means that you can search through multiple accounts at once, and if you want, you can replace what you find with new information. For example, it's not uncommon to enter the names of payees in slightly different ways over the course of several months, you could have checks written to your favorite drugstore written as "Right Aid" and "RiteAid." Or you could have placed some prescription transactions in the "Medical" category and others in a category called "Prescriptions." At the end of the year, you want all of these transactions to show up under the correct name (RiteAid) and a single category. Global Find and Replace is just the ticket.

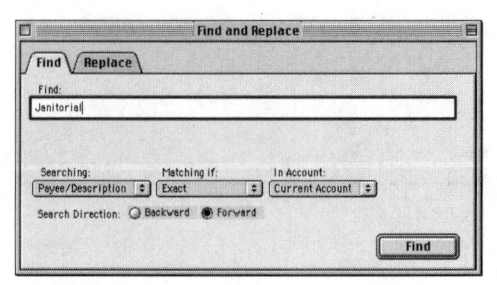

Figure 4.17 Enter the text that you wish to search for in the Find field.

To find a transaction:

1. Open the account register in which you want to find a transaction.

2. Choose Edit > Find, or press ⌘F. The Find dialog box appears (**Figure 4.17**).

3. In the Find field, enter the text that you wish to search for. Make choices from the "Searching," "Matching if," and "In Account" pop-up menus to narrow your search. You can also choose to search Backward or Forward using the Search Direction radio buttons.

4. Click the Find button again to find the next occurrence of your search text.

5. When you're done with your search, click the Close box in the Find window.

✔ Tips

- The Find window floats over the register in which it is searching, so you might need to move one or the other windows to see the results of your search.

- Finding is most useful when you're entering a transaction and wish to be reminded of the details of a previous transaction.

- When you're looking for multiple transactions, you'll get a better overview by switching to the Reports section and running a QuickReport. See Chapter 12 for more information about reports.

- Most searches tend to be made on date or Payee, but you can search for a wide variety of criteria by using the Searching pop-up menu. Check this menu when you're looking to find a transaction based on some unusual criteria, such as Address, or Amount.

To replace a transaction:

1. Open the account register in which you want to find a transaction.

2. Choose Edit > Replace, or press ⌘R. The Find and Replace dialog box appears (**Figure 4.18**).

3. In the Find field, enter the text that you wish to search for.

4. In the Replace with field, enter the text that you wish to replace in the register.

5. Make choices from the "Searching," "Matching if," and "In Account" pop-up menus to narrow your search. You can also choose to search Backward or Forward using the Search Direction radio buttons.

6. Click the Find button to find the first occurrence of what you're searching for. Quicken displays the found item in the register.

7. Click the Replace button to replace the text in the found occurrence. If you want to replace all occurrences of the found text, click the Replace All button. If you prefer to step through each occurrence and decide if you want to replace on a case-by-case basis, use the Replace & Find button.

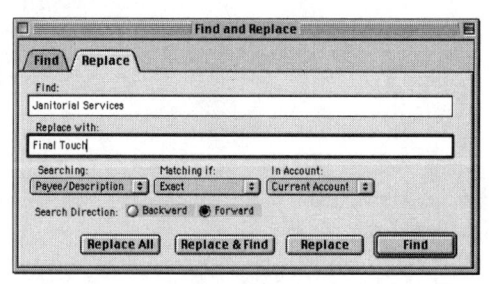

Figure 4.18 Enter the replacement text in the Replace with field, and refine your search using the pop-up menus.

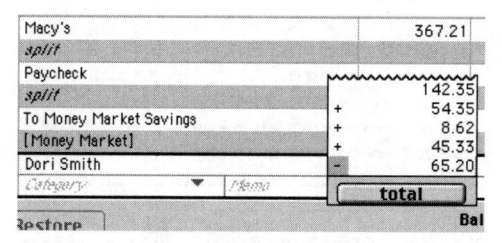

Figure 4.19 Enter the numbers you wish to calculate, pressing an operator key between each number.

Using Data Entry Helpers

Two other useful data entry tools you should know about are QuickMath and QuickEntry. QuickMath lets you make simple mathematical calculations right in the account register, and QuickEntry allows you to enter transactions without even opening Quicken.

QuickMath

QuickMath gives you a simple "paper tape" calculator right in the account register. If you want to make calculations while entering a transaction—for example adding up a bunch of checks while you're filling out the deposit transaction—QuickMath will make it easier.

To use QuickMath:

1. Begin entering a transaction in an account register.

2. For any field in which you can enter an amount, press an arithmetic operator key (+, –, *, /, or =) to pop up a "paper tape." You can enter numbers here as you would on an adding machine (**Figure 4.19**).

3. Enter the numbers you wish to calculate, pressing an operator key between each number. When you have entered all your numbers, click the Total button at the bottom of the paper tape (or press Enter). Quicken does the calculation and places the result in the amount field.

✔ Tip

- You can use the arithmetic operator keys on either the keyboard or (if you have it) the keyboard's numeric keypad.

QuickEntry

If you enter transactions every day (and even if you don't), QuickEntry can reduce the time it takes. QuickEntry is a small application that opens quickly and lets you enter data into all of your bank, credit card, and cash account registers. You enter transactions into QuickEntry in exactly the same way you would into Quicken. QuickEntry data is stored in your Quicken data file and added to your Quicken registers the next time you open the Quicken program. You can't have QuickEntry and Quicken open at the same time, since they share the same data file.

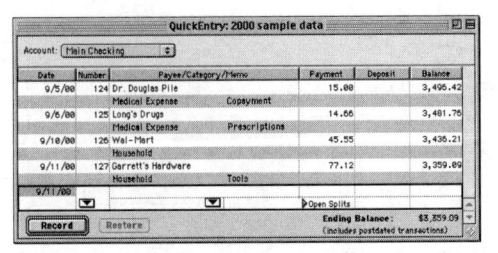

Figure 4.20 Choose QuickEntry from the Apple menu to open the QuickEntry window.

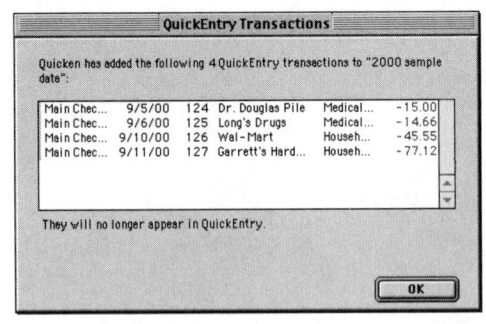

Figure 4.21 Click the OK button, and Quicken will add the QuickEntry transactions to your register.

To use QuickEntry:

1. Choose QuickEntry from the Apple menu.

   The QuickEntry window appears (**Figure 4.20**).

2. Choose the account to which you want to enter data from the Account pop-up menu.

   After you make the change, the Ending Balance for that account is displayed in QuickEntry's lower-right corner.

3. Enter transactions as you would in any Quicken register, clicking the Record button after each entry.

4. When you're done making entries, choose File > Quit.

5. The next time you open your Quicken data file, the QuickEntry Transactions window will appear (**Figure 4.21**), recapping the entries you made in QuickEntry. Click OK, and Quicken adds the QuickEntry transactions to your Quicken registers and removes those entries from QuickEntry.

ALL ABOUT QUICKFILL

If your financial situation is anything like mine, you find yourself repeating similar transactions over and over. For example, you probably make a rent or mortgage payment every month and deposit your paycheck biweekly or once a month. You probably also pay many of the same bills every month—to the phone company, to your electric utility, to your supermarket for groceries, whatever. You could simply type in all of that stuff again and again and again, but why bother? That's the kind of repetitive dog work for which computers were designed. You can let your computer remember and enter the boring stuff by using the QuickFill feature in Quicken.

QuickFill watches over your shoulder as you type information into an account register or onto a check. When the information you're typing matches a previous transaction, QuickFill enters the rest of the transaction for you. QuickFill can remember all or part of a transaction, so you can use it to remember and enter transactions whose amounts stay the same every month (such as your rent or mortgage payment) or transactions that can change each month (like the electric bill).

In this chapter, you'll learn how to use QuickFill to make entering transactions easier and how to memorize, edit, enter, and delete QuickFill transactions.

How QuickFill Works

Let's face it—there's nothing especially fun or glamorous about entering your transactions into an account register. In fact, it can be downright dull. QuickFill is an important tool that helps you get information into Quicken fast and with less boredom.

Every time you enter a transaction in your account register or on a check, Quicken adds the information to the QuickFill Transaction list. Then, when you create a new entry, Quicken compares the information in the QuickFill list to what you're typing. As soon as it finds a match, QuickFill fills in the rest of the transaction for you. If QuickFill's guess is correct, all you'll probably need to do is change the amount of that particular check. If QuickFill guesses wrong, just keep typing and your entry will replace QuickFill's guess.

You can also manually add transactions to QuickFill's list by selecting a transaction and manually "memorizing" it. You can view, use, edit, or delete QuickFill transactions via the QuickFill Transactions window (**Figure 5.1**).

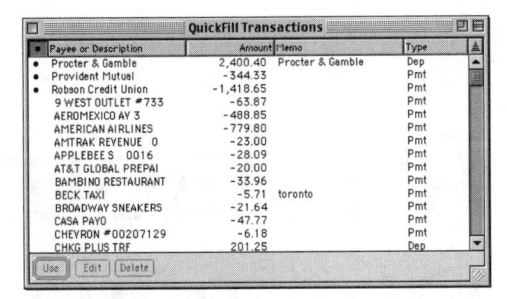

Figure 5.1 The QuickFill Transactions list helps you save a tremendous amount of time and keystrokes.

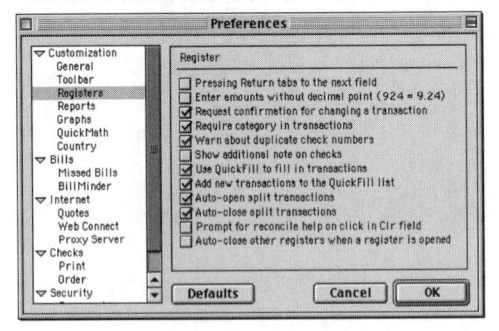

Figure 5.2 You can turn QuickFill on or off in the Register panel of the Preferences window.

✔ Tips

- If you hold down (Option) when you tab from the Payee field to the Amount field, Quicken removes its QuickFill guesses from the Amount and Category fields.

- Keep in mind that Quicken won't add information to the QuickFill list from the account registers in the Investing section.

- You can turn QuickFill on or off, and you can turn off the automatic updating of the QuickFill list. To do so, choose Edit > Preferences to open the Preferences window. Click the Register category. Then click on or off the check boxes next to "Use QuickFill to fill in transactions" and "Add new transactions to the QuickFill list" (**Figure 5.2**).

All About QuickFill

Figure 5.3 Quicken indicates locked transactions by adding a black dot to the left of the transaction in the QuickFill list.

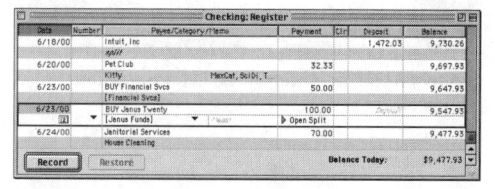

Figure 5.4 Quicken indicates which transaction is selected in a register by adding a border around it.

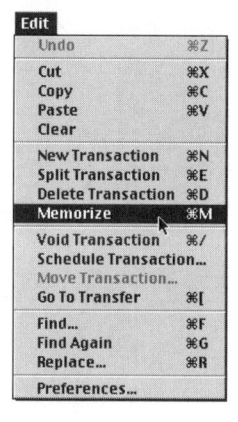

Figure 5.5 Choose Memorize from the Edit menu, or press ⌘M.

Memorizing Transactions

Usually you won't need to do anything to memorize a transaction and add it to the QuickFill Transactions list. Quicken will do it for you automatically. See for yourself: You have already entered some data into Quicken, so open the QuickFill Transactions list by choosing Lists > QuickFill Transactions (or by pressing ⌘T) to see the automatically memorized transactions.

Sometimes, however, you'll want to manually memorize a transaction, usually because you want to lock or unlock it. The black dots that appear at the left of the transactions in **Figure 5.3** indicate locked transactions. You can unlock transactions so that QuickFill will memorize any changes, or you can lock them so that the QuickFill entry will not update should you make any changes to the register entry.

Unlocked transactions are typically used for transactions that are written to the same payee but with different details. For example, you might often write checks to Safeway when you go grocery shopping, but the amount and even the category might vary with every check.

Locked QuickFill transactions are useful for checks written to the same payee for which the details rarely change, such as a car payment. You can still change the amount in the register or on the check, but that won't affect the memorized amount stored in a locked QuickFill transaction.

To manually memorize a QuickFill transaction:

1. In your account register, select a transaction by clicking it. Quicken adds a border around the transaction you selected (**Figure 5.4**).

2. Choose Edit > Memorize (**Figure 5.5**), or press ⌘M.

53

Using QuickFill Transactions

QuickFill usually works unobtrusively, automatically popping in information as you enter transactions in account registers or on checks. But you can also use the QuickFill Transactions list manually to help you add transactions by keeping the list open while entering data.

Why would you want to do this? Here's one example. I use three telephone lines in my house, one personal, the other two business-related, so I track expenditures on all three separately. Naturally, the lines are all maintained by the same phone company, so the payee is the same. If I used QuickFill in the usual fashion, I couldn't track which QuickFill transactions cover the personal line and which ones cover the business lines. So I open the QuickFill Transactions window, where each transaction includes a Memo field indicating the type of phone line to which the transaction applies.

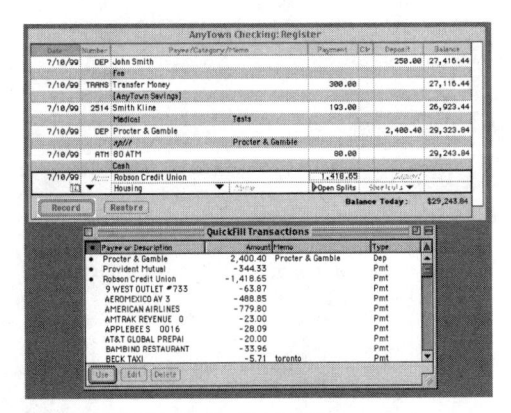

Figure 5.6 You can enter QuickFill transactions manually.

To use the QuickFill Transactions list to help enter transactions:

1. With your account register open, choose Lists > QuickFill Transactions, or press ⌘T. The QuickFill Transactions window opens (**Figure 5.6**).

2. Scroll through the QuickFill Transactions list until you find the transaction that you want to use.

3. Click the transaction to highlight it.

4. Click the Use button to transfer the contents of the transaction to the open account register. Or, drag a transaction from the QuickFill Transactions window and drop it on the account register. Or even simpler, double-click the transaction to enter it in the account register.

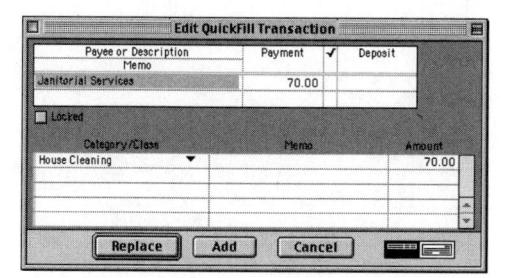

Figure 5.7 You can edit a transaction in the Edit QuickFill Transaction window.

Editing QuickFill Transactions

You can change any part of a QuickFill transaction, although you won't usually need to. Most often, you'll clear the amount of a transaction and then lock the transaction so that in future transactions with the same payee, you'll simply fill in the amount of the check.

To edit a QuickFill transaction:

1. Open the QuickFill Transactions window.

2. Click to select the transaction that you want to edit.

3. Click the Edit button at the bottom of the QuickFill Transaction window.
   The Edit QuickFill Transaction window appears (**Figure 5.7**).

4. Make any needed changes in the Payee or Description, Payment, Category/Class, Memo, or Amount fields. Notice that you can use split transactions here (see Chapter 4).

5. To replace the transaction with your changes, click the Replace button. Or to create a new QuickFill transaction with the edited information, click the Add button. Or to back out of the window without saving changes, click the Cancel button.

To lock or unlock a QuickFill transaction:

1. Follow steps 1 through 4 above.

2. To lock a transaction, click the "Locked" check box in the Edit QuickFill Transaction window. To unlock the transaction, clear the "Locked" check box.
   The QuickFill Transactions list indicates locked transactions by adding a black dot next to them (refer to **Figure 5.3**).

Deleting QuickFill Transactions

You might choose to get rid of a QuickFill transaction because it lists a payee that you dealt with only once or to eliminate duplicate entries.

To delete a QuickFill transaction:

1. In the QuickFill Transactions window, click the transaction that you want to eliminate.

   Quicken highlights the memorized transaction.

2. Click the Delete button at the bottom of the QuickFill Transactions window.

3. Click Yes when Quicken asks you to confirm the deletion.

✔ Tips

- If you leave a QuickFill transaction unlocked, Quicken replaces the amount of the check in the transaction every time you use the QuickFill entry. The next time you use that QuickFill entry, you'll see the amount of the last check you wrote to that payee. This makes it easy to tell if your spending with that payee has changed drastically. If it has, you have a chance to either rethink your spending pattern or check for an error in the current month's bill. I once found a $75 error in a utility bill in this fashion.

- If a loan transaction is listed in your QuickFill Transactions list, you won't be able to edit it from the QuickFill Transactions window. You'll need to go to the Loans window (choose Lists > Loans). For more about changing loan information, see Chapter 14.

Writing and Printing Checks

Just to avoid any possible confusion, this chapter is about writing checks that you intend to print from Quicken on preprinted check forms. Checks that you write by hand should be entered into Quicken in your checking account register, as shown in Chapter 4. And I'll cover paying bills with electronic "checks" in Chapter 11.

If you don't already use Quicken to print your checks on preprinted check forms, you should definitely reconsider—you're missing out on a lot of convenience. Consider: When you write checks by hand in your regular checkbook, you first fill out the check. Then you'll have to type all the same information into Quicken's check register. That's a lot of double work.

Using Quicken to print your checks can also help you avoid errors. Before I started printing checks, I'd discover (usually after chasing numbers for a good half-hour when balancing my checkbook) that I had typed an incorrect amount for a handwritten check into the Quicken register. But when you write a check in Quicken in the first place, there's no chance of a pesky typo wasting your time later, because Quicken automatically enters each check amount into its register. It makes checkbook balancing much faster.

Chapter 6

Writing and Editing Checks

There's no mystery to writing checks in Quicken; rather than give you some whizzy data entry form, carefully optimized for maximum data entry ease, Quicken goes with the familiar. When you write a check in Quicken, it's a lot like writing a check by hand. There's almost nothing new to learn. But read the section below anyway, OK?

To write a check:

1. Open the Write Checks window by choosing Activities > Write Checks, by pressing ⌘J, or by clicking the Checks button on the task bar (**Figure 6.1**). The Write Checks window for your main checking account appears (**Figure 6.2**).

2. In the Write Checks window, today's date is entered for you and highlighted. If you want to change the date, type in a new date.

   or

   Click the Calendar button in the Write Checks window, and a small calendar will pop up (**Figure 6.3**). Click the new date in the small calendar window to add that date to the check.

3. Type in the name of the payee. As you type, QuickFill will anticipate and fill in the payee's name if what you're typing is similar to a name that appears on a previously written check. (See Chapter 5 for more about QuickFill.)

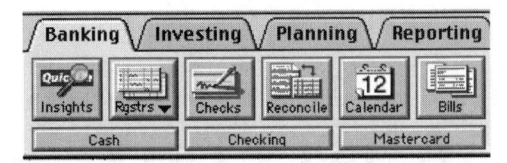

Figure 6.1 Click the Checks button in the task bar to open the Write Check window.

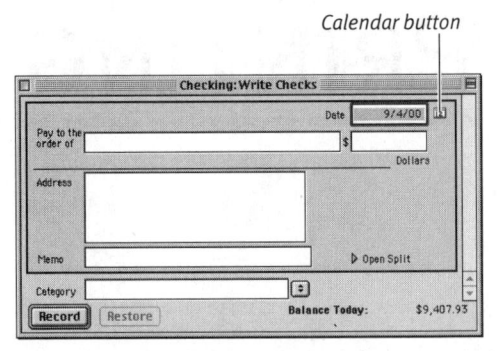

Figure 6.2 The Write Checks window looks like a real paper check, and you fill it out in much the same way.

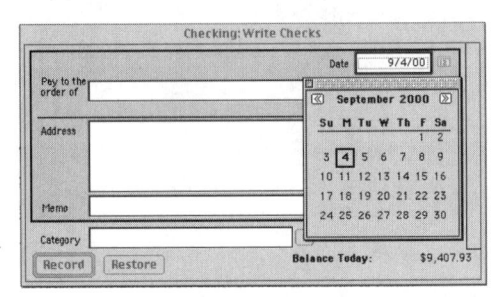

Figure 6.3 You can choose a date for the check from the calendar pop-up window.

58

Writing and Printing Checks

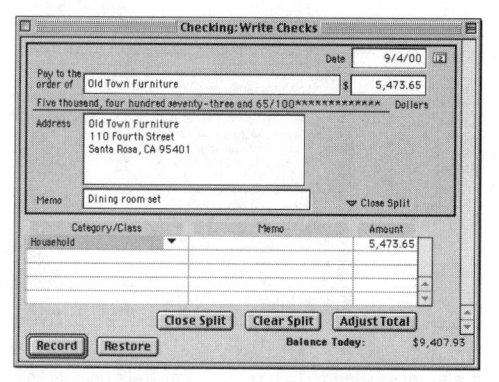

Figure 6.4 Your completed check should look something like this (though only checks with split categories will normally have the split lines displayed).

4. QuickFill puts in the same amount that appeared in the last transaction with the payee unless the QuickFill entry is locked; this is handy for checks that you write each month for the same amount. Press [Tab] to move on if the amount is correct. If it's not correct, fill in the amount of the check.

   On the next line, Quicken turns the amount you entered into its text form. (For $42.76, for example, Quicken enters Forty-two and 76/100.)

5. Enter the name and address of the payee in the Address field (optional). To copy and paste the payee's name into the first line of the Address field, press the single quotation mark ([']) key.

6. Fill in the Memo field to record a memo about this check (optional).

7. If QuickFill entered the appropriate payee in step 3, it probably filled in the Category field correctly as well, and you can move on to the next step. Otherwise, type in the appropriate category or use the Category pop-up menu to select one. You can use split transactions if you need to.

8. Click the Record button, or press [Enter]. The completed check should look similar to that shown in **Figure 6.4**.

✔ Tips

- The Write Checks window is usually the one for your main checking account (you can tell which account you're using because the name of the account shows up in the title bar of the Write Checks window), but you can force it to appear for other accounts from which you can write checks. Just open the register for that account before you open the Write Checks window.

59

- If you mail your printed checks in a windowed mailing envelope (a surprisingly inexpensive and time-saving idea), the Memo line may be visible through the window. Adding confidential account numbers to the Memo line would be unsuitable. You can use another space to add these numbers. Choose Edit > Preferences, click the Register icon, and click "Show additional note on checks" (**Figure 6.5**). A note line will appear on the check (**Figure 6.6**). You can fill in this note line only from the Write Checks window; the account register doesn't show it. This note line also won't appear through the envelope window.

- To memorize transactions in the Write Checks window as well as in the account register, choose Edit > Memorize or press ⌘M.

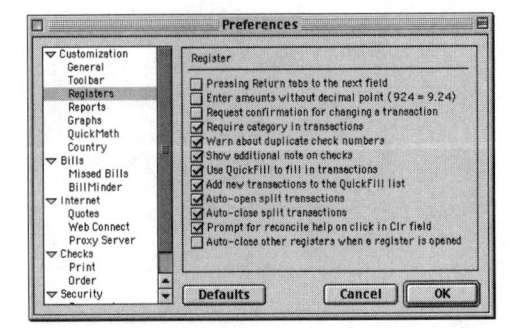

Figure 6.5 Use the Register section of Quicken's preferences window to turn on a note field on checks.

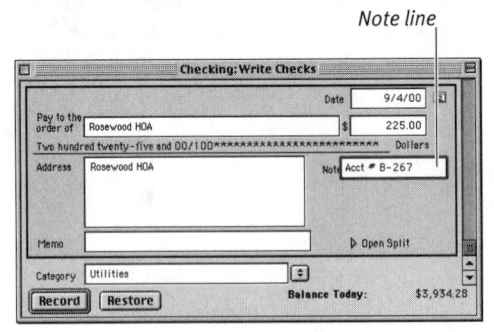

Figure 6.6 Type your account number on a check in the note line.

To edit a check:

1. Use the vertical scroll bar in the Write Checks window to scroll through checks you've written in the current session.

2. Find the check, and edit the information.

3. Click the Record button or press Enter to save your work.

✔ Tip

- If you prefer, you can edit the check by making changes in the account register. (See Chapter 4 for how to use the account register.) After you print a check, it disappears from the Write Checks window and is entered in the account register. Note that the check is accessible only from the account register after it has been printed.

To delete a check:

1. Scroll in the Write Checks window until you find the check you want to delete.

2. Choose Edit > Delete Transaction, or press ⌘D. Quicken will pop up a dialog box asking you if you're sure you want to delete this check.

3. Click the Yes button to confirm the deletion.

✔ Tips

- You can neither delete a check nor edit check information from the Write Checks window after the check has been printed. If you need to change or delete check information after you have printed a check, you must access the information from the account register. See Chapter 4 for more information.

- Looking to void a check? You have to do that in the account register. See "Changing Transactions" in Chapter 4 for more information.

Table 6.1

Source for computer checks		
COMPANY	PHONE NUMBER	URL
ASAP Checks	888-852-4325	www.asapchecks.com
Checks for Less	800-245-5775	www.checksforless.com
Intuit	888-241-0502	www.intuitmarketplace.com
NEBS	800-225-6380	www.nebs.com
PC Checks	800-322-5317	www.pcchecks.com

Ordering Checks

You can buy checks preprinted with your name, address, bank name and account number, check numbers, and any other information required by your bank. These checks are designed for use in laser printers and inkjet printers (you can also order continuous checks for dot-matrix printers, if you still have one of those older units), and they generally come in one of three styles:

- Standard Checks are sized for use in a business-size envelope and come three to a page **(Figure 6.7)**. Most people use these checks.

- Voucher Checks are good for payroll and accounts payable use; you get one check per page, with two check stubs that you can keep or send out with the check as needed **(Figure 6.8)**. For personal use, you always end up keeping a paper receipt. (Which makes no sense to me; I want to store as little paper as possible. But whatever works for you.)

- Wallet Checks are smaller than standard checks (so that they can, not surprisingly, fit into your wallet) and include a stub for recording check information when writing a check by hand **(Figure 6.9)**.

After you decide which style makes the most sense for you, have your current checkbook ready (you'll need it for the bank information and your account number) and order your checks. But where to get computer checks? One place is from Intuit itself, although they tend to charge quite a bit more than some other companies. Many other business supply companies can provide checks. Prices vary wildly, depending on special sales and the phases of the moon, so a bit of comparative shopping on the companies' Web sites can save you some money. See **Table 6.1** for some suggestions for computer checks.

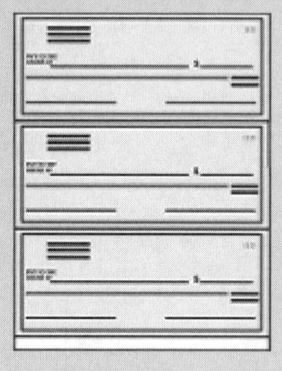

Figure 6.7 Standard checks are the ones used by most people, because they're the most convenient and least paper-wasteful.

Figure 6.8 Voucher checks are good if you must keep a paper trail of check stubs. But for most of us, the less paper, the better.

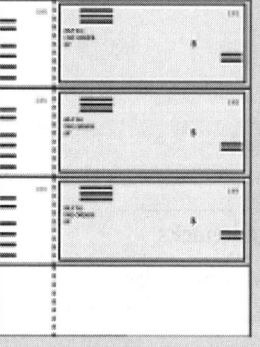

Figure 6.9 Wallet-style checks make sense if you want to carry some of your computer checks with you.

Writing and Printing Checks

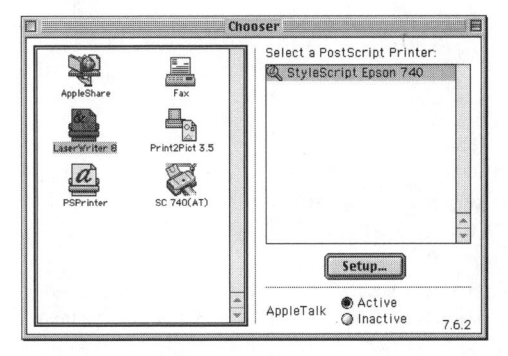

Figure 6.10 Select which printer you want to use from the Chooser window. For most printers, Quicken's default settings will do just fine.

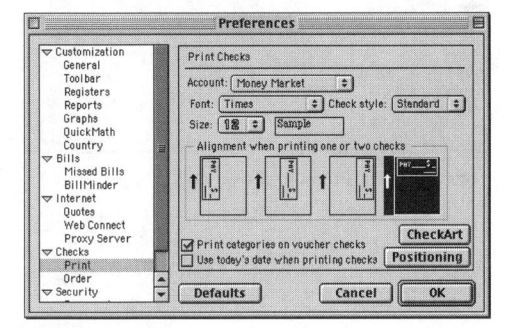

Figure 6.11 In the Print Checks Preferences window, you can create different check printing settings for each account.

Getting Ready to Print

After you have entered your checks for printing in the Write Checks window or in the account register, you're almost ready to print. But first you must set up Quicken to use your checks.

To set up Quicken to print:

1. From the Apple menu, select Chooser.
2. In the Chooser window (**Figure 6.10**), select the printer you want to use, and then close the window.
3. In Quicken, choose Edit > Preferences.
4. From the Checks category in the scrolling list on the left, choose Print (**Figure 6.11**).
5. Each bank account can have its own Print Checks settings. From the Account pop-up menu, choose the account to which you want these settings to apply.
6. Choose the font and font size you want printed on your checks.
7. Pick a style (standard, voucher, or wallet) from the Check Style pop-up menu.
8. Depending on how your particular printer feeds paper, choose one of the four alignments when printing one or two checks.
9. If you're using voucher checks, check the "Print categories on voucher checks" check box.
10. Click the OK button to save your settings for this checking account.

GETTING READY TO PRINT

63

Printing Checks

Now that you've set up Quicken's printing functions, it's finally time to print. Note that most of the setup needs to be done only once; you'll just be printing merrily away.

To print checks:

1. Make sure the checks are in your printer tray and positioned correctly for printing. You might want to run a test on some plain paper before you print on real checks for the first time.

2. Verify that your printer is turned on and that it is online.

3. Open the account from which you want to print checks.

4. Choose File > Print Checks, or press ⌘P (**Figure 6.12**). The Print Checks window appears (**Figure 6.13**), telling you how many checks are ready to print.

5. The starting check number should match the first number of the checks that you put in the printer. If it doesn't match, change it. (In subsequent times that you print, Quicken will remember the number of the last check that you printed and automatically add the next number in this space.)

6. Add a date in the "Checks dated through" box to print all checks written up to this date. You'll probably use this option most often.

    or

    Click the Selected Checks radio button to open the Select Checks to Print dialog box (**Figure 6.14**). In the Print column, put a checkmark next to the checks that you want to print, and then click OK.

7. In the Print Checks window, click Print to open the printer dialog box.

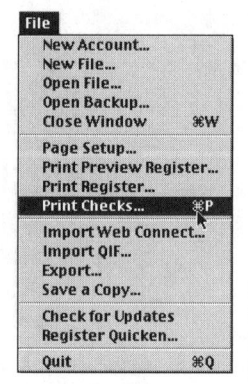

Figure 6.12 Choosing Print Checks from the File menu is your entrée to check-printing bliss.

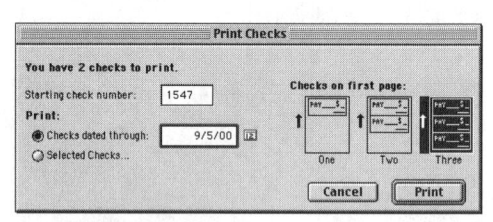

Figure 6.13 The Print Checks window lets you know how many checks are set to print.

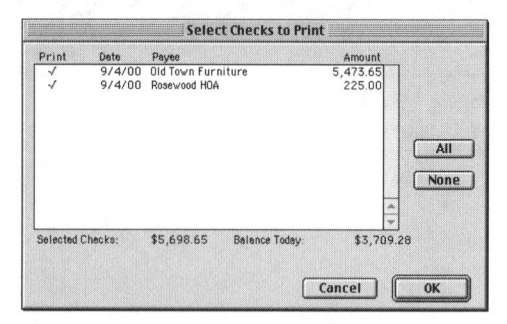

Figure 6.14 If you only want to print particular checks, use the Select Checks to Print dialog box.

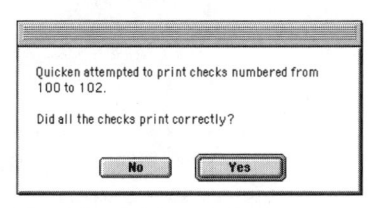

Figure 6.15 Quicken needs reassurance that your checks printed correctly. Soothe it by clicking the Yes button.

Writing Checks by Hand

When you're away from home, you can write checks with the checkbook that your bank provided when you opened your account, or you can use your preprinted computer checks and fill them out by hand. I like to use my regular bank checkbook and enter the information into Quicken when I return home. I differentiate between the checks that Quicken prints and ones I handwrite by using two widely different sets of check numbers for each kind of check. For example, I started my computer checks at 1000 and my handwritten checks start in the 4000 range. Quicken has no problem dealing with different sets of check numbers.

8. Click the Print button in the printer dialog box to start printing checks.

9. After the checks have been printed, Quicken will ask you whether all the checks printed correctly (**Figure 6.15**). If they did, click Yes and Quicken will enter the check numbers into the account register.

   If any of the checks did not print correctly (usually because of a printer problem), click No and Quicken will ask you to type in the number of the first incorrectly printed check. Fix the printer problem and start again at step 4 above to print the remaining checks.

✔ Tips

- To stop printing in the middle of a print job, press ⌘ . (period).

- You can reprint a check at any time (if a payee loses a check, for example). Just replace the check number in your register with the word PRINT, and click the Record button. Then print the check normally.

- Quicken's User Manual includes a chart showing Mac printers and how to position checks in their printer trays for correct printing.

- In the past year or so, the prices for good-quality inkjet printers have dropped dramatically. Prices are so low (under $100, in some cases!) that you can now consider obtaining and dedicating a printer just for printing checks. That way, you never have to mess around with changing from regular paper to checks, and you never have to accidentally print a letter on the checks that you left in your printer. All you would have to do is switch printers in the Chooser.

USING THE CALENDAR

When a bill gets paid is often as important as the amount of the payment. Because many of your financial transactions are time-sensitive, Quicken gives you a tool that lets you see your transactions over time: the Financial Calendar. With the Calendar, you can schedule future transactions and set up recurring transactions that need to be paid on a regular schedule, such as mortgage payments or utility bills. Scheduled transactions can be entered automatically, saving you the drudgery of data entry. The Calendar can also remind you of upcoming payments and give you a quick visual overview of how you spend your money each month.

Two other Quicken features work with the Financial Calendar: the Scheduled Transactions list and Billminder. Scheduled transactions are memorized transactions (see Chapter 5) that get entered automatically when they're due. Billminder pops up when you start your computer and reminds you of scheduled transactions.

Chapter 7

Working with the Calendar

To display the calendar, choose Activities > Calendar, or click the Calendar button in the task bar (**Figure 7.1**). The Financial Calendar will appear (**Figure 7.2**). The current day is automatically highlighted and each financial transaction you've made in the current month is listed in black text on its respective date. Scheduled transactions that have not yet been paid are listed in blue text.

The controls at the top of the Financial Calendar let you change the month or year that is displayed. Controls at the bottom of the calendar let you view transactions for your accounts and enter new transactions.

To add a new transaction:

1. In the Calendar, select the date on which you wish to schedule a transaction.

2. At the bottom of the Calendar window, click the New Transaction button. The Enter Transaction window appears (**Figure 7.3**). If you choose a future date, the same window appears, this time labeled Schedule Future Transaction.

Figure 7.1 Click the Calendar button to display...well, the calendar.

Month pop-up menu — *Previous month* — *Next month* — *Year pop-up menu*

Account selection — *Current day*

Figure 7.2 If you like, you can do all your data entry in the Financial Calendar.

Write checks — *Account register mode* — *Online payments*

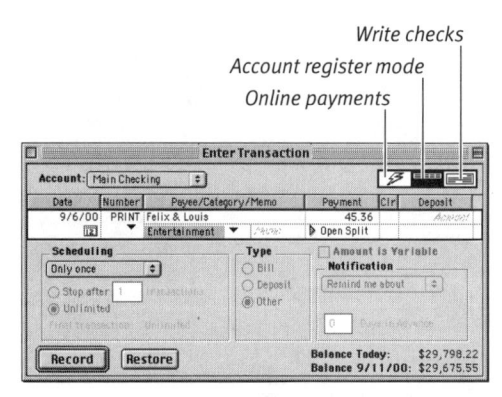

Figure 7.3 The Enter Transaction screen's default mode acts like an account register.

68

Using the Calendar

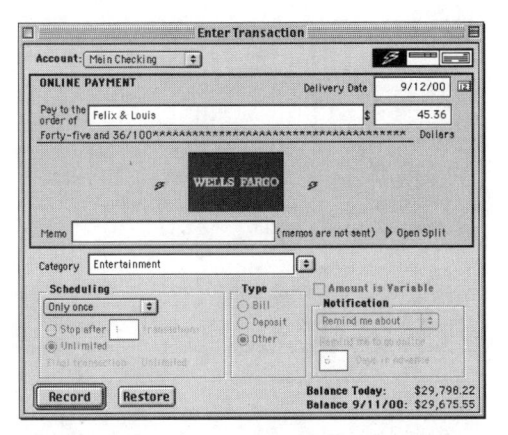

Figure 7.4 If you'd rather pay your bills online, you can do so in the Enter Transaction window's online payment mode.

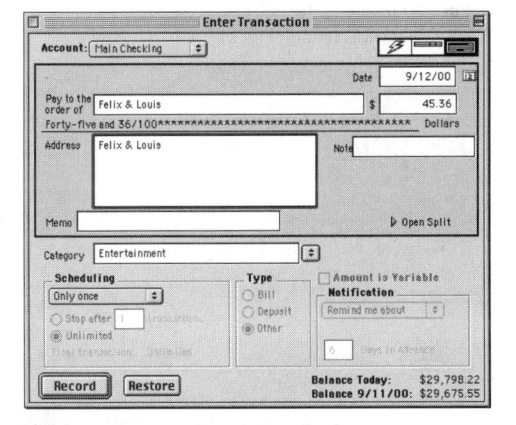

Figure 7.5 If you prefer printing checks, you can use write checks mode.

3. Using the buttons in the upper-right corner of the Enter Transactions window, choose the mode in which you want to enter the transaction.

   By default, the Enter Transaction screen is set to account register mode, in which you can enter a transaction just as you enter a transaction into an account register. If you plan to create transactions that will be sent via online bill payment and have already enabled online bill payment (see Chapter 11), you can switch to that mode, as shown in **Figure 7.4**. Or you can enter Calendar transactions in the familiar write checks mode, as shown in **Figure 7.5**.

4. Click the Account pop-up menu to see the Account list. Choose the account against which you'll apply the transaction.

5. By default, the current date appears in the Date field. You can leave this date as is or change it to another date (past or future).

6. In account register mode, with the cursor in the Number field, press the Plus key ([+]) on your keyboard to enter the next check number. If you plan to print the check, you could instead type PRINT in the Number field.

7. Enter the payee's name.

   As you're typing, QuickFill looks at names it has learned. If it finds a match, it adds the name. If this name is incorrect, you can simply change it.

8. In the Payment field, enter the amount if QuickFill hasn't already.

9. Type in the category or click the down arrow in the Category area to select the category of the transaction.

(continued)

10. Enter a memo about the transaction (optional).

11. If necessary, split the transaction. See Chapter 4 for more about splitting transactions.

12. If this is a one-time transaction, leave the frequency pop-up menu in the Scheduling area set to "Only once." If this will be a recurring transaction, select how often it will recur from the Scheduling pop-up menu (**Figure 7.6**).

13. Setting a recurring transaction makes the rest of the Scheduling controls active (**Figure 7.7**). In the Duration area, select either the "Unlimited" or the "Stop after [blank] transactions" radio button and fill in the blank.

    In the Type area, click the Bill, Deposit, or Other radio button.

    If the transaction has a variable amount, click the "Amount is Variable" checkbox. Quicken will present the scheduled transaction with a blank amount but will fill in all of the other information for you.

14. In the Notification pop-up menu, choose either "Remind me about" or "Automatically enter." Whichever you choose, to enter the information in advance of the selected date, fill in the "Days in Advance" field with a number.

15. Click Record to save the transaction.

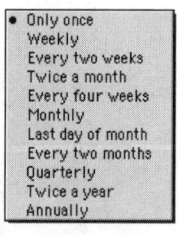

Figure 7.6 The Scheduling pop-up menu allows you to select how often a transaction will recur.

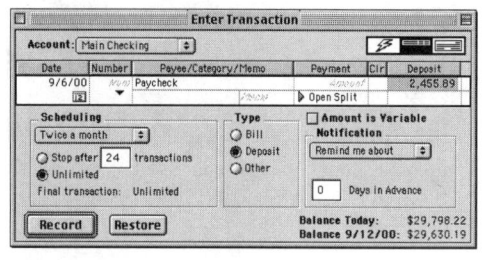

Figure 7.7 In any of the entry modes, you can schedule a transaction to recur.

✔ Tip

- When you want to move around in the Calendar, the same shortcut keys work as when entering dates in an account register. For a list of these shortcut keys, see **Table 4.1** in Chapter 4.

Using the Calendar

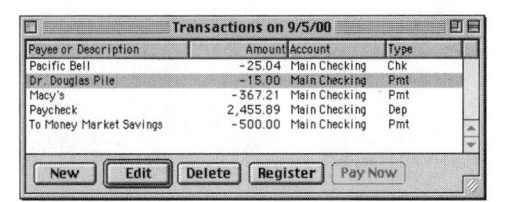

Figure 7.8 Double-click a day in the Calendar window to open the Transactions window that lists all transactions scheduled for or that occurred on that day.

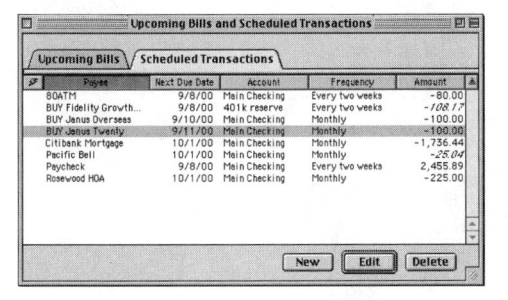

Figure 7.9 You can view upcoming bills and transactions in the Scheduled Transactions window.

To edit a transaction:

1. In the Financial Calendar, double-click the day that contains the transaction that you want to edit. The Transaction window for that day appears, as shown in **Figure 7.8**.

2. Double-click the transaction that you want to edit. The Edit Transaction window, which looks and acts exactly like the Enter Transaction window, appears.

3. Make any changes you want, and then click the Record button.

To view scheduled transactions:

1. Choose Lists > Scheduled Transactions. A window appears showing you your upcoming transactions (**Figure 7.9**). The window shows recurring transactions with their frequency, so rather than listing every future instance of a transaction that happens twice a month, it only lists the transaction's next due date and "Twice a month" in the Frequency column.

2. You can create a new scheduled transaction or edit or delete existing transactions using the buttons at the bottom of the Upcoming Bills and Scheduled Transactions window.

71

To delete a transaction:

1. In the Financial Calendar, double-click the day that contains a transaction that you want to delete. The Transaction window for that day appears (**Figure 7.8**).

2. Click the transaction to select it.

3. Click the Delete button in the Transactions window.

4. Quicken will ask you to confirm the deletion. Click the Yes button to delete the transaction.

5. Close the Transactions window.

✔ Tip

- Remember that entering or deleting a transaction in the Calendar also adds or gets rid of it in an account register.

Using the Calendar

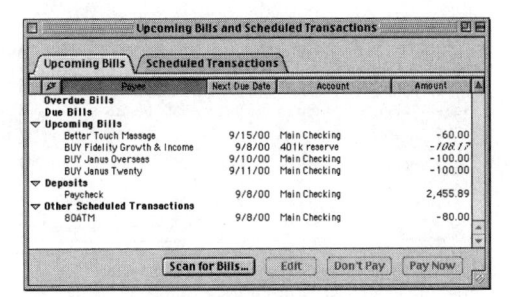

Figure 7.10 The Upcoming Bills and Scheduled Transactions window is where you'll begin scanning your transactions for possible scheduling.

Figure 7.11 Select one the transactions in the Bill Candidates window, and then click the Schedule button.

Scheduling and Paying Your Bills

One of the best new features in Quicken 2001 is the way that it proactively scans the transactions in your account registers, taking note of which ones occur on a regular basis. Quicken then offers to turn those recurring transactions into scheduled transactions. The idea is to automate those recurring transactions so that you don't accidentally forget to pay some bills.

People upgrading from prior versions of Quicken will notice that while converting your data into Quicken 2001 format, the program scans for recurring payments and offers to let you turn them into scheduled transactions. Naturally, if you're new to Quicken, there won't be any recurring payments in your data file, and you won't get the offer.

When you have your bills scheduled, you can work in the Upcoming Bills and Scheduled Transactions window to edit, pay, or skip paying a bill.

To schedule your bills:

1. Choose Lists > Bills, or press ⌘B. The Upcoming Bills and Scheduled Transactions window appears (**Figure 7.10**).

2. Click the Scan for Bills button. The Bill Candidates window appears (**Figure 7.11**).

   In the Bill Candidates window, payment amounts that remain the same in every transaction appear in plain text and transactions where the amount has varied appear in italics.

73

Chapter 7

3. Select one of the transactions in the Bill Candidates window.

4. Click the Schedule button. The Schedule Future Transaction window appears (refer to **Figure 7.7**), with most of the information already filled in.

   Make any changes necessary, and then click the Record button.

   A dialog box will appear asking you if you want to schedule all transactions or only future transactions (**Figure 7.12**). You'll usually only want to schedule future transactions. Make your choice, and then click OK. The transaction will be added to the Scheduled Transactions list and will also show up in the Upcoming Bills list.

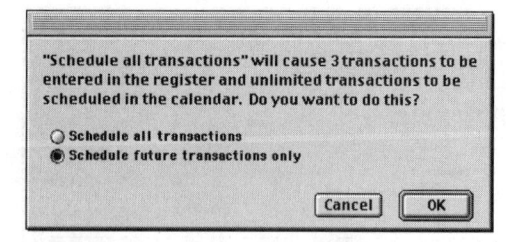

Figure 7.12 You can choose whether you want to schedule all or just future transactions.

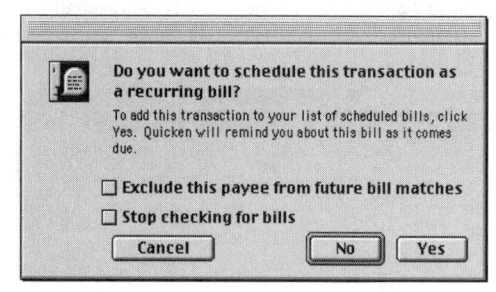

Figure 7.13 Especially if you're new to Quicken, it will offer to schedule transactions quite often. You can expect to see this dialog box less as time goes on.

✔ **Tips**

- The Upcoming Bills window and scheduled transactions replace the transactions groups feature in previous versions of Quicken. If you used transactions groups in Quicken 98 or 2000, they will be automatically converted into scheduled transactions when you first open your data file in Quicken 2001.

- You can sort the list of transactions in the Bill Candidates window by clicking any of the column headers. Clicking the sort triangle to the right of the column headers reverses the sort direction.

- As you enter transactions, you'll find that Quicken is always on the lookout for possible recurring bills. After you put the same (or similar) transaction into Quicken a few times, you'll see the dialog box in **Figure 7.13**, asking you if you want to turn the transaction into a bill. Clicking Yes opens the Schedule Future Transactions window. You can also tell Quicken to ignore this payee in the future or even to stop checking for bill matches altogether.

Using the Calendar

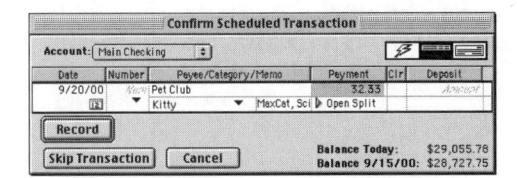

Figure 7.14 Once you've decided to pay a scheduled transaction, you'll need to confirm it.

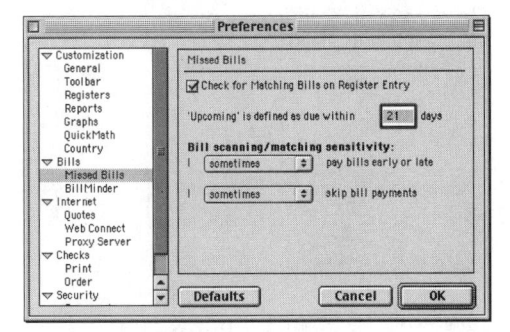

Figure 7.15 Set Quicken's sensitivity to Missed Bills in this Preferences panel.

To pay your bills:

1. Choose Lists > Bills, or press ⌘ B. The Upcoming Bills and Scheduled Transactions window appears.

2. If necessary, click the disclosure triangle to view the transactions in any of the categories.

3. Select the transaction that you wish to pay.

4. Click the Pay Now button. The Confirm Scheduled Transaction window appears (**Figure 7.14**).

5. Click the Record button, or if you made a mistake, click the Cancel button.

✔ Tips

- If you don't want to pay a particular bill this month, you can select it and click the Don't Pay button in the Upcoming Bills and Scheduled Transactions window. It has the same effect as clicking the Skip Transaction button in the Confirm Scheduled Transaction window.

- If you feel that Quicken is suggesting transactions as bill candidates a bit too often, you can fine tune the program's sensitivity. Choose Edit > Preferences, and then click the Missed Bills category (**Figure 7.15**). You can turn off bill matching, set how far in the future Quicken should look for upcoming bills, tell Quicken how often you pay bills early or late, or skip bill payments altogether.

SCHEDULING AND PAYING YOUR BILLS

Chapter 7

Adding Calendar Notes

In addition to showing transactions, the Calendar can also contain notes, kind of like yellow sticky notes, that contain virtually any information—from personal notes to to-do lists to additional notes on the financial transactions for that day.

To create a calendar note:

1. In the Calendar window, select a date to which you wish to add a note.
2. At the bottom of the Calendar window, click the Add Note button. The note window for that date appears.
3. Enter the text for the note (**Figure 7.16**).
4. Close the window to save the note.
5. Quicken adds a small note icon to the day in which you created the note (**Figure 7.17**). To read the note in the future, double-click the note icon.

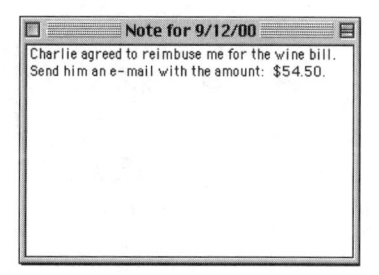

Figure 7.16 You can include any text you want in the Calendar's note window.

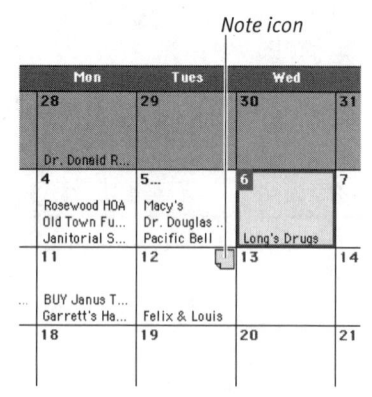

Figure 7.17 Double-click the note icon to recall your note.

Using the Calendar

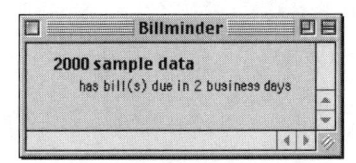

Figure 7.18 Billminder reminds you of pending—and overdue—transactions.

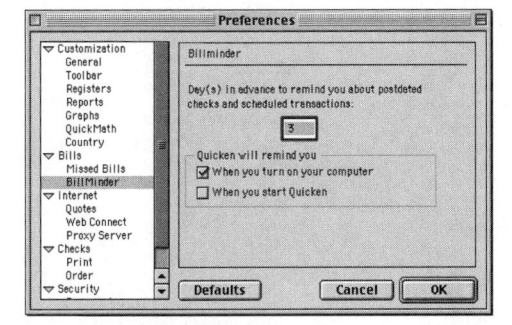

Figure 7.19 You can control the way Billminder works from the Preferences panel.

Using Billminder

Billminder is a feature that you can set to alert you of scheduled transactions as soon as you start up your Mac. (Don't worry, you can turn it off if you want.) Quicken doesn't have to be running for Billminder to do its job. Once Billminder pops up (**Figure 7.18**), you can either run Quicken and deal with the reminders or skip the reminders until the next time you start up the application.

To turn Billminder on:

1. Choose Edit > Preferences to open the Preferences dialog. Scroll down to the Billminder section (**Figure 7.19**).

2. Check either or both of the boxes in the Quicken will remind you area.

3. Set the days in advance field to whatever lead time you'd like. Click OK.

USING QUICKEN INSIGHTS

Quicken offers you a lot of control over your finances, and a virtual avalanche of supporting data that you can use to assess where you are in terms of reaching your financial goals. But this wealth of information, while useful, can also be overwhelming. It can take a long time to plow through several reports and registers to get the big picture of your investments, assets, and liabilities.

Quicken 2001's Insights feature organizes all of your financial information onto one page. From this home page, you can get the big financial picture and evaluate how you are doing in any personal finance area without having to rummage through different reports. The Insights page includes tables, graphs, and hypertext links called Actions that let you perform a whole range of Quicken tasks.

In this chapter, you'll learn how to use and customize Quicken's Insights page to get the information that you need.

Using the Insights Page

The Insights page is kind of a one-stop-shopping presentation of your whole Quicken file. There are up to 13 areas in the window, ranging from a summary of your accounts to graphs of your Net Worth and your Income and Expenses (**Figure 8.1**). Insights can be set up to present as much or as little information as you want in a variety of different forms.

Each of the areas on the page is presented as a main display—either a list or a graph—and some Observations and Actions that allow you to do something with the information in front of you.

On the Insights page, you can use the various Actions options to customize the individual items, editing lists, changing date ranges, and so on.

Using Quicken Insights

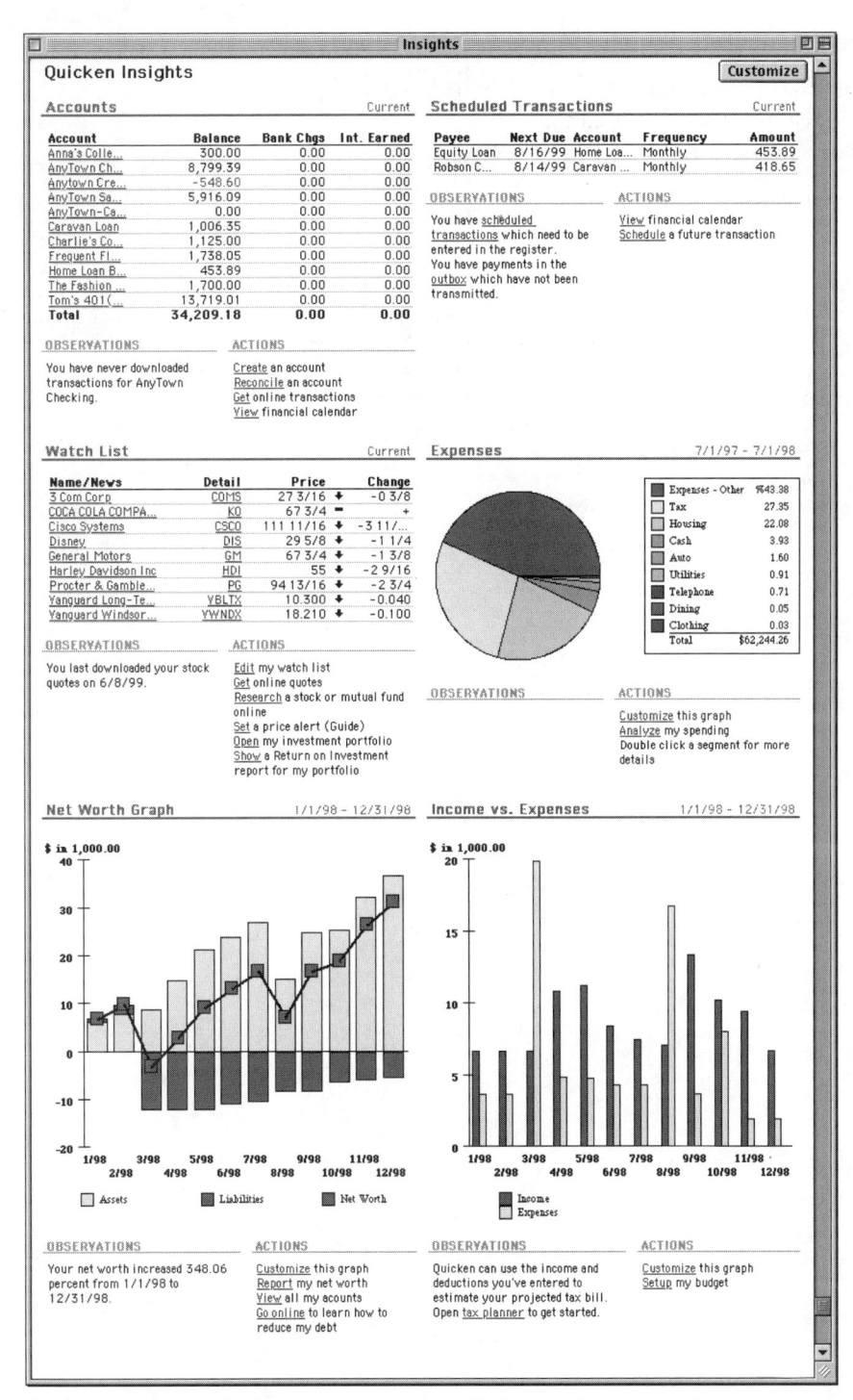

Figure 8.1 Quicken Insights presents huge amounts of information in a compact form.

Chapter 8

To customize the Insights page:

1. Open Insights by choosing Activities > Insights or by clicking the Insights button on the toolbar (**Figure 8.2**).

2. In the upper-right corner of the window, click the Customize button.

3. In the Customize Insights window (**Figure 8.3**), you can move items from the Available list to the Selected list and arrange the latter on the page with the Move Up and Move Down buttons.

4. When you're satisfied, click Done.

Figure 8.2 The Insights button on the toolbar takes you directly to the Insights page.

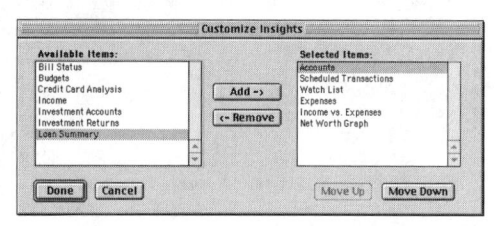

Figure 8.3 You can move items on or off the page from the Customize Insights dialog box.

Using Quicken Insights

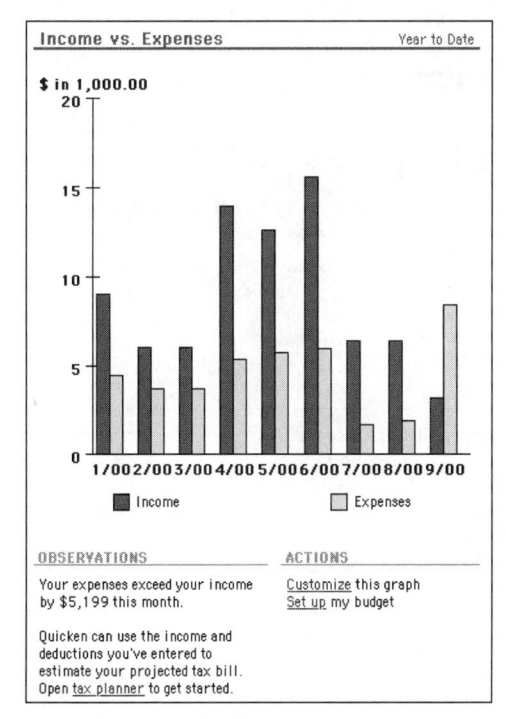

Figure 8.4 You can click this bar graph to reveal more information, and the links below it can be useful as well.

Adding to Your Insights Page

From the Customize Insights window, you can choose any of the following for your own personal Insights. Putting these on the page gives you immediate access to them and makes it much easier for you to move among your various accounts.

- **Accounts** presents a list of all your Quicken accounts with their current balances, bank charges, and interest earned. It includes Actions to create new accounts, reconcile your accounts, get online transactions, and open your Financial Calendar.

- **Bill Status** provides you with a list of upcoming bills, currently due bills, scheduled deposits, other scheduled transactions, and (hopefully not!) past due bills.

- **Budgets** gives you a rundown on how well you are keeping to your budget and helps you analyze your spending and even go online to learn how to reduce your debt.

- **Credit Card Analysis** shows your current charges, credit limits, and balances.

- **Expenses** shows a pie chart of your expenses by category and a detailed breakdown of your expenditures at the touch of a button.

- **Income** tracks your various categories of income and compares them to the same period last year. It links to the Investment Returns area and to a calculation of your net worth.

- **Income vs. Expenses** (**Figure 8.4**) is a bar graph that compares these two key measures of financial well-being on a monthly (or other period) basis. It also links you to the budget setup window and the tax planner.

83

Chapter 8

- **Investment Accounts** gives a capsule view of your money invested and links to your portfolio and to the online quote feature of Quicken.

- **Investment Returns** analyzes the performance of your investments.

- **The Loan Summary** section charts the balances and interest rates as well as the principle paid and the payments remaining on each of your loan accounts. It includes links to the Scheduled Transactions window to make payments and to the Web, where you can shop for mortgage rates.

- **The Net Worth Graph** area (**Figure 8.5**) graphs the change in your financial picture over time with the option of creating various detailed reports.

- **Scheduled Transactions** presents the information from the window of the same name in the main body of the Quicken program and provides a direct link to the Financial Calendar. Sometimes it gives you a gentle reminder that "you have scheduled transactions that need to be entered in the register."

- **The Watch List** (**Figure 8.6**) is a group of stocks and funds that you don't yet own but that you have chosen to track online. Insights provides access to an extensive range of analytic tools and online research on the Quicken Web site.

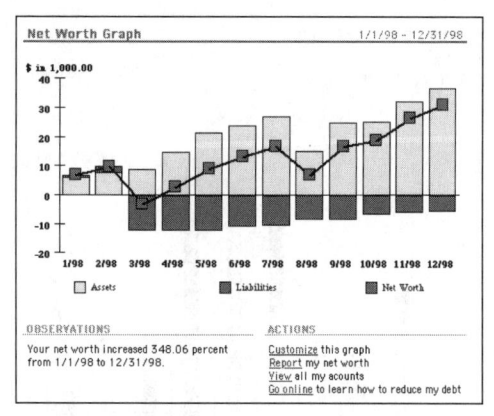

Figure 8.5 The Net Worth graph contains a lot of useful information.

Figure 8.6 The Watch List allows you to quickly download current prices and news items for a preset list of securities.

Using Quicken Insights

Diving Beneath the Surface

The amount of information you can access through the Insights page is not immediately obvious, but the mouse is a remarkably powerful tool here.

Clicking an underlined link in the Actions area triggers that function; in this way, Insights acts like a Web page, because clicking a link makes something happen. If the display area contains a graph, clicking a graph segment shows you the dollar amount of that segment, and double-clicking it opens a more detailed graph of the underlying data. You can keep drilling down through your data in this fashion until you get to the individual register transactions that are the basis for those fancy charts you began with.

The following is an example of drilling down through your financial data in the Insights window, using the Expenses pie chart as a starting point. You can begin on any of the other charts in the Insights window, of course.

To go deeper into the Insights page:

1. You can customize the chart by clicking on the Customize this Graph link at the bottom of the window and making your choices in the Customize Expense Comparison Graph window (**Figure 8.7**).

    In the first view (**Figure 8.8**), last year's expenses have been divided into 11 categories, including that always useful "Other."

2. Move the cursor over one of the segments (in this case, Taxes) (**Figure 8.9**) to turn it into a magnifying glass. Hold down the mouse button and up pops the dollar figure for the segment.

(continued)

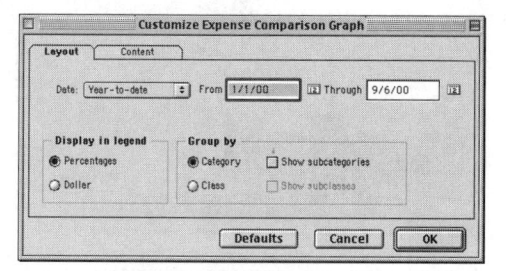

Figure 8.7 You can customize individual components of the Insights window in the windows that open from the main window.

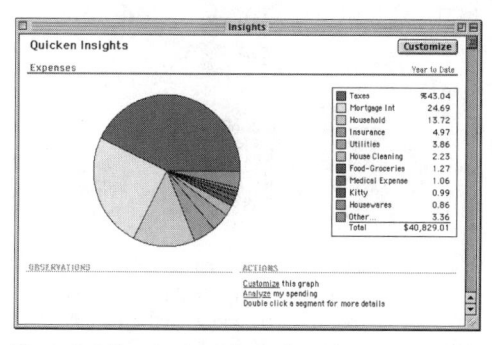

Figure 8.8 The pie chart shows how your expenses are distributed over a number of categories.

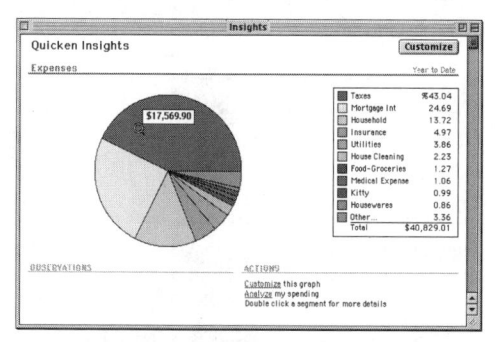

Figure 8.9 The magnifying glass shows the dollar figure represented by the pie slice.

85

Chapter 8

3. Double-click on another category (Kitty). Quicken zooms in and produces a bar graph of the month-to-month expenditures for that category (**Figure 8.10**).

   Again, the magnifying glass shows the dollar value of any individual month (**Figure 8.11**).

4. Double-click to bring up a detail report for the month (**Figure 8.12**).

5. Double-click a line of that report to go all the way back to the register in which the item is entered (**Figure 8.13**).

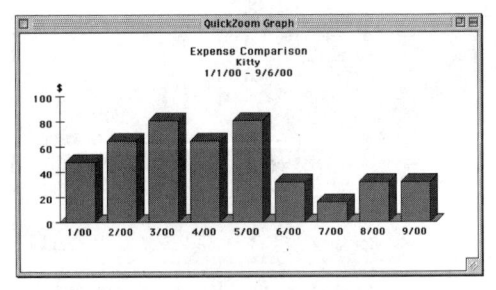

Figure 8.10 Double-clicking a segment of the pie chart opens a bar chart with details on that one segment.

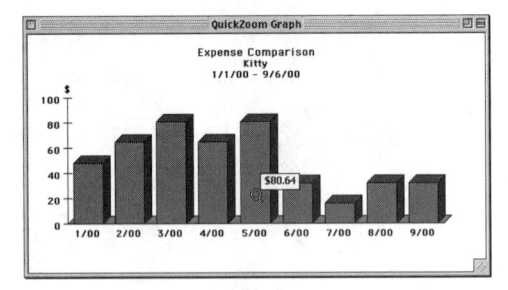

Figure 8.11 The magnifying glass shows the dollar value of each bar when the mouse button is held down.

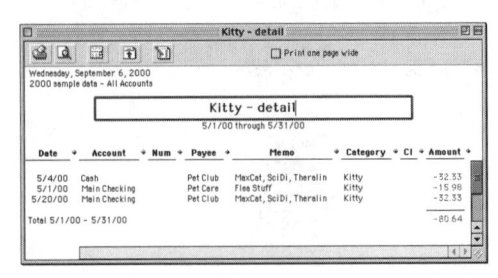

Figure 8.12 A double-click opens a report page for the month.

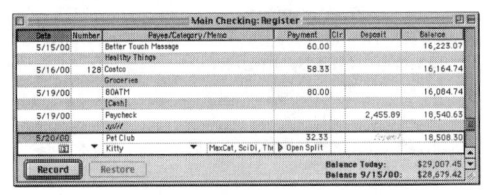

Figure 8.13 Double-clicking a line item in the report takes you all the way back to the original register entry.

Using Quicken Insights

On to the Internet

From other areas on the Insights page, you can jump to the Internet for more information and updates. Here are a few examples:

♦ Several of the investment-related areas link directly to the Quicken Quotes server (**Figure 8.14**), to download current prices for your Portfolio or Watch List, or through the Research Security dialog box (**Figure 8.15**) to Quicken.com's investment page on the Internet (**Figure 8.16**). For more about using Quicken and the Web, see Chapter 19.

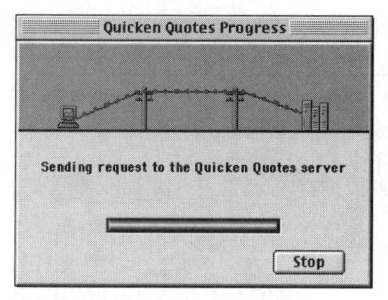

Figure 8.14 The Quicken Quotes server—and detailed security quotes—are just a click away.

Figure 8.15 You can find out more about an individual stock by clicking the Research link below the Watch List. You'll get the Research Security dialog shown here, which will produce detailed information about the security.

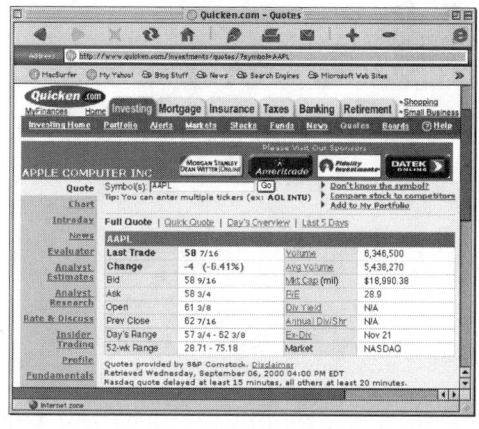

Figure 8.16 The Quicken.com quote page is a treasure trove of investment information.

Chapter 8

- The Net Worth and Loan Summary areas both have links to Quicken's mortgage page (**Figure 8.17**), which has a wealth of information and links to participating lenders.

- Budgets links to an online Debt Reduction Planner on Quicken.com's site (**Figure 8.18**) on the off-chance that your budget is not quite what it ought to be.

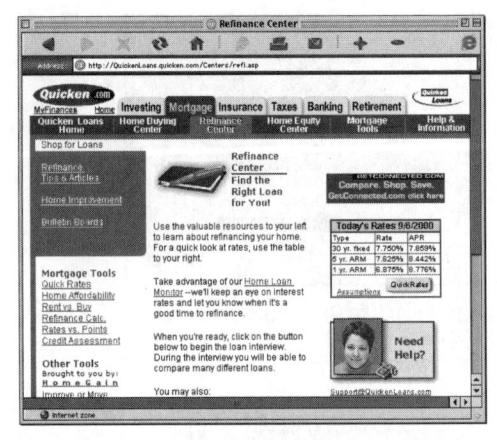

Figure 8.17 The Mortgage page has links to all kinds of tools, services, and assorted links.

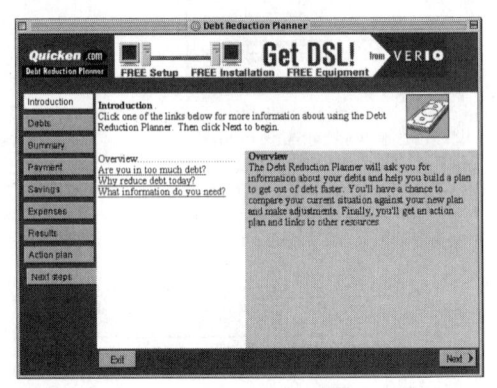

Figure 8.18 The Debt Reduction Planner is another example of the planning tools you can access on the Quicken.com Web site.

BALANCING YOUR ACCOUNTS

9

Balancing your checkbook is one of Those Chores—things that everyone knows you need to do, that everyone claims to do regularly, but that surprisingly few people actually accomplish. And who can blame them? Balancing your checkbook by hand is a pain, especially if you have slacked off for a few months and need to catch up.

Tracking your checking account and balancing your checkbook is the No. 1 reason that people buy Quicken: to do it for them. Quicken does a great job of reconciling accounts, and a chore that took an hour to do by hand is easy to do in just a few minutes.

Quicken isn't limited to just reconciling your checkbook, however. You can balance your savings, Money Market, or credit card accounts, too. In addition to balancing accounts, you can update balances in cash, asset, or liability accounts to reflect transfers of funds, payments made, or interest received.

In this chapter, you'll learn how to reconcile accounts, update account balances, and resolve any differences between the bank's records and your own.

Chapter 9

Balancing Accounts

You'll use the same procedure to balance a checking account, savings account, or Money Market account. First you enter your bank statement balance, and then you match transactions on your bank statement with transactions in your Quicken account register.

Balancing a credit card account works in almost the same way—except that if a balance is due on the credit card, Quicken will ask whether you want to make a payment at the end of the reconciliation process.

Before you begin, you should make sure that you have entered all transactions that occurred between the date of your last statement and the date of your current statement.

If you need to reconcile for more than one month, you first need to reconcile your account with the bank statements for each of the prior months before you try to reconcile the current month's statement.

To balance a checking, savings, or money market account:

1. Open the register for the account you want to balance by clicking its button (**Figure 9.1**) on the toolbar or by choosing Lists > Registers and selecting it on the list (**Figure 9.2**).

2. Click the Reconcile button in the toolbar (**Figure 9.3**), or choose Activities > Reconcile.

   The Reconcile Startup window appears (**Figure 9.4**).

3. Check to make sure that the beginning balance on your bank statement matches the amount in the Beginning Balance box in the Reconcile Startup window. If the amounts don't match, you'll need to click the Cancel button and fix the problem.

Figure 9.1 Click the account button on the toolbar to open the register.

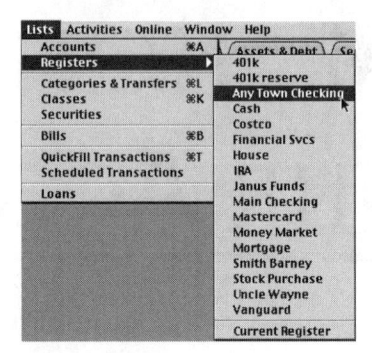

Figure 9.2 Select the account you wish to reconcile.

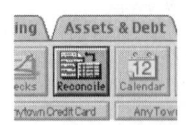

Figure 9.3 Click the Reconcile button to open the Reconcile Startup window.

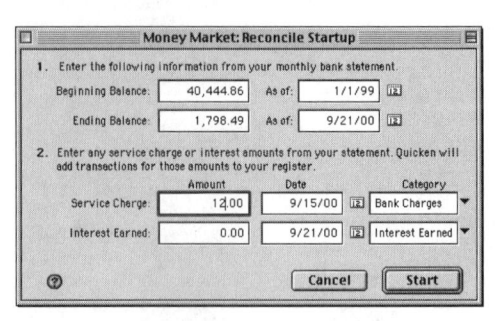

Figure 9.4 Check to make sure that the beginning balance on your bank statement matches the amount in the Beginning Balance box.

Balancing Your Accounts

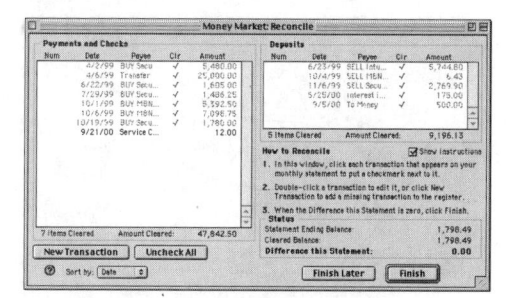

Figure 9.5 Click each transaction that has cleared on your bank statement in the Reconcile window.

Figure 9.6 Click the OK button in the Reconcile Complete window.

4. Enter the Ending Balance from your bank statement.

5. Enter the amount, date, and category of service charges or interest transactions.

6. Click the Start button to open the Reconcile window (**Figure 9.5**).

7. Click each transaction that has cleared on your bank statement.

   A checkmark appears next to each cleared transaction.

8. Double-click any transaction in error in the Reconcile window to open the account register and edit it. To add a missing transaction, click the New Transaction button at the bottom of the window to open the account register and make the addition.

9. As you check off each transaction, Quicken updates the "Difference this Statement" figure in the lower-right corner of the window. When you've checked off all the transactions, that figure should be zero. If it is, click the Finish button.

   If a difference amount still appears, skip to "Correcting Differences" later in this chapter to find out how to correct the problem.

10. If you balance successfully, the Reconcile Complete window appears (**Figure 9.6**). Click the OK button, and you're done!

✔ Tips

- At the bottom of the Reconcile window (refer to **Figure 9.5**), the Sort by pop-up menu lets you sort items in the lists by number or by date.

- Reconciliation problems occur for a variety of reasons, but it's usually because a previous month was not reconciled. See the Quicken User Manual for details on fixing beginning balance problems.

Chapter 9

To balance a credit card account:

1. Credit card accounts are balanced in almost the same way as checking, savings, or Money Market accounts. Follow steps 1 through 10 in the preceding section using a credit card account.

2. If you balance successfully, the Reconcile Complete window appears, which looks a bit different for credit card accounts (**Figure 9.7**).

3. If you want a make a payment on your credit card at this time, click the Yes button. The Pay Credit Card Bill window appears (**Figure 9.8**).

4. From the scrolling list of accounts, choose the account you wish to pay from, and then choose the means of payment using the Handwritten, Printed, or Electronic radio button.

5. Click the Pay button.

   Quicken enters the payment in the register for the account you selected. If you clicked Printed, Quicken will write a check for the payment (**Figure 9.9**).

Figure 9.7 Just as with your checking account, after you balance your credit card account successfully, the Reconcile Complete window appears.

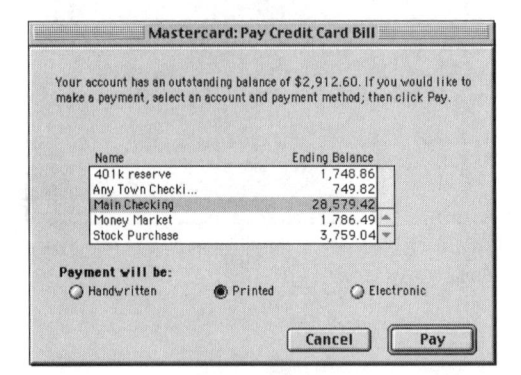

Figure 9.8 Click the Pay button to make a payment to your credit card account.

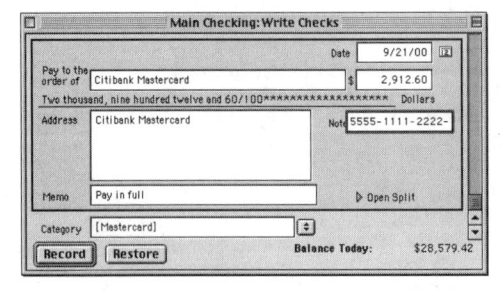

Figure 9.9 Quicken will write a check to pay off all (or a portion, if you change the check's amount) of your credit card account.

Correcting Differences

In the Reconcile window, if the "Difference this Statement" amount is not zero, it means that your account is not balancing for the current statement period. This usually occurs for one of two reasons: either a wrong number of payment or deposit items have been checked or some of the checked items have incorrect dollar amounts.

To find the mistakes:

1. Count the number of credit items on your bank statement, and then count the number of deposits shown in the Reconcile window. If the number doesn't match, you've found the problem.

   or

   Compare the number of checks and payments on your bank statement against the number of debit items in the Reconcile window.

   You might not have recorded an item in the register, or you might have duplicated a transaction, entered a payment as a deposit or a deposit as a payment, or marked an item cleared by mistake.

2. If the number of items is correct but the statement still doesn't balance, you have a problem with the dollar amount of one or more of your items. By hand or using a calculator, add up all the transactions shown under "Payments and Checks."

3. Compare the total with the total of debits on the statement.

   If the numbers don't match, you have a problem with the dollar amount of the debits.

4. Add up all the transactions shown under "Deposits" and compare them to the total of deposits on the statement.

   If those numbers don't match, there's a discrepancy in your deposit figures.

Letting Quicken Fix the Problem

If the dollar amount of an unreconciled balance is small, you may decide that it's not worth the time it takes to track down the mistake. In that case, you can let Quicken enter a register adjustment, which will force your account to reconcile.

If you click the Finish button in the Reconcile window while there is still a difference, Quicken will pop up the Adjust Ending Balance window (**Figure 9.10**). If you want Quicken to enter an account adjustment, click the Adjust Register button. If you want to take another whack at finding the mistake, click the Return to Reconcile button.

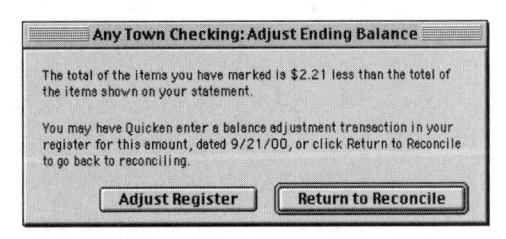

Figure 9.10 To have Quicken enter a balance adjustment for an account that just won't balance, click the Adjust Register button.

✔ Tips

- The most common mistake in this area is transposing two digits during data entry.

- If you're off by a small amount that is a round number (for example, $8.00, rather than $3.87), it's likely that you missed a bank service charge. Check your statement carefully for charges you don't normally see, such as those for check printing or using another bank's ATM.

- Using Online Banking (see Chapter 11) makes balancing your checkbook and other accounts even easier, because you download your bank and credit card statements directly into Quicken's account registers.

- Know when to quit. Unless you're the type who obsesses endlessly about that $2.53 you can't seem to account for, just let Quicken make the account adjustment. My rule of thumb is that if I can't balance after 15 minutes of trying, and the amount is under $20, I'll throw in the towel and make a balance adjustment. Adjust that rule to your own comfort level.

Dealing with Credit Cards

10

Credit cards are an incredibly convenient way to make purchases. They make it easy to buy things now and pay for them later. The price you pay for this convenience, of course, is the interest your credit card company charges as compensation for the loan of its money. And as purchases and interest charges mount, it's all too easy to get to the point where your credit card debt becomes overwhelming.

If you're already at the point where you are uncomfortable with the size of your debt load, you should use Quicken's Debt Reduction Planner to develop a plan to get out of debt. See Chapter 17 for more about the Debt Reduction Planner.

One way to make sure that your credit card debt doesn't spin out of control is to track it carefully on a monthly basis. That means categorizing your card charges so that you know where you're spending your money and reconciling your credit card accounts to make sure that spending doesn't slip by unnoticed.

It's also a good idea to take advantage of Quicken's built-in tools that let you know if you spend more than you want to in a particular category, help you find the best credit card rate, and help you set account limits.

Tracking Credit Card Transactions

Quicken offers two methods for tracking credit cards. The first method is to use the associated register for a credit card account to track each transaction separately (**Figure 10.1**). This method lets you see all the transactions within the credit card account, including the current balance; you can create more comprehensive reports about your spending; and it's easier to find and correct data entry errors. However, it does require a little more data entry (although if you arrange to download your credit card statement over the Internet, there's almost no data entry at all).

The other way to handle your credit card transactions is for those of you who always pay your bill in full each month. You would enter the credit card payment into your checking account register, creating a split transaction with a separate line for each purchase you made this month (**Figure 10.2**). This method saves a little bit of data entry and keeps all of your transactions within your checking account. You have to be a little more clever about selecting reports to display your spending, and if you run a balance, you won't be able to track that balance in Quicken; you'll need to refer to your paper statement. You also won't have any easy way to track credits to your credit card account.

I favor the first method of tracking. Sure, it's a bit more data entry, but if I do happen to run a balance for a particular month, I know just what that balance is. And it's much simpler to see where my purchases occurred without having to go into my check register and open each split transaction. Pick a method based on your spending and payment habits and on the importance of debt tracking in your situation.

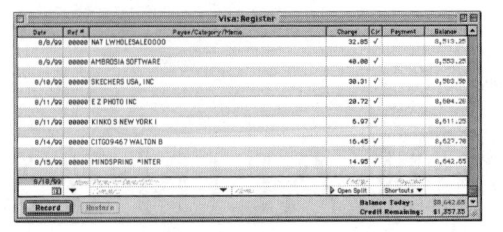

Figure 10.1 The best way to handle credit card transactions is to make all of your entries in a separate credit card account.

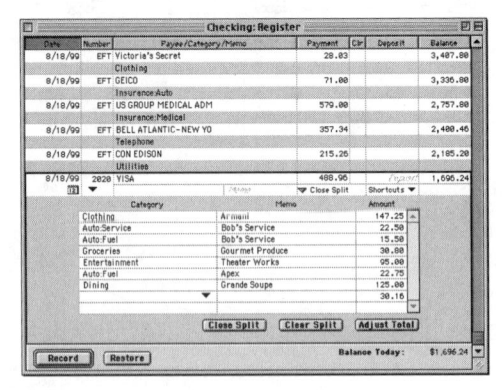

Figure 10.2 Another way to track credit cards is to make payments in your checking account register, creating split transactions to track the categories for your charges.

Dealing with Credit Cards

Figure 10.3 The Credit Card account button on the toolbar gives you direct access to your credit card register.

Figure 10.4 This pop-up calendar makes it easy to select a transaction date.

To enter a credit card transaction in a credit card account:

1. Click the button for your credit card register on the toolbar (**Figure 10.3**) or choose Lists > Registers > Credit card register from the menu to open the credit card account register.

2. If the credit card account you want isn't displayed, scroll the account tabs below the register until the account is visible and then click that tab to display the register.

3. The credit card account register appears (refer to **Figure 10.1**) with the current date filled in and the Date field highlighted. You can change the date by typing in a new date or by clicking the calendar icon underneath the date (**Figure 10.4**).

4. Press Tab to move to the Ref # field. This is usually unused in a credit card account (you might see a reference number entered here if you download your credit card statement), so press Tab again to move to the Payee field.

5. Enter the payee (for a charge) or the name of your credit card company (for a payment).

6. Enter the charge or payment amount.

7. Assign a category to the transaction by typing it into the Category field. The QuickFill feature fills in the category name from the pop-up menu after you enter the first few letters.

   or

   Use the pop-up menu in the Category field to select the category.

   (continued)

Chapter 10

8. Enter a memo about the transaction (optional).

9. Click the Record button (or press `Enter` on the keyboard).

   Quicken saves the transaction and adds it to the register (refer to **Figure 10.1**).

To enter credit card transactions in your checking account register:

1. Open the checking account register.

2. Enter the date, the check number, the name of your credit card company, and the total payment amount.

3. Click the Split button in the register. The Split Transaction window appears. Enter each charge to your account in the split lines.

4. Enter the category for the first charge in the first Category field in the split, either by typing in the category or by choosing it from the pop-up menu.

5. Type the name of the store or merchant in the first Memo field. If needed, also enter a description of the charge here.

6. Type the amount of the charge in the first Amount field. Quicken subtracts that amount from the total and puts the remainder in the next Amount field.

7. Enter the next category, merchant, and amount on the next line. Repeat this until you have allocated the entire payment or deposit amount and there is no unallocated figure remaining at the bottom of the amount column (refer to **Figure 10.2**). Click the Record button to save the transaction, which is now properly allocated to multiple categories.

Dealing with Credit Cards

Figure 10.5 Start the process of setting credit card limits in the Account list.

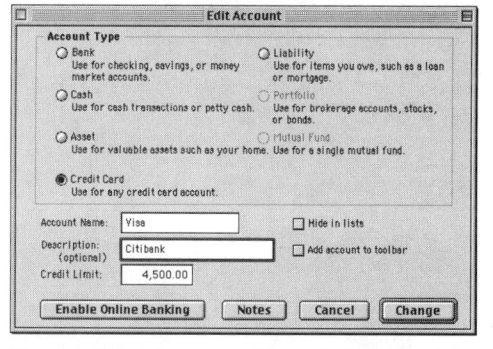

Figure 10.6 Update your credit card limit in the Edit Account window.

Controlling Credit Card Debt

Credit card debt is a particularly troubling form of debt; that piece of plastic is so easy to use that your level of debt can creep up without your even noticing it, and it is only rarely used for the kind of goods and services that can be considered investments. Furthermore, the interest rates on cards tend to be extremely high.

If you have entered a credit limit for your card, Quicken's credit card account registers show both the current balance and the Credit Remaining at the bottom. It is easy to see when you are approaching your limit, and when the Credit Remaining figure goes into the red (literally), you know it's time to take urgent action.

To enter your credit limit for a credit card account:

1. Choose Lists > Accounts. The Accounts list opens (**Figure 10.5**).

2. Click a credit card account to select it.

3. Click the Edit button at the bottom of the Account list window.

   The Edit Account window appears (**Figure 10.6**).

4. Enter the credit limit in the Credit Limit window, and then click Done.

✔ Tip

- One way to control your credit card debt is not to spend as much for debt service. That means using Quicken.com to find the best interest rates on credit cards; there's no reason to spend more money than necessary on interest. See Chapter 19 for more information on using Quicken.com.

Controlling Debt by Budgeting

Perhaps the most useful tools Quicken offers for controlling debt—and credit card debt in particular—are the Budget and Budget Monitoring functions. Obviously, spending more money than you are taking in is going to drive you deeper into debt, and more than likely, that means more and more dependence on credit cards. Using Quicken, you can set up both an overall budget for your accounts and individual budgets for specific categories and accounts. As I stated in the Introduction, I'm not a big fan of budgets overall, since I don't think—and studies bear me out—that most people adhere to their budgets. But you can use the Budget Monitoring tools to keep a close eye on your credit card use.

QuickBudget uses the data in your file to set up a starting point that you can then modify.

To set up a budget:

1. Choose Activities > Budgeting > Budget Setup, or click the Budget button on the Planning tab of the toolbar.

    The Create Budget window opens (**Figure 10.7**).

2. Click the Selected categories radio button, choose the categories you want to include in the budget from the resulting Select Categories dialog box, and then click OK to return to the Create Budget window.

3. Select the radio button for Use QuickBudget to open the QuickBudget window (**Figure 10.8**).

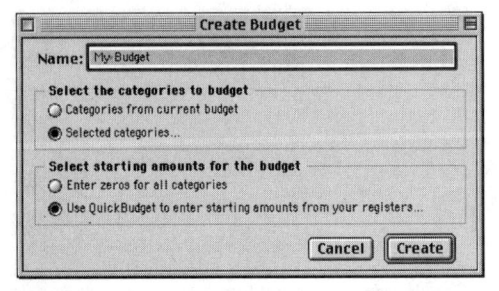

Figure 10.7 The Create Budget window sets up the categories for your budget.

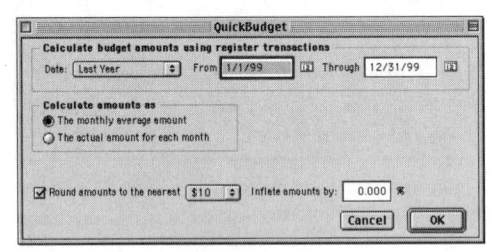

Figure 10.8 The QuickBudget option makes it easy to get the budget process started.

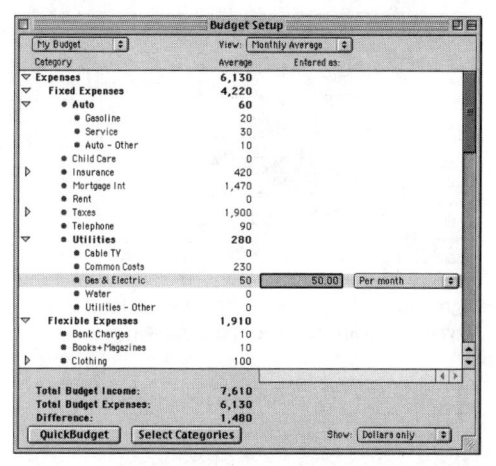

Figure 10.9 The Budget Setup window is a bit intimidating at first but easily managed in the end.

4. You can probably leave the settings as they are for the first pass, so click OK. Then Click Create in the Create Budget window.

   The Budget Setup window (**Figure 10.9**) opens with a long column of figures, many of them zeros.

5. Click any line and edit it by typing a new figure in the field that opens. You can delete the line by choosing Edit > Delete Item From Budget or by pressing ⌘D. When you are done, you can close the window by clicking the close box in the upper-left corner.

6. You can create additional budgets using these steps by choosing New Budget from the pop-up menu in the upper left of the window.

✔ Tip

- By setting up very specific budgets—for example, areas where you tend to overspend for discretional items like clothing, dining, and entertainment—you can keep a tight rein on your spending habits.

Using the Budget Monitor to Track Your Expenditures

One of Quicken's best tools for keeping your spending on track is the Budget Monitor. This gives you color-coded bars for each budget category that you wish to track; the color of the bar tells you if your spending this month is within budget, is getting out of hand, or should be cause for alarm.

To use Budget Monitoring:

1. Choose Activities > Budgeting > Budget Monitoring.

   The Budget Monitoring window opens (**Figure 10.10**).

2. From the pop-up menus across the top of the window, choose the budget and time period you want to look at.

3. Click the Set Up Monitoring button at the bottom-left corner of the window.

   The Set Up Monitoring window (**Figure 10.11**) opens.

4. Select the categories or category groups you want to view, and then click OK.

   The Budget Monitoring window will display a bar for each category or group chosen. The bars are colored green for Good, yellow for Caution, red for Danger.

5. Position the cursor over one of the bars and hold down the mouse button. The dollar figure for the category appears (**Figure 10.12**).

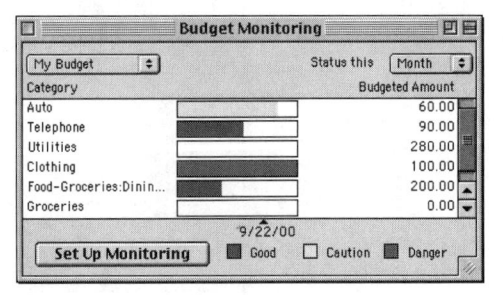

Figure 10.10 The Budget Monitoring window shows how well you are keeping to your budget.

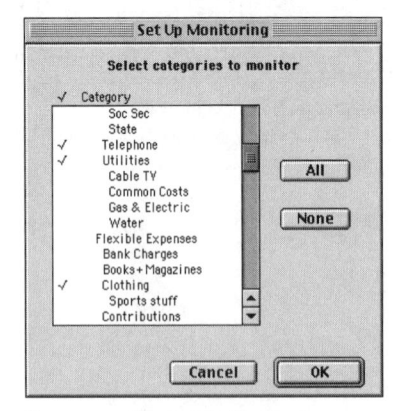

Figure 10.11 The Set Up Monitoring screen controls which categories are displayed.

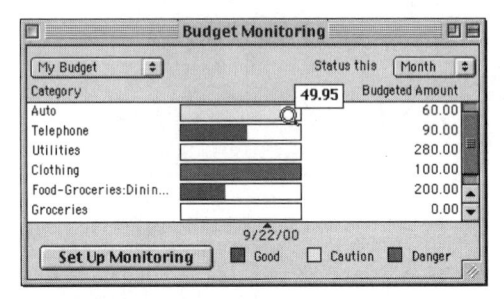

Figure 10.12 You can read the dollar figure for each bar by clicking it with the mouse.

Online Banking and Bill Paying

Using your computer to download bank statements and pay bills is a new and, to some people, a scary way of dealing with your bank. Yet it can save you a lot of time and a bit of money.

Banking online saves you time spent recording your checks, ATM withdrawals, or credit card transactions by hand. Instead, you download them from your bank, review the transactions to catch any possible errors and make sure they are properly categorized, and then add them to your account registers with the click of a button. Because the information is current as of the close of the previous banking day, you can monitor your cash flow more closely. This lets you make sure, for example, that deposits are credited to your account before you write checks and helps you to avoid expensive bounced check charges. You can balance your checkbook in minutes every time you download your statement, instead of the much longer time it takes when working with a paper statement. Best of all, there's never any waiting in line when you're online.

Online bill payment lets you transfer money from your checking account directly to your creditors. You don't have to write or print checks, stuff envelopes, find stamps, or go to the post office. You simply enter a payment instruction in an account register and have Quicken send it over the phone lines to your bank, which then transfers the money.

Applying for Online Banking

To use online banking, you must first have access to the Internet. You'll need an Internet Service Provider (ISP) and a modem or another connection (such as a DSL line or a cable modem) to the Internet. Information from Intuit's Web site about how to apply for online banking will be displayed on the Web browser you've set in your computer's Internet Control Panel.

You must contact your bank or other financial institution to get online access for checking, savings, and credit card accounts. Not all financial institutions support online banking, and some support it only for certain account types, such as checking but not credit card accounts. Even if your financial institution doesn't support online banking, you can still use online bill payment through Intuit. If you have accounts at more than one financial institution, you'll need to apply to each one separately.

Each financial institution sets its own fees for online banking. The fee amount varies from bank to bank, so it's a good idea to shop around for the best deal. You can find the most complete list of banks and their online banking fees on Intuit's Web site at http://www.quicken.com. Look for the Banking section, and then look for the Online banking link. You can also access the list from within Quicken 2001 by choosing Online > Financial Institutions (see **Figure 11.1**). You should click the Update List button, which will make Quicken connect to the Internet and download the latest list of financial institutions (nearly 700 when I wrote this). The Apply button in the Financial Institutions list opens your Web browser and takes you to the selected financial institution's Web page.

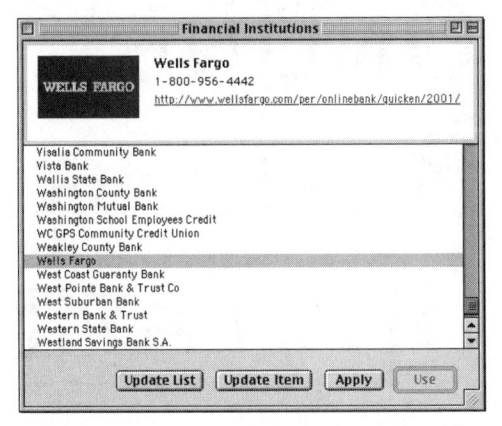

Figure 11.1 The Financial Institutions list, updateable via Quicken.com, gives you online contact information (and phone numbers) for the hundreds of financial institutions that support online banking through Quicken.

Online-enabled account

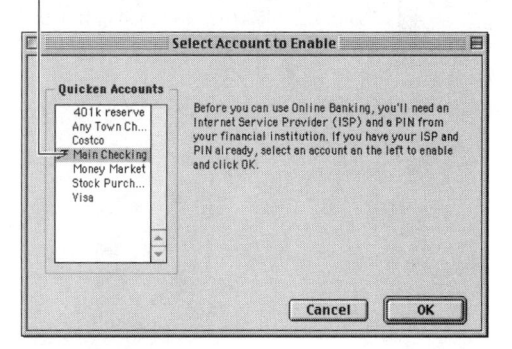

Figure 11.2 Select the account you want to set up for online service.

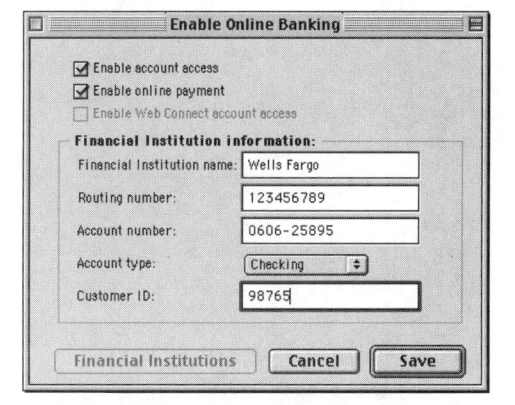

Figure 11.3 Check the boxes to enable electronic banking, and fill in the form below.

After you have signed up for online banking, your financial institution will send you a kit with information to help you set up your Quicken accounts for online banking. You'll also receive an initial personal identification number (PIN), which you should change in your first online banking session.

To enable a Quicken account for online use:

1. Choose Online > Enable Online Banking > Online Banking.

   The Select Account to Enable window appears (**Figure 11.2**).

2. Select the account you want to set up for online service, and then click OK.

   The Enable Online Banking window appears (**Figure 11.3**).

3. Click the Enable account access checkbox if you'll be using this account to download statements. Click the Enable online payment checkbox to use the account for bill payments.

4. Refer to the information kit you received from your financial institution to enter the financial institution name, routing number, account number, account type, and Customer ID, exactly as listed in the kit.

5. Click the Save button. You return to the Select Account to Enable window, which now shows a lightning bolt next to the account name, which indicates that it is enabled for online services.

6. Repeat steps 2 through 5 to enable other accounts.

Chapter 11

Going Online

The first time that you go online, it's a good idea to just download your current transactions. This gets you used to the process and lets you update your account registers. During this first session, your bank may prompt you to change your PIN.

Figure 11.4 Click the Download button to open the Download Transactions window.

To download transactions:

1. Click the Download button in the toolbar (**Figure 11.4**), or choose Online > Download Transactions.

   The Download Transactions window appears (**Figure 11.5**).

2. If you have online accounts at more than one financial institution, choose the financial institution you want from the pop-up menu below the institution's logo on the left side of the window.

Financial institutions pop-up menu
Downloaded transactions
Accept √ Items button
Last online balance
Account pop-up menu
Account register

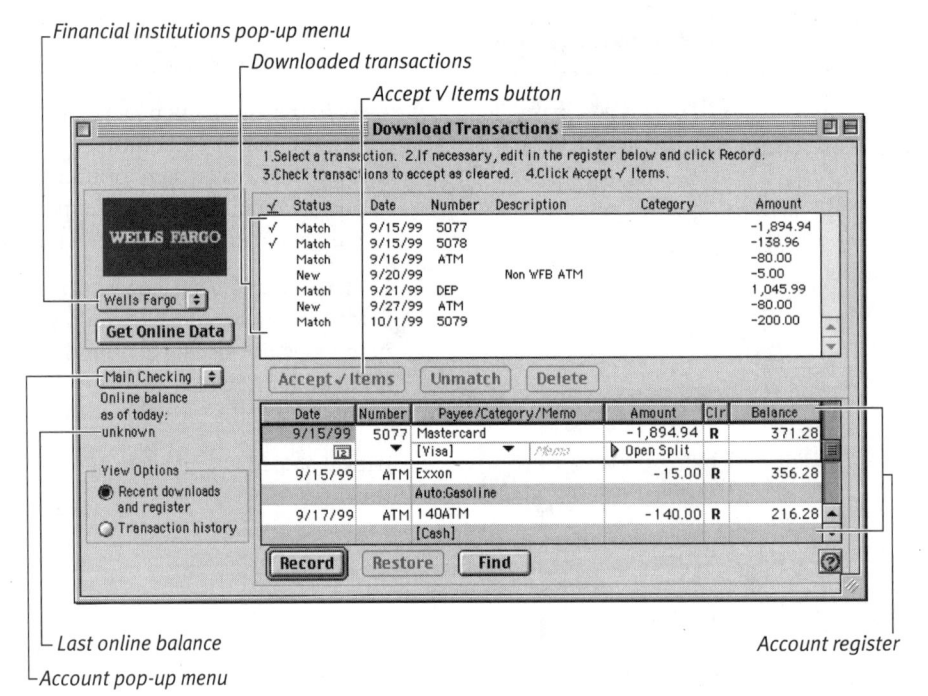

Figure 11.5 Start your online transactions from the Download Transactions window.

Online Banking and Bill Paying

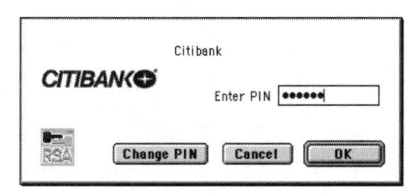

Figure 11.6 Enter your PIN, and click the OK button.

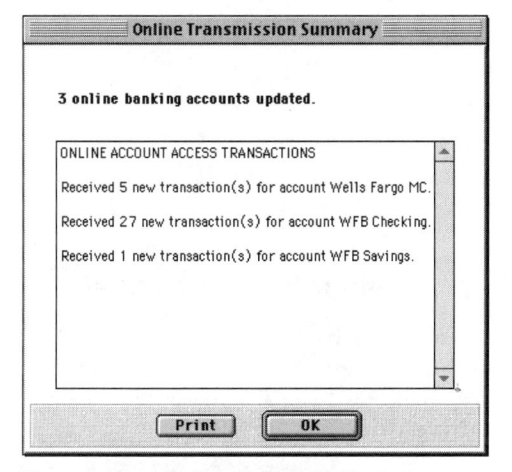

Figure 11.7 Review the information in the Online Transmission Summary window, and then click OK.

3. Click the Get Online Data button.

   Quicken connects to the Internet and then asks for your PIN (**Figure 11.6**).

4. Enter your PIN, and then click the OK button.

5. Review the information in the Online Transmission Summary window (**Figure 11.7**), and then click OK.

   Quicken displays the downloaded transactions in the top half of the Download Transactions window. You can sort the downloaded transactions by clicking one of the column titles.

   Quicken compares the downloaded transactions with transactions that are already in your account register. If the transactions correspond, the word "Match" appears next to the downloaded transaction in the Download Transaction window.

6. Click each matched transaction to place a checkmark next to it, signifying that it is ready to be cleared in your register.

   If Quicken doesn't find a match for a downloaded transaction, the transaction appears in the list in the Status column marked "New." Quicken marks a transaction as New when you haven't yet entered that transaction in your account register or when the check number or amount differs from the transaction that you entered.

7. For these New transactions, you'll need to enter the missing payee and/or category information. Select the New transaction in the transaction list.

   Quicken displays the transaction in the register at the bottom of the Download Transactions window.

   (continued)

107

8. Make your changes in the register, and then click the Record button. The transaction's status will change to "Match." Click the newly matched transaction to place a checkmark next to it.

9. Repeat steps 7 and 8 for every New transaction.

10. Click the Accept ✓ Items button.

    Quicken adds the checked items to the account register marked cleared and removes them from the transaction list in the Download Transactions window.

✓ Tips

- Your financial institution may label ATM transactions and service charges as EFT, which stands for Electronic Funds Transfer.

- Quicken doesn't close the Internet connection after it finishes downloading, so if you're using a dial-up connection with a modem, you must close it manually.

- You can edit your transactions to change the category either before or after updating your register, but it's usually easier to do it in the Download Transactions window.

Is Online Banking Secure?

Since online banking and online bill payment transactions travel over the Internet, it's perfectly reasonable to wonder if your financial data can be intercepted and used by criminals. Quicken's security measures make it extremely unlikely.

The first line of defense is the Personal Identification Number (PIN) that you must enter whenever you use online banking or bill payment. When you first sign up for online banking, your bank sends you a PIN that you can (and should) change. After you change it, you're the only one who knows that PIN. For extra security, you should change your PIN on a regular basis.

For additional security, Quicken encrypts all transferred information—back and forth. Encryption is a technique that scrambles data before it is sent using a mathematical algorithm. At the other end, your bank unscrambles the data. (For those more technically inclined, Quicken uses 128-bit DES [Data Encryption Standard] encryption along with SSL [Secure Sockets Layer] transfer protocols.)

Paying Bills Online

To make online bill payments with Quicken, you'll first need to set up the payment recipients in the Payee list. To send a payment, you just select a payee from the list, create the payment instruction, and send it to your financial institution.

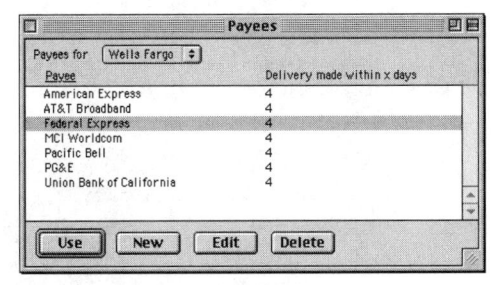

Figure 11.8 Click the New button to open the Set Up Payee window.

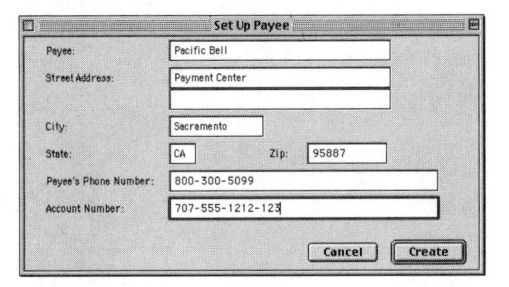

Figure 11.9 Enter the new payee's information and account number.

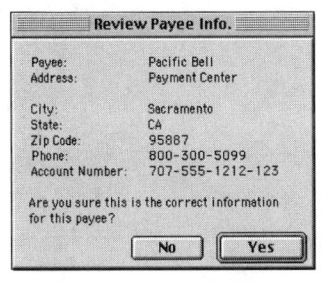

Figure 11.10 Review the payee information, and if correct, click Yes to store it in the Payees list.

To set up a payee:

1. Choose Online > Payments > Online Payees or select Online Payees from the EPay menu on the Banking section of the toolbar.

   The Payees window appears (**Figure 11.8**).

2. Click the New button.

   The Set Up Payee window appears (**Figure 11.9**).

3. Enter the payee's name, address, and phone number.

4. Enter the account number that the payee uses to identify you. If the payee doesn't use account numbers, enter your name.

5. Click the Create button. Quicken will present a dialog box asking you to review and verify the payee information (**Figure 11.10**). If it is correct, click the Yes button; otherwise, click the No button and correct the payee information.

   After you verify the information, Quicken adds the new payee to the Payee list.

Chapter 11

To create and send an online payment:

1. Open the register you want to use to make the payment.

2. Use the EPay button in the Banking section of the toolbar (**Figure 11.11**) to select Enter Payment, or choose Online > Payments > Enter Payment from the main menu. The Enter Online Payment window appears (**Figure 11.12**).

3. Choose Online > Payments > Online Payees to open the Payees window.

4. In the Payees window, select one of the payees, and then click the Use button. The payee's name is transferred to the Enter Online Payment window.

5. Fill in the amount and the category of the payment in the Enter Online Payment window.

6. If you plan to create more online payments in the current session, click the Put in Out Box button. Quicken stores the payment in a list of instructions to send to your financial institution the next time you connect. If this is the only payment you are making, you can click the Send Now button and Quicken immediately connects online, prompts you for your PIN, and sends your payment instruction.

7. If you put payments into the Out Box, click the Out Box button in the Banking section of the toolbar (**Figure 11.13**). The Out Box appears (**Figure 11.14**).

8. Review the items in the Out Box, and if you're satisfied, click the Send Now button. Quicken connects to your financial institution and sends the payments.

Figure 11.11 Click the EPay button in the banking section of the toolbar to open the Enter Online Payment window.

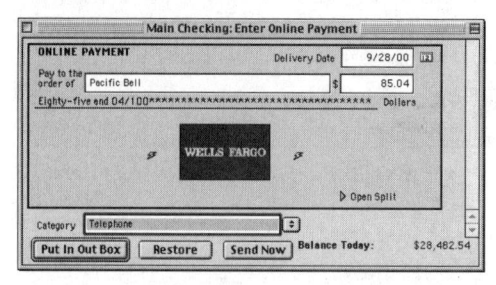

Figure 11.12 The Enter Online Payment window looks like a check. Fill it in with QuickFill's help.

Figure 11.13 Click the Out Box button in the toolbar to review transactions in the Out Box.

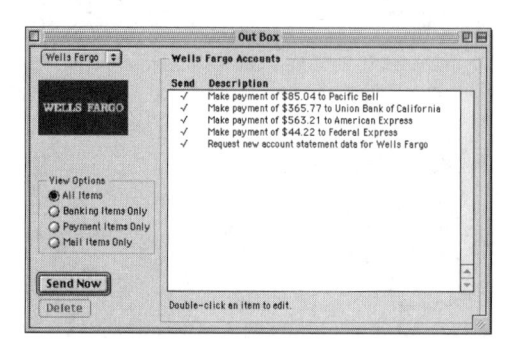

Figure 11.14 If you're satisfied with the pending online transactions, click Send Now.

✔ Tips

- If your payee is set up to receive electronic funds transfers, payment is transferred directly from your account to your payee's account. This usually takes less than two business days. If the payee doesn't accept EFTs, your financial institution prints a check and sends it to the payee by U.S. mail. It's important that you allow sufficient time for the payment to get to the payee to avoid a late charge. So make sure that you schedule payments at least three or four days before a payment due date.

- Don't forget that a payee will often need a day or two after receiving a check to process the payment and credit your account.

12

CREATING REPORTS

I have to admit that before I started using Quicken, my financial house was not exactly in order. Like many people, I had built up a bit too much credit card debt; I balanced my checkbook twice a year, whether it needed it or not; and although I knew that money was coming in and money was going out, I didn't know just where all that money was going.

Quicken's reports, one of its most powerful tools, went a long way toward solving my financial problems by giving me a comprehensive picture of my finances. After using Quicken for just a few months, I had a good record of how much I was spending and where I was spending it. I could also see how much I was spending on interest, which really gave me the impetus to pay off those bills.

One of the best features of Quicken reports is that you can use them to look at your financial data in different ways. You can view your finances in as much or as little detail as you need, and you can pull out just the information that you want. For example, at tax time, I pull a report to show all of my tax-deductible expenditures for the previous year, all neatly categorized and totaled. My accountant appreciates it (anything would be better than that shoe box of loose receipts I use to drop on his desk), and because using the reports takes less of his time, it saves me money.

Using Reports

Quicken comes with a variety of report templates that cover most of the questions you have about your finances. You can customize those reports to zero in on just the information that you want.

You can get six kinds of reports from Quicken: EasyAnswer reports, QuickReports, Standard reports, Memorized reports, Shortcut reports, and Register and List reports.

You use a slightly different method to create each kind of report. You can move among different kinds of reports by using the tabs at the top of the Reports window. The scrolling window at the left side of the window displays the names of Quicken's report templates. When you click the name of a report template, Quicken shows you a sample of that report on the right side of the Reports window.

Using EasyAnswer Reports

EasyAnswer reports give you quick answers to eight basic questions, such as "Where did I spend my money?" and "What are my investments worth?"

To create an EasyAnswer report:

1. Click the Reports button in the Reporting tab of the toolbar (**Figure 12.1**) or choose Activities > Reports & Graphs > Reports to open the Reports window (**Figure 12.2**).

2. Click the EasyAnswer tab. Quicken displays the EasyAnswer report window (**Figure 12.3**). This window shows eight basic questions that you can ask about your finances. Select the radio button for the question that you want to ask.

3. If necessary, adjust the date range by choosing a new time frame from the pop-up menu next to the radio button that you clicked.

4. If you picked a question that requires it, choose a category from the pop-up menu next to the question to narrow your report.

5. Click the Create button. Quicken displays the report on your screen (**Figure 12.4**).

Figure 12.1 Click the Reports button on the toolbar to open the Reports window.

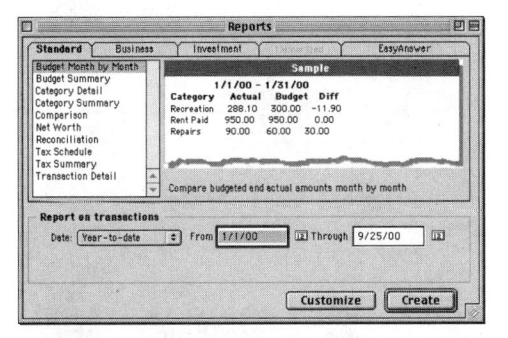

Figure 12.2 The Reports window gives you access to a wide variety of report templates.

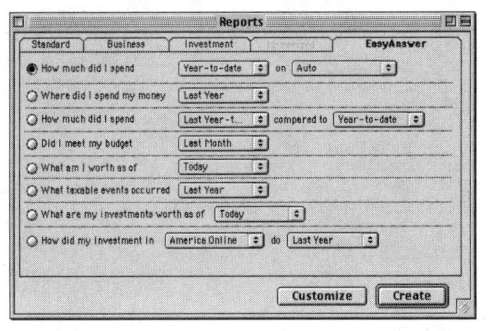

Figure 12.3 EasyAnswer reports offer quick and basic information about your finances.

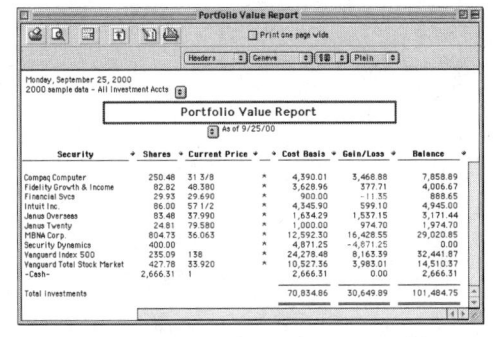

Figure 12.4 An example of a Quicken report. This one answers the question, "What are my investments worth as of...?"

115

Using QuickReport

A QuickReport is a transaction detail report that offers only a few options; it's designed to give you fast information for one specific payee, category, account, or security.

To create a QuickReport:

1. Click the QuickReport button in the Reporting tab of the toolbar (**Figure 12.5**) to open the Create QuickReport dialog box (**Figure 12.6**).

2. Choose the source for the report from the pop-up menu. Your choices are Payee & Description, Category, Class, Memo, Account, or Security.

3. Type in your search criteria.

4. Choose the date range for the QuickReport from the pop-up menu next to Date.

5. Click OK. Quicken grinds through its data file and presents a transaction report based on your criteria (**Figure 12.7**).

Figure 12.5 Click the QuickReport button in the toolbar to open the QuickReport dialog box.

Figure 12.6 Enter information in the Create QuickReport dialog box for fast report results.

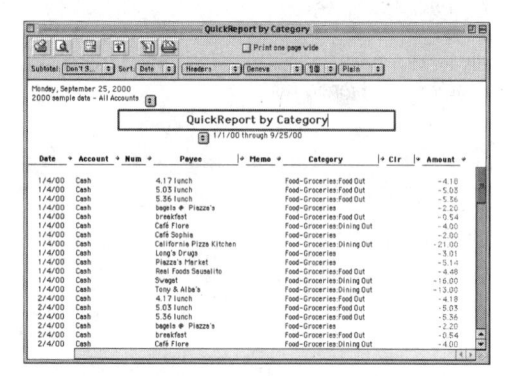

Figure 12.7 A transaction report created with the QuickReport feature. In this report, we searched for all transactions from last year-to-date where the category was Groceries.

Creating Reports

Magnifying glass cursor

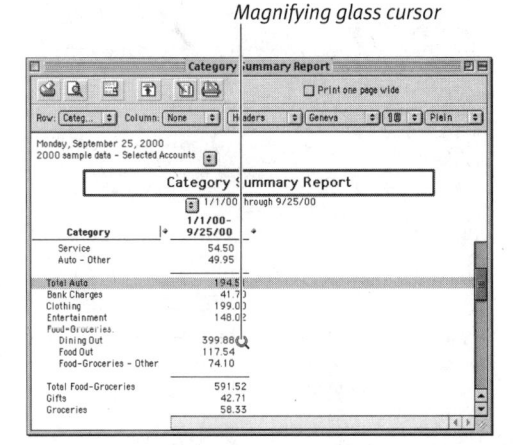

Figure 12.8 When the cursor turns into a magnifying glass, you can zoom in for more detailed information by double-clicking.

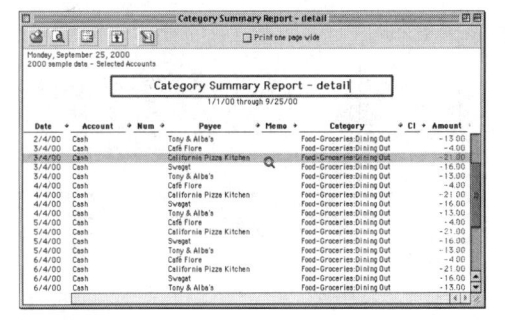

Figure 12.9 The detail transaction report produced by zooming in on a category—in this case, Groceries.

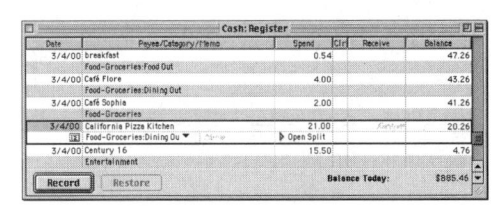

Figure 12.10 Zooming further, the final detail shows the original transaction in the account register.

Zooming in on the Details

You can use QuickZoom to examine the information in your reports in greater detail. If you're viewing a report that summarizes the amounts from a category, you can double-click an amount and QuickZoom will take you to another report that shows more detail about the item you selected. But if you use QuickZoom in a transaction report, Quicken opens the register and shows you the original transaction.

To use QuickZoom:

1. Create a report summarizing expenses by category. (That's just an example; you can actually create any sort of report you wish.)

2. In the open report window, move the cursor over one of the amounts in the report until the cursor turns into a magnifying glass (**Figure 12.8**).

3. Double-click the amount of a category. A new transaction report window opens showing you the detailed transactions for the category (**Figure 12.9**).

4. To view an original transaction, double-click an amount in the detailed transaction report window. The account register for the transaction opens, with the transaction selected (**Figure 12.10**).

117

Chapter 12

Using Standard Reports

Standard reports give you basic information, such as details of transactions, net worth, and category transaction reports. In the tabs at the top of the Reports window, Quicken lists Standard, Business, and Investment report types. All three of these types are generated in the same fashion.

To create a Standard report:

1. Click the Reports button in the Reporting tab of the toolbar or choose Activities > Reports & Graphs > Reports to open the Reports window.

2. Click the Standard, Business, or Investment tabs at the top of the Reports window. The window will switch to the area you clicked (**Figure 12.11**).

3. In the scrolling pane on the left side of the window, select a template for a report that you want to create. On the right side of the window, Quicken shows you a sample of the kind of report you select.

4. If necessary, change the date range of the report by changing the value of the Date pop-up menu or by typing a date or dates in the date field in the Reports window.

5. Click the Create button to generate the report (**Figure 12.12**).

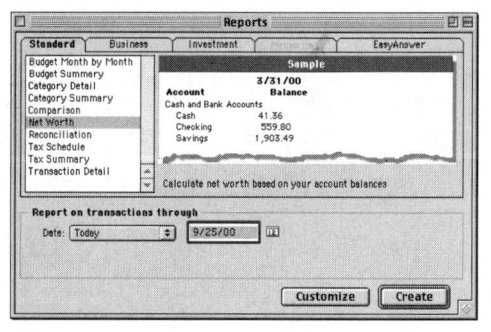

Figure 12.11 You can change the date range of a report by typing in a new date or by choosing a new value in the Date pop-up menu.

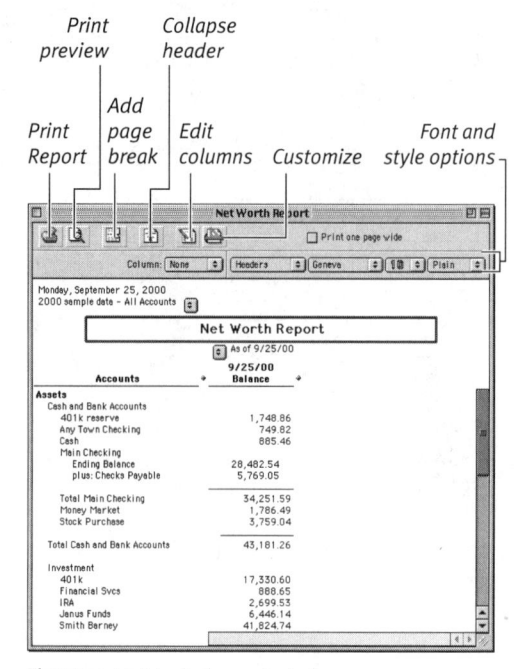

Figure 12.12 A typical report window.

Customizing Reports

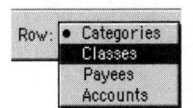

Figure 12.13 Select an option from the Row pop-up menu to change the contents of the rows of report.

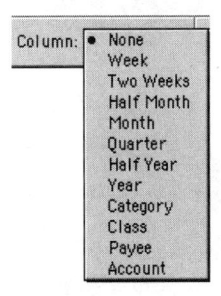

Figure 12.14 Select an option from the Column pop-up menu to choose the contents of the columns in the report.

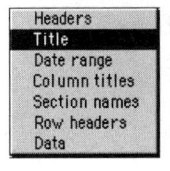

Figure 12.15 These pop-up menus let you change the look of the text in each part of a report.

You can customize reports in Quicken in two ways: by creating a custom layout of a Standard report or by creating an entirely new custom report.

To customize report layouts:

1. Follow steps 1 through 6 in the previous section, "To create a Standard report."

2. In the Report window, choose one or more of the following formatting options (not all of the options below will be available in all reports):

    - Change the contents of the rows in a report by choosing from the Row pop-up menu (**Figure 12.13**).
    - Choose the contents of the columns in the report by selecting an option from the Column pop-up menu (**Figure 12.14**).
    - Change the look of the text in the report with the font, font size, and style pop-up menus (**Figure 12.15**).
    - Click the "Print one page wide" check box to resize the report to fit on one page.
    - Edit the report title by selecting it and typing in a new one.
    - Resize the width of the columns in the report by clicking and dragging the diamonds between each column head. Drag the rules under each column head to rearrange the columns in the report.

(continued)

✔ Tip

- You can also customize the look of the report by clicking one of the three icons in the Report window (**Figure 12.16**). To add a page break, select a row in the report and click the Page Break icon. Click the Collapse Header icon to remove the header from the printed document. Click the Edit Columns icon to open a window that allows you to select which columns to include in your report (**Figure 12.17**).

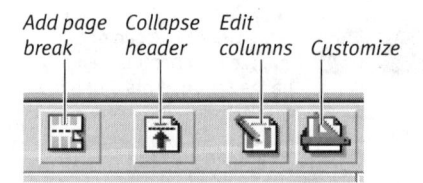

Figure 12.16 Use these icons to customize the overall look of the report.

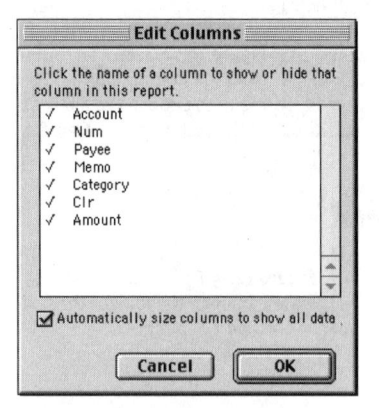

Figure 12.17 The Edit Columns window lets you choose which columns to include in a report.

Creating Reports

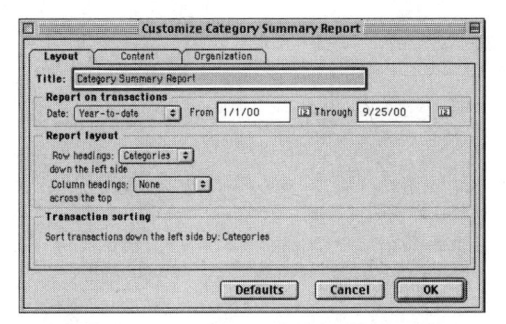

Figure 12.18 The Layout tab lets you set the basic report parameters.

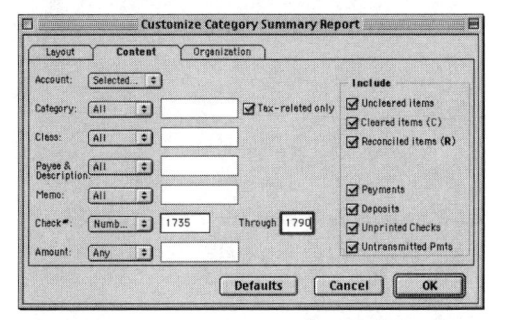

Figure 12.19 Narrow the report's information in the Content tab.

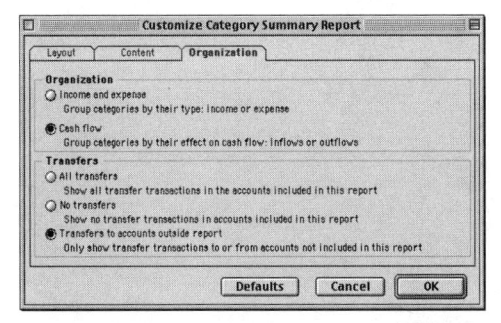

Figure 12.20 The Organization tab lets you switch between two different ways to view your report.

To create a custom report:

1. Follow steps 1 through 4 in "To create a Standard report" to choose a report template.

2. Click the Customize button at the bottom of the Reports window. The Customize Report window appears.

3. Make changes in one or more of the following areas:
   - The Layout tab (**Figure 12.18**) of the Customize Report window lets you specify row and column headings as well as the date range for the report.
   - The Content tab lets you choose which information will appear in the report (**Figure 12.19**). You can narrow the focus of your report to show only the items of your interest.
   - The Organization tab (**Figure 12.20**) allows you to organize the look of a report either as an income and expense report or by cash flow.

CUSTOMIZING REPORTS

121

Using Memorized Reports

Tweaking reports until they're just the way that you want them can take some effort, and it would be a waste of your time if you had to re-create a custom report every time. Instead, you can save custom settings and reuse them. These are called Memorized reports.

To memorize a report:

1. Create a custom report.

2. Choose Edit > Memorize, or press ⌘M. The Memorize Report Template window appears (**Figure 12.21**).

3. Enter a name and a description for the report. If you click the "Use current date" check box, Quicken will create future reports using the current date, rather than the dates that you specified when you customized the report.

4. Click the Memorize button.

To use a Memorized report:

1. Click the Reports button in the taskbar.

2. In the Reports window, click the Memorized tab (**Figure 12.22**).

3. Click the memorized report that you want to use. Optionally, change the date range at the bottom of the Reports window.

4. Click the Create button.

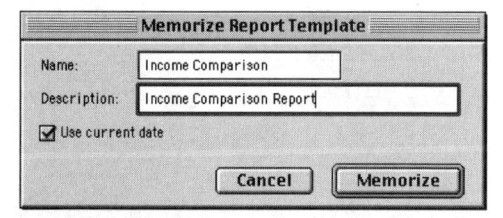

Figure 12.21 Enter the name of a report to be memorized in the Memorize Report Template window.

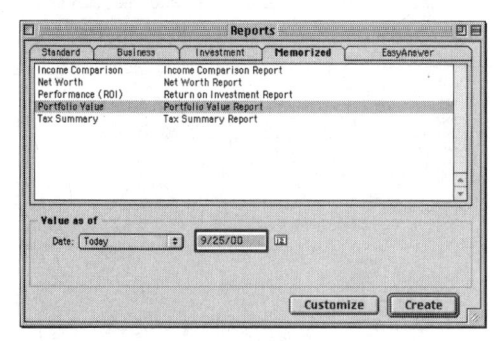

Figure 12.22 Choose a report that you have already memorized from the Memorized tab in the Reports window.

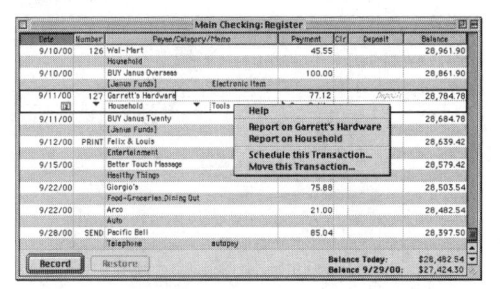

Figure 12.23 The Shortcuts pop-up menu in the account register lets you get fast reports on a transaction.

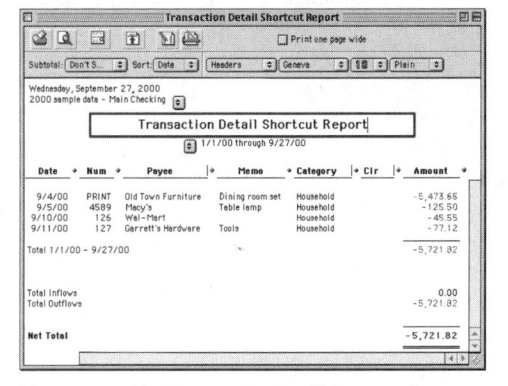

Figure 12.24 The Transaction Detail Shortcut Report gives you quick year-to-date information about the payee or category of a transaction.

Using Shortcut Reports

Shortcut reports are found in the account registers. They are simple year-to-date transaction reports of all occurrences of a selected payee or category.

To create a shortcut report:

1. Open an account register.

2. Scroll through the register until you find the transaction on which you want a report. Click the transaction to select it.

3. Control-click the transaction. The Shortcuts contextual menu appears in that transaction (**Figure 12.23**). Click the Shortcuts menu, and choose either "Report on [payee name]" or "Report on [category name]." Quicken generates the report (**Figure 12.24**).

✔ Tip

- Besides getting the shortcut reports, you can also use the contextual menu in registers to add the transaction to the Scheduled Transactions list or you can move the transaction to another register. The latter option is useful when you accidentally enter a transaction in the wrong register. Rather than delete the errant transaction and reenter it, just move it to the correct register.

Printing Reports

Quicken makes it easy to print reports and lists of all kinds, whether from the Reports section or from other areas of the program, such as account registers or lists.

To print a report:

1. Click the Reporting button in the activity bar.

2. Click the Reports button in the toolbar to open the Reports window.

3. Create a Standard or Memorized report as described earlier in this chapter, or choose an existing report.

4. Choose File > Print Report. The printer dialog box will appear.

   or

   Click the Print button at the top of the Reports window. The printer dialog box will appear, as shown in **Figure 12.25**.

5. Click the Print button to print your report.

✔ Tip

- Note that Quicken, unlike almost every other Macintosh program, doesn't use ⌘P as the shortcut key for its printing needs. That shortcut key is reserved for Print Checks.

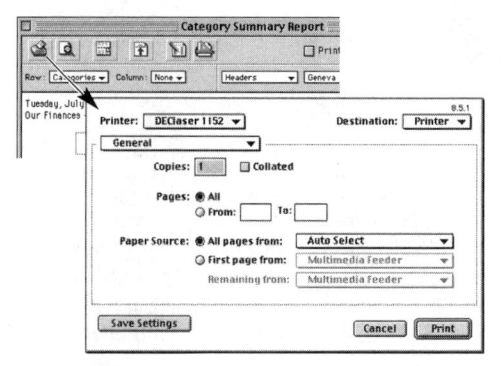

Figure 12.25 To print any Quicken report, choose File > Report or click the Print button at the top of the Reports window and click Print.

Creating Reports

Figure 12.26 Sometimes it's handy to have a hard copy of all or part of a transactions register. That's easily accomplished simply by choosing Print Register from the File menu.

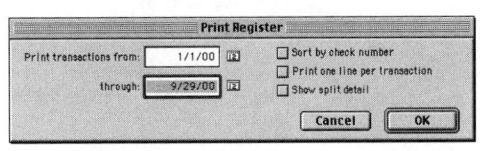

Figure 12.27 You can print out an entire history of your transactions from a given register or specify a range of dates using the two pop-up calendars or entering the dates in the windows.

Register and List Reports

These aren't exactly reports in the same sense as the the other five types. With these reports, Quicken simply allows you to print the current list or account register. But sometimes that's all you need.

To print an account register or a list:

1. Open the account register or list that you want to print.

2. If you're printing a register, choose File > Print Register (**Figure 12.26**). The Print Register window will appear (**Figure 12.27**). Enter the date range of the register entries you wish to print, and then click OK. If you are printing a list, the menu item will be called File > Print [List Name] ([List Name] is the name of the list you have open.)

3. The printer dialog box will appear.

4. Click Print.

125

13

CREATING GRAPHS

When it comes to getting a good overview of your finances, reports are good but graphs are better. Graphs can often illustrate relationships in your finances that numeric reports don't make clear.

Quicken can display your financial data as bar graphs, line graphs, and pie charts to help you quickly analyze your income and expenses, develop budgets, and determine your net worth.

In addition to their informational benefits, graphs can give you an important emotional boost, as I discovered while working to pay off my consumer debt. I created a bar graph that showed how much debt I owed. Every month, as I made payments, I'd check the graph to see how much the debt bar had shrunk. It felt great to see the downward trend in graphic form as I worked toward my goals—and it felt even better the month that the bar finally hit the zero mark.

As with reports (see Chapter 12 for more about reports), Quicken comes with a variety of templates to get you started using graphs. You can create custom graphs to answer particular questions about your finances. Quicken has three main types of graphs: EasyAnswer graphs, Standard graphs, and Memorized graphs.

127

Chapter 13

Using EasyAnswer Graphs

EasyAnswer graphs address basic questions about your finances.

To create an EasyAnswer graph:

1. Click the Graphs button in the Reporting tab of the toolbar (**Figure 13.1**). The Graphs window appears (**Figure 13.2**).

2. Click the EasyAnswer tab. Quicken shows you the EasyAnswer Graphs window (**Figure 13.3**).

3. Select the radio button to indicate the question that you want to ask.

4. If necessary, choose a new time frame from the pop-up menu next to the radio button that you clicked.

5. If your question requires a category selection, choose one from the pop-up menu next to the selected question.

6. Click the Create button. Quicken displays the graph on your screen (**Figure 13.4**).

Figure 13.1 Click this button to open the Graphs window.

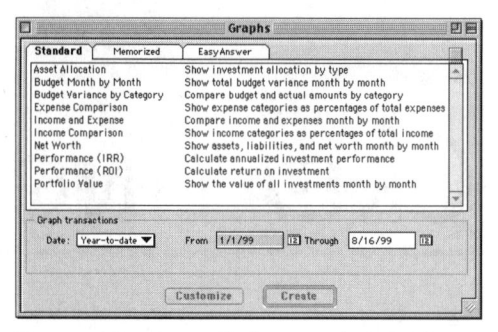

Figure 13.2 You create all of your graphs in Quicken from the Graphs window.

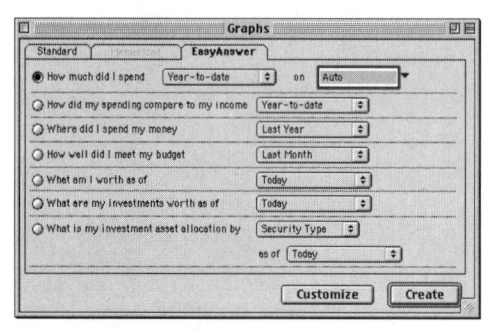

Figure 13.3 Use the EasyAnswer Graphs screen to get fast financial graphs.

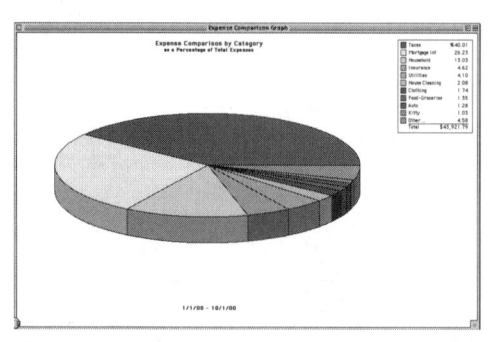

Figure 13.4 Quicken displays a completed graph. This graph shows expenses by category.

128

Creating Graphs

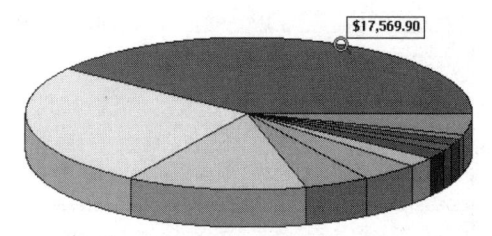

Figure 13.5 Click and hold the mouse button on a section of the graph. The cursor becomes a magnifying glass to show the dollar value of the graph segment.

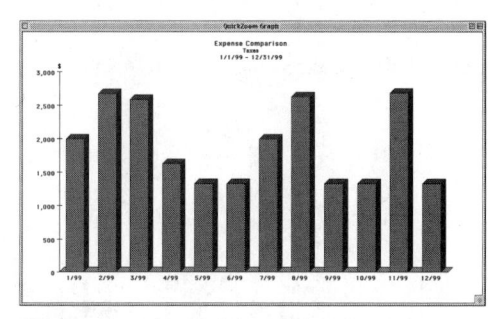

Figure 13.6 Double-click the graph segment to open a more detailed graph.

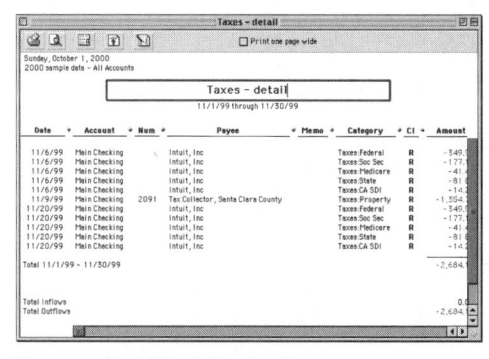

Figure 13.7 Double-click a detail segment to see a report showing you the original transactions that were used to create the graph.

To use QuickZoom to get details:

1. Move the cursor over one of the colored areas on an existing graph. The cursor will turn into a magnifying glass. Click and hold the mouse button to see the dollar value of that segment of the graph (**Figure 13.5**).

2. Double-click a segment of the graph to open another graph showing you more detail (**Figure 13.6**).

3. For even more detail, double-click a segment of the detailed graph. A report window opens, showing you the original transactions that make up the graph segment (**Figure 13.7**).

USING EASYANSWER GRAPHS

129

Chapter 13

Using a Standard Graph

Standard graphs provide such information as your net worth, the value of your investment portfolio, and details about your income and expenses. You can customize Standard graphs to suit your own needs.

To create a Standard graph:

1. Click the Graphs button in the Reporting section of the toolbar to open the Graphs window.

2. Click the Standard tab.

   Quicken shows you the Standard Graphs window (**Figure 13.8**).

3. Select the type of graph that you want to create.

4. If necessary, change the date range of the graph by changing the value of the Date pop-up menu or by typing in a date or dates in the date fields in the Standard Graphs window.

5. Click the Create button to generate the graph (**Figure 13.9**).

✔ Tip

- Use QuickZoom with any type of graph to view more detailed information about your finances.

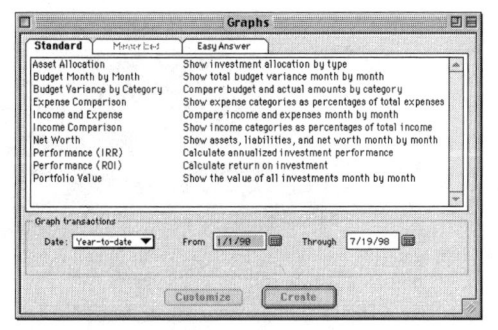

Figure 13.8 Quicken provides a variety of standard graphs.

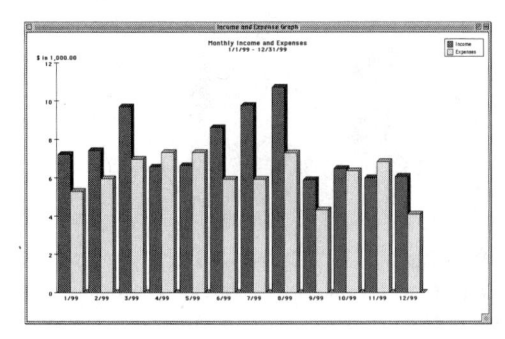

Figure 13.9 You can customize a standard income and expense graph to suit your needs.

Creating Graphs

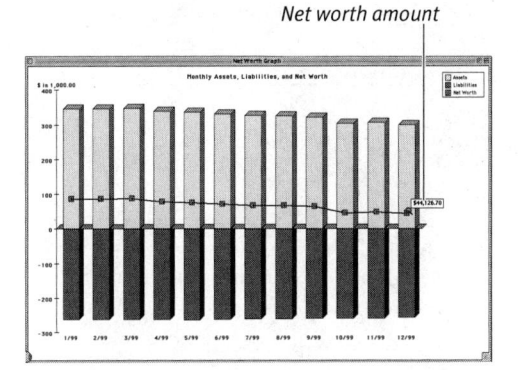

Net worth amount

Figure 13.10 Hold down the mouse button over the Net Worth square to see your current net worth dollar value.

Creating a Net Worth Graph

Net Worth graphs are a bit complicated. Your net worth is calculated by subtracting your liabilities from your assets. These bar graphs show your assets above the zero line and your liabilities below the zero line, with your net worth showing as a small red square (hopefully above the zero line!).

To create a Net Worth graph:

1. Click the Graphs button in the toolbar to open the Graphs window.
2. Click the Standard tab.
   Quicken shows you the Standard Graphs window.
3. Select the Net Worth template on the Standard tab.
4. If necessary, change the date range.
5. Click the Create button.
   Quicken generates your Net Worth graph (**Figure 13.10**).

131

Customizing Graphs

Quicken's standard graph templates are adequate in most cases, but you'll sometimes want to create a custom graph to get some specific information. For example, you might want to compare your income against your spouse's income or (if you're really looking for marital trouble) compare your expenses.

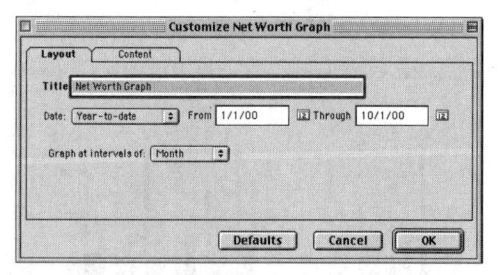

Figure 13.11 You can customize your graphs from this window.

To create a custom graph:

1. Click the Graphs button on the Reporting section of the toolbar.

2. Click the EasyAnswer or Standard tab in the Graphs window, and then select the kind of graph you wish to create.

3. Click the Customize button.
   The Customize Graph window appears (**Figure 13.11**).

4. Click the Layout tab. If you wish, change the title and date range of the graph.

5. Click the Content tab. Use one or more of the three pop-up menus to narrow the scope of the graph.
   For example, you can use the Account menu to limit the graph to show data from one or more accounts. Similarly, the Category and Class pop-up menus allow you to select those criteria.

6. Click the OK button to create your custom graph.

✔ Tips

- If you have already created a graph, you can customize it by clicking the Customize button in the lower-left corner of the Graphs window.

- If you decide you don't like the changes that you made in the Customize Graph window, click the Defaults button to return all the settings back to their initial values.

Creating Graphs

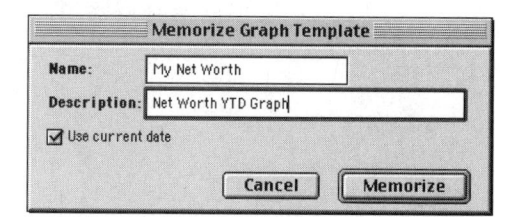

Figure 13.12 After you have customized a graph, you can memorize it and give it a unique name.

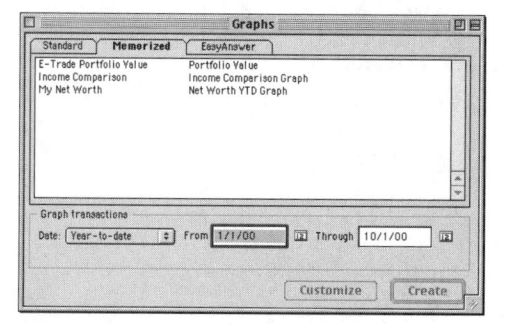

Figure 13.13 Choose a previously memorized report from the Memorized tab of the Graphs window.

Using Memorized Graphs

Once you have customized a graph, chances are you're going to want to use it again. Memorized graphs are custom graphs that you have saved for later reuse.

To memorize a graph:

1. Create a custom graph as described above.

2. Choose Edit > Memorize, or press [#][M]. The Memorize Graph Template dialog box appears (**Figure 13.12**).

3. Enter a name and a description for the graph. If you click the "Use current date" check box, Quicken will create future graphs using the then-current date rather than the dates that you specified when you customized the graph.

4. Click the Memorize button.

To use a memorized graph:

1. Click the Graphs button in the toolbar.

2. In the Graphs window, click the Memorized tab (**Figure 13.13**). Select a graph that you previously memorized. Optionally, change the date range at the bottom of the Graphs window to see information pertaining to a particular range.

3. Click the Create button.

To delete a memorized graph:

1. Click the Graphs button in the toolbar.

2. In the Graphs window, click the Memorized tab. Select a graph that you previously memorized.

3. Choose Edit > Delete Graph, or press [#][D].

4. Click the Yes button when Quicken asks you to confirm the deletion.

133

Printing Graphs

Most of the time, you'll be displaying your graphs onscreen, but on occasion you'll want to print them out to show others. You might want to print an income graph to dazzle a loan officer, for example, or to demonstrate to your doubting parents what a financial whiz you've become.

To print a graph or chart:

1. Open or create a graph or chart.
2. Choose File > Print Graph (**Figure 13.14**). The printer dialog box appears.
3. Click the Print button to print the graph or chart.

Figure 13.14 You can print any type of Quicken graph simply by choosing Print Graph from the File menu while the graph is displayed on-screen.

Working with Loans and Mortgages | 14

Loans come in two flavors: either you are borrowing money from another person or from a financial institution or, perhaps a happier sort of loan, you are lending money to someone else. Quicken handles both kinds of loans with aplomb, creating an account for each new loan.

When you are borrowing money, Quicken tracks how the loan is *amortized*, or paid off, to show you the interest you are paying, the remaining principal, and the length and amounts of your payment schedule. When you set up this kind of loan, Quicken automatically creates a *liability* account.

When you loan money to someone else, Quicken sets up a payment schedule and creates an *asset* account.

Chapter 14

Creating Loans

To set up a loan account, Quicken needs information about the terms of the loan and the lender or borrower. Then Quicken creates the loan payment schedule and the principal asset or liability account.

To create a loan (when you're the borrower):

1. Click the Loans button in the Assets & Debt section of the toolbar (**Figure 14.1**), or select Lists > Loans.

    The Loans window appears (**Figure 14.2**).

2. Click the New button.

    The Loan Interview window appears (**Figure 14.3**).

3. Select the radio buttons in the Loan Interview window as appropriate for the loan that you're creating.

4. Click the Continue button to open the Set Up Loan window (**Figure 14.4**).

5. In the Set Up Loan window, enter the name of your lender.

6. Enter the payment amounts. Enter your monthly (or quarterly, annual, etc.) payment in the Principal + interest field. If you're creating a real estate loan and extra fees are added to the loan, such as PMI and property taxes, enter those amounts too.

7. Enter the date of your first payment.

8. Indicate the frequency of the payment. If this loan will be paid on a schedule other than monthly (the default), change the setting of the Frequency pop-up menu.

9. Enter the total number of payments.

Figure 14.1 Click the Loans button to begin creating a loan.

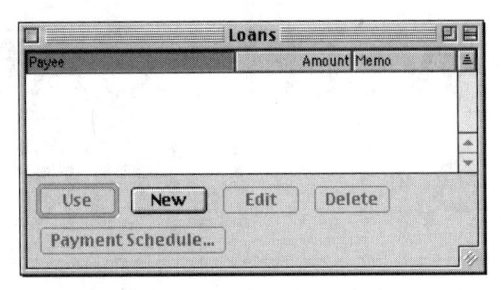

Figure 14.2 The Loans window shows the loans you've entered and lets you start a new loan account.

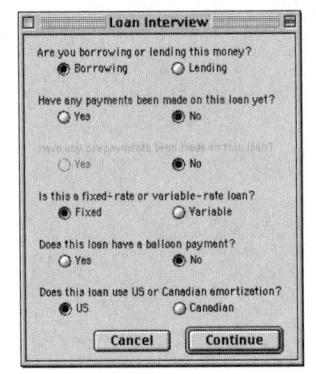

Figure 14.3 Quicken learns about the kind of loan that you want to set up in the Loan Interview window.

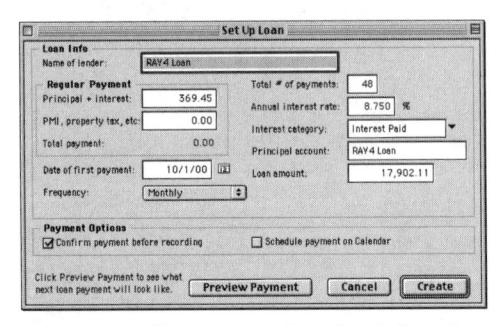

Figure 14.4 You'll enter most of your loan information in the Set Up Loan window.

Working with Loans and Mortgages

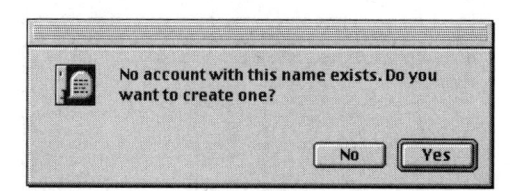

Figure 14.5 Quicken confirms that you want to set up a new liability account.

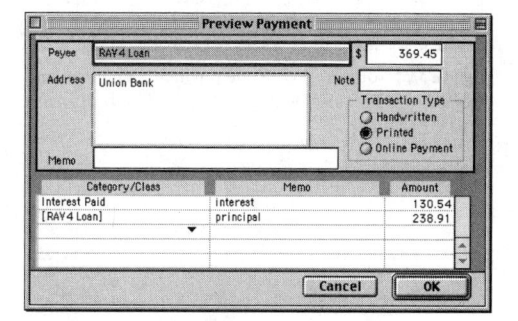

Figure 14.6 The Preview payments window lets you make sure that your loan is set up correctly before the final creation step occurs.

10. Enter the annual interest rate.

11. Choose an expense category to track the interest paid on the loan.

12. Enter a name for the principal liability account that you'll use to track this loan. Quicken pops up a dialog box confirming that you want to create a new liability account (**Figure 14.5**). Click the Yes button.

13. Enter the total loan amount.

14. In the Payment Options area, click the "Confirm payment before recording" check box if any of these conditions apply:

    ♦ You want to review or change the payment information every time you make a payment.

    ♦ You plan to make prepayments to reduce your principal and pay off the loan faster.

    ♦ The loan has a variable interest rate.

15. Click "Schedule payment on Calendar" if you want to be automatically reminded about your loan payment.

16. To make sure that everything looks good before you finish creating the loan, click the Preview Payment button to open the Preview Payment window (**Figure 14.6**).

17. After you've viewed the information, click OK to return to the Set Up Loan window.

18. If the loan information looked OK, click the Create button. (If not, make your corrections now.)

    If you clicked the "Schedule payment on Calendar" check box, the Calendar window will open to let you schedule your payment. (See Chapter 7 for information on the Financial Calendar.) Your new loan will appear in the Loans window.

CREATING LOANS

To view your payment schedule:

1. Choose Lists > Loans or click the Loans button in the toolbar to open the Loans window.

2. In the Loans window, click the loan for which you want to see a payment schedule.

3. Click the Payment Schedule button in the Loans window.

   The Payment Schedule window for that loan appears (**Figure 14.7**).

✔ Tips

- The term of a loan must be at least 12 months for Quicken to be able to calculate the interest, principal, and payment information.

- For variable-rate loans, you can change the interest rate when you make a payment or whenever your loan's interest rate changes.

- In the Preview Payment window, the principal and interest amount applies to the next scheduled payment only. That's because Quicken calculates the correct amounts of these numbers every time you make a payment.

- You can specify whether you want to pay your loan with a handwritten check, an online banking transaction, or a printed check by selecting the appropriate radio button in the Preview Payment window.

Date	Pmt	Principal	Interest	Balance
		8.750%		17,902.11
10/1/00	1	238.91	130.54	17,663.20
11/1/00	2	240.66	128.79	17,422.54
12/1/00	3	242.41	127.04	17,180.13
1/1/01	4	244.18	125.27	16,935.95
2/1/01	5	245.96	123.49	16,689.99
3/1/01	6	247.75	121.70	16,442.24
4/1/01	7	249.56	119.89	16,192.68
5/1/01	8	251.38	118.07	15,941.30
6/1/01	9	253.21	116.24	15,688.09
7/1/01	10	255.06	114.39	15,433.03
8/1/01	11	256.92	112.53	15,176.11
9/1/01	12	258.79	110.66	14,917.32
10/1/01	13	260.68	108.77	14,656.64
11/1/01	14	262.58	106.87	14,394.06
12/1/01	15	264.49	104.96	14,129.57

Figure 14.7 You can review the payment schedule for any loan by clicking the Payment Schedule button in the Loans window.

Working with Loans and Mortgages

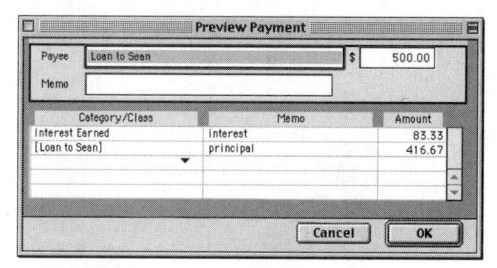

Figure 14.8 When you're the lender, the Preview Payment window is much simpler.

To create a loan (when you're lending):

1. Click the Loans button in the toolbar. The Loans window appears.

2. Click the New button. The Loan Interview window appears.

3. Select the Lending radio button and any others that are appropriate for this loan, and then click the Continue button.

4. Fill out the information in the Set Up Loan window.

5. Click the Preview Payment button. As you can see in **Figure 14.8,** the Preview Payment window is small and uncomplicated when you're the lender.

CREATING LOANS

139

Chapter 14

Making Loan Payments

To make a loan payment, you first recall the loan payment from the Loans list and enter it in the register of the bank account from which you're making the payment. Quicken then calculates the principal and interest amounts and updates the loan balance.

Of course, you don't have to do this manually if you have a fixed-rate loan. It's easy to schedule the loan payment for automatic entry using the Calendar (as discussed in Chapter 7).

To make a loan payment:

1. Open the account register or the Write Checks window for the bank account from which you will make the loan payment.

2. Choose Edit > New Transaction, or press ⌘N.

3. Choose Lists > Loans. The Loans window appears.

4. Select the loan for which you want to enter a payment and click the Use button, or simply double-click the loan.

   The Payment window appears (**Figure 14.9**).

5. If you need to make any adjustments in the Payment window, enter them now. For example, if you have a variable-rate interest loan, you should enter the current interest rate. You can also enter a prepayment if you want to pay off the loan faster.

6. Click the OK button.

   Quicken will enter the loan payment in the account register.

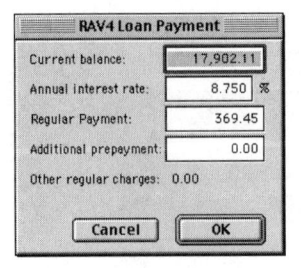

Figure 14.9 You can change the interest rate or add a prepayment amount in the Loan Payment window.

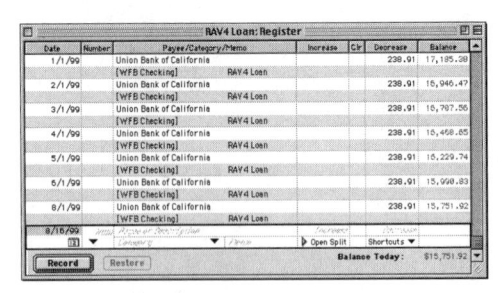

Figure 14.10 You can view the history of your loan at any time by opening the account register for the loan from the Accounts list.

✔ Tips

- To see the history of a loan, open the account register for the loan from the Accounts list. Your register should resemble the one shown in **Figure 14.10**.

- Loan payments are entered as split transactions. Open the split to see what portion went toward interest and what went to pay down the principal.

Setting Up Investment Accounts

15

"Investing? Who needs it? Why, I'm only [fill in some number under 30] years old; I won't need to worry about retirement for a long time."

Sound familiar? When you're in your teens or twenties, retirement is a lifetime away. Ironically, that is just the time that you should begin investing, because you'll have nearly 50 years of compound interest working for you. Professional financial planners like to show if you save just $100 per month starting when you're 20, you can easily retire with more than a million dollars. But if you wait until you're 30 and make the same investments, you end up with only about a third as much when you're 65.

(If you're already past your twenties and thirties, don't despair—it's never too late to start preparing for your future.)

For the vast majority of us, the key to comfortable living in future years and a successful retirement is a solid and consistent savings and investment program. Quicken lets you update current market values and see whether you're earning or losing money on your investments.

In this chapter, you'll learn how to set up and add to an investment portfolio and how to set up a mutual fund account in Quicken. So don't wait; get started on saving for the future today.

Using Investment Accounts

You can use a variety of account types within Quicken to track your investments (see **Table 15.1**). Here are the four choices:

- Use a regular bank account for investments with a constant share price or no share price. For example, a certificate of deposit (CD) earns interest, but because the interest rate is fixed when you buy the CD, the value doesn't go up or down according to a fluctuating market.

- Asset accounts are used to keep track of things that you own, such as personal property, real estate, or other tangible items. For example, if you have a valuable stamp or wine collection, you might track its value in an Asset account so that the collection shows up as part of your net worth. You can reassess and update the value of the collection in the Asset account from time to time.

- A Portfolio account tracks one or more securities. (A security is an investment vehicle, such as a stock, bond, mutual fund, money market fund, certificate of deposit, precious metal, or collectible.) Your Portfolio account can include a mix of securities, and you can use the account to track transactions and provide the total market value for your portfolio. It's a good idea to have one Portfolio account for each broker or other financial institution you use to handle a group of investments. For example, if you use an online broker like E-Trade and a traditional broker like Merrill Lynch, you should have a separate Portfolio account for each brokerage. Quicken's many reporting options can show you how your portfolio is performing.

Setting up Investment Accounts

- ◆ Each Mutual Fund account tracks a mutual fund. It's easier to use than the Portfolio account if all you want to do is track a single mutual fund. (Of course, you can have as many Mutual Fund accounts as you wish, each tracking a different mutual fund.)

✔ Tip

- One drawback of using a bank account or an Asset account is that it cannot track the rate of return on an investment. To track a return rate, you'll need to use a Portfolio or Mutual Fund account.

Table 15.1 If you're not sure which kind of account to use for your investments, take a look at Table 15.1 to see Intuit's recommendations.

Selecting the proper account type for your investment

Investment Type	Account Type
Securities for which you want to track a cash balance, such as stocks, bonds, or mutual funds; or a collection of investments in a brokerage account	Portfolio
A single mutual fund with no cash balance	Mutual Fund
Money Market funds	Bank (if you write checks against the fund) or mutual fund (if you need to track the rate of return)
Certificates of deposit	Bank
Real estate	Asset
IRA accounts, Keogh accounts, variable annuities	Portfolio
Unit trusts	
Real estate investment trusts or partnerships	
Treasury bills	Portfolio or asset
Fixed annuities, 401(k)m 403(b), pensions	
Collectibles or precious metals	

Chapter 15

Setting up Your Portfolio

Before you get started setting up your portfolio accounts, you need to decide how much investment history you want to include in your records. You have three options: a complete history, just this year's information, or what I call the "Aw-the-heck-with-it" method—just enter your current investment holdings. (For a detailed rundown of the pros and cons of each method, see the Quicken User Guide.)

If you choose the complete history option, you'll need to enter the initial purchase price for each security and all subsequent transactions. On the plus side, all your reports are complete and Quicken can accurately calculate capital gains. On the minus side, if you been investing for several years, that's a lot of data to enter. However, Intuit recommends this option, and so do I.

If you decide to enter just this year's data, you'll enter the investment balances as of the end of last year and then enter all of the transactions for each security since the beginning of this year. With this method, the information you need to find and enter is more recent and probably easier for you to obtain. Reports that deal with events from this year will be accurate, and if you sell a security, Quicken will be able to track which lots of that security you should sell to minimize or maximize your short-term capital gains. This method's disadvantage is that Quicken will not know the original cost of the security (called the cost basis), so you can't get accurate long-term capital gains or realized gain reports.

Setting up Investment Accounts

Figure 15.1 Click the Accounts button to set up a new account.

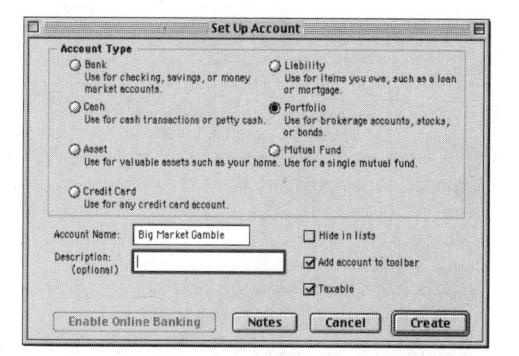

Figure 15.2 You can create a new portfolio from the Set Up Account window.

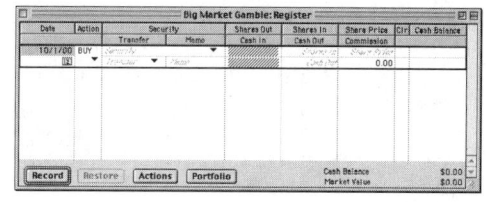

Figure 15.3 When you set up a new portfolio account, Quicken opens an associated account register.

The "Aw-the-heck-with-it" method is the fastest, and reports that cover events after today will be accurate. You just enter in your current investment holdings. On the other hand, data for this year and past years will be incomplete, and you won't be able to get reports for capital gains or realized gains. This is a significant drawback, so think twice before you decide to use this method.

To create a portfolio account:

1. Click the Accounts button in the Banking section of the toolbar or select Lists > Accounts to open the Accounts list (**Figure 15.1**). Click New.

   The Set Up Account window appears (**Figure 15.2**).

2. Select the Portfolio radio button.

3. Enter the name of the Portfolio account in the Account Name box.

4. In the Description box, add a short description of the account (optional).

5. If the account is taxable, make sure that the Taxable box is checked. If this account is going to be tax-free, clear the Taxable box.

6. Click the Create button.

   Quicken opens a new account register for the new portfolio account (**Figure 15.3**).

SETTING UP YOUR PORTFOLIO

145

Chapter 15

To add securities to your portfolio:

1. Click the Portfolio button at the bottom of the new account register. The Portfolio window will appear (**Figure 15.4**), containing the account you just created.

    If you previously created other investment accounts, they will appear in the Portfolio window as well. All investment accounts are listed in a single Portfolio window.

2. Click the Add Security button at the bottom of the Portfolio window.

    The Security Name dialog box appears (**Figure 15.5**).

3. Type in a name for the new security, and then click OK.

4. Quicken pops up a dialog box that says it can't find that security (**Figure 15.6**). Click the Set Up button.

    The Set Up Security window appears (**Figure 15.7**).

5. In the Symbol box, enter the stock ticker symbol for the security.

6. In the Type box, choose one of the options from the pop-up menu (Bond, CD, Mutual Fund, or Stock).

7. In the Goal box, choose one of the options from the pop-up menu (College fund, Growth, High-risk, Income, or Low-risk).

8. Ignore the "Notify if price is" boxes.

9. If the security is taxable, make sure the "Taxable" box is checked. Make sure that the "Hide in lists" box is not checked.

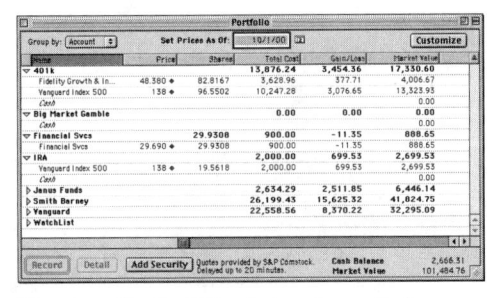

Figure 15.4 The Portfolio window shows all of your investment accounts.

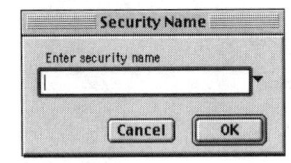

Figure 15.5 To add a security to your portfolio, enter its name.

Figure 15.6 Click the Set Up button to reassure Quicken that you want to create a new security.

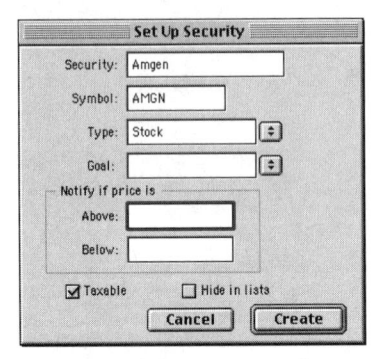

Figure 15.7 Use the Set Up Security window to enter details of the new security.

Figure 15.8 Select an option from the Add Security dialog box to tell Quicken that you own the security or that you're just keeping an eye on it.

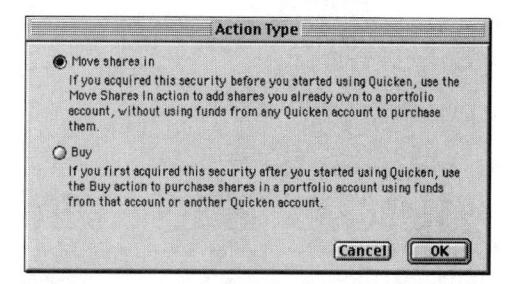

Figure 15.9 You must indicate that you acquired the security before you began using Quicken or that you'll be transferring funds from another Quicken account to purchase the security.

10. Click the Create button.

    The Add Security dialog box appears (**Figure 15.8**).

11. If you own the security, select the "Add shares to account" radio button and click OK. The Action Type List window appears.

    or

    If you don't own the security but want to track its performance, select "Add security to WatchList." Then click OK.

    In the WatchList area, you can add securities that interest you but that you don't yet own to track how they do. If you choose this option, setup for that security is complete.

12. If you selected the "Add shares to account" radio button in step 11, the Action Type dialog box (**Figure 15.9**) appears. You must tell Quicken whether you acquired the security before or after you started using Quicken. Select "Move shares in" to add shares that you already owned without using funds from any Quicken account to purchase those shares. Click OK and the Move Shares In window appears.

    or

    Select the "Buy" radio button to purchase shares with funds from another Quicken account. Click OK to open the Buy dialog box, and then go to step 15.

13. In the Move Shares In window, enter the date, the number of shares in the security that you own, the price you bought the shares for, and a memo (optional).

14. Click the Record button. The security shows up in the Portfolio window.

(continued)

147

Chapter 15

15. If you selected "Buy" in step 12, the Buy dialog box appears (**Figure 15.10**). Fill in the date, the number of shares, the price you bought the shares for, the broker commission (if any), and the source of funds (must be another Quicken account). Click the Record button and the security will show up in the Portfolio window.

✔ Tips

- If you leave the Source of Funds field blank when purchasing a security, Quicken deducts the money for it from the Portfolio account.

- If you leave the Destination of Funds field blank when selling a security, Quicken credits the proceeds of the sale to the Portfolio account.

- When you buy stocks, you always want to keep track of the purchase price and commission so that later, when you sell them, you can gauge your profit, loss, or capital gains tax liability.

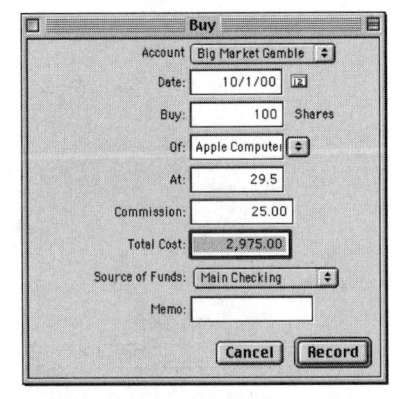

Figure 15.10 Here you note the source of funds from which you bought your shares.

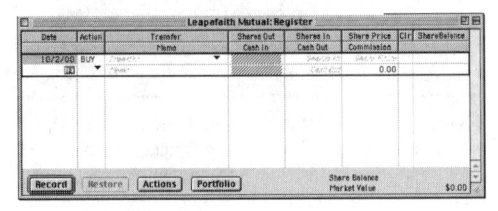

Figure 15.11 Quicken maintains an account register for mutual funds, as with every other kind of account.

To add a mutual fund account:

1. Click the Accounts button in the toolbar or select Lists > Accounts from the menu to open the Accounts list. Click New.

   The Set Up Account window appears (as shown in **Figure 15.2**).

2. Select the Mutual Fund radio button.

3. Enter the name of the mutual fund in the Account Name box.

4. In the Description box, add a short description of the mutual fund (optional).

5. If the mutual fund is taxable, make sure that the "Taxable" box is checked. If this is a tax-free fund, clear the "Taxable" box.

6. Click the Create button.

   Quicken opens an account register for the new mutual fund account (**Figure 15.11**).

MANAGING YOUR INVESTMENTS

After setting up your investment portfolio (see Chapter 15), you need to manage your investments on an ongoing basis. That means updating the share prices of your securities and making entries whenever you buy or sell an investment.

Getting up-to-date quotes on stocks, bonds, and mutual funds is easy with the Internet. If you have a modem and access to the Internet, Quicken can download securities prices and enter them directly into your Portfolio window.

Quicken 2001 can also download historical prices for securities.

Quicken also allows you to view and manually enter security prices in either the Portfolio window or the Security Detail window.

Chapter 16

Portfolio Maintenance

You use the Portfolio window to get an overview of your investments, and it's an important tool for analyzing how well your investment strategy is working. You'll want to update the prices of your securities on a fairly regular basis; how often, of course, will depend on how active an investor you are. Active traders will want to update daily; buy-and-hold investors will probably be happy updating once a week.

Figure 16.1 Click the Portfolio button to open the Portfolio window.

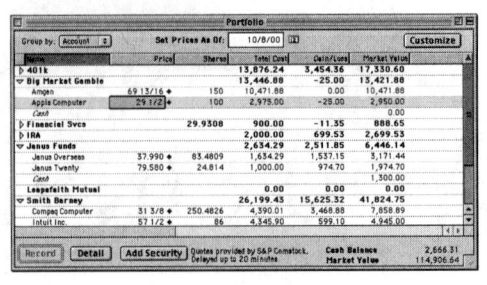

Figure 16.2 You can use the Portfolio window to view all of your investments.

To manually update prices in the Portfolio window:

1. Click the Portfolio button in the Investing section of the toolbar (**Figure 16.1**) to open the Portfolio window (**Figure 16.2**).

2. At the top of the Portfolio window, you'll see a date next to "Set Prices As Of." The default is today's date; if you're updating securities prices as of another day, change this date.

3. Select a security in the Portfolio window by clicking it, and then enter a share price for the displayed date by clicking at the appropriate spot in the Price column, as shown in **Figure 16.2**. You can enter a price either as a decimal number or as a fraction.

4. Click the Record button (or press [Return] or [Enter]) to save the new price.

    Quicken will recalculate the value of that security and your whole portfolio.

✔ Tips

- In the Price column, you can increase or decrease the price by ⅛ share (0.125) by pressing the plus ([+]) or hyphen ([-]) key.

- If the prices in the Portfolio window appear to be incorrect, press ⌘[Option][U] to force a recalculation of your entire Portfolio.

150

Managing Your Investments

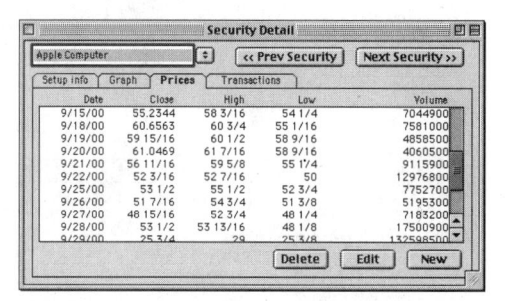

Figure 16.3 The Security Detail window provides a wealth of information about a security.

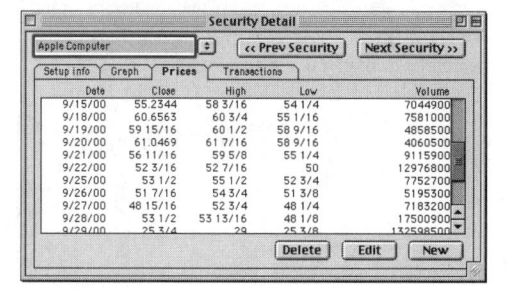

Figure 16.4 You can view the price history of the security from the Prices tab of the Security Detail window.

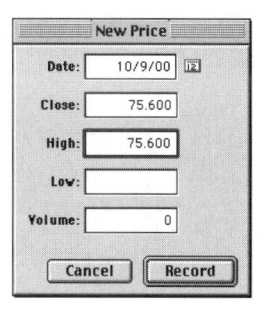

Figure 16.5 Change a stock price in the New Price dialog box.

To manually update prices in the Security Detail window:

1. In the Portfolio window, double-click a security name, or click the Detail button at the bottom of the window. A Security Detail window will appear (**Figure 16.3**).

2. Click the Prices tab (**Figure 16.4**).

3. Make necessary changes to the prices:

   ◆ To enter a new price, click the New button and fill out the New Price dialog box (**Figure 16.5**); then click the Record button.

   ◆ To change a price, click the Edit button, fill out the Edit Price dialog box (which looks almost identical to the New Price dialog box), and then click the Change button.

   ◆ To delete a price, select the price that you wish to delete and click the Delete button. Quicken will ask you to confirm the deletion. Choose OK to confirm.

PORTFOLIO MAINTENANCE

151

Chapter 16

To download price quotes:

1. Click the Quotes button in the toolbar (**Figure 16.6**).

   Quicken will connect to the Internet and download the latest prices of your securities.

2. The Download Summary window (**Figure 16.7**) opens, showing how many quotes were downloaded and when. Click "View Latest Prices."

   A Quicken Quotes window shows you the downloaded price information for every security in your Portfolio (**Figure 16.8**). At the same time, your portfolio is automatically updated.

✔ Tips

- You can download prices as many times per day you wish, but Quicken stores only one price per day.

- The stock symbols in your setup must be exactly the same as those used by the markets. If the message "Ticker not found" appears in your Quicken Quotes window, check to make sure that your stock symbols are correct. To enter or edit a stock symbol, see "To add securities to your portfolio," in Chapter 15.

- Stocks, options, and indexes are updated constantly during the business day, although the quotes you get online are delayed by about 20 minutes. Prices for mutual funds are updated only once per day at 6 p.m. Eastern time.

- You can sort the Quicken Quotes window by clicking any of the column names in the window. This is useful for things like seeing which of your securities had the highest trading volume or which ones changed the most in value.

Figure 16.6 Click the Quotes button to download security quotes.

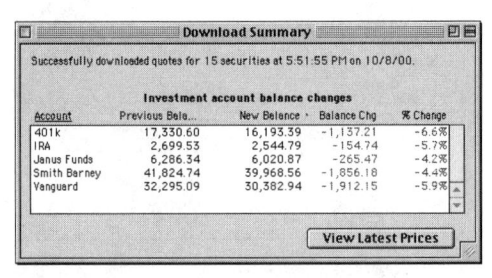

Figure 16.7 The Download Summary window opens when the quotes have been downloaded.

Figure 16.8 The Quicken Quotes window shows the downloaded information for your portfolio.

Figure 16.9 Click the Historical Price button on the toolbar.

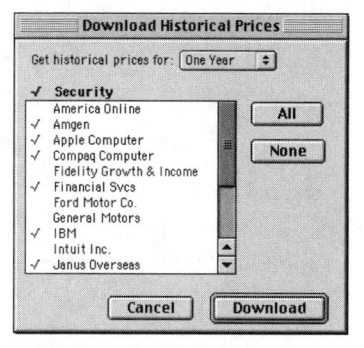

Figure 16.10 The Download Historical Prices dialog box lets you choose which securities you want to research.

Using Quicken.com's Investment Tools

In the Investment area, Quicken.com offers a broad spectrum of tools that should prove very useful to the investor. Many of these features are discussed in Chapter 19.

One of Quicken's strengths is its integration with the Internet. As working online has become more and more the norm, Intuit has shifted many of its functions to the Internet, which keeps the product up to date with market trends and changing technologies.

Quicken allows you to download not only today's prices from the Quicken.com server but up to five years of historical information for both stocks and mutual funds. This is an invaluable tool for making decisions about your investment strategies.

To download historical prices:

1. Choose Online > Historical Prices, or click the Historical Price button (**Figure 16.9**) on the Investing section of the toolbar.

   The Download Historical Prices dialog box opens (**Figure 16.10**).

2. Choose the securities you want to research from the list of stocks in your portfolio, and select the time period for which you want quotes. Then click Download.

   Quicken logs onto the Internet and downloads the information you specified and adds it to your portfolio data.

3. To view the information, open the Security Detail window, as described previously.

Buying and Selling Securities

Most of the transactions in your investment accounts will involve buying or selling securities, but Quicken can handle virtually any sort of investment transaction. **Table 16.1** shows the transactions available in Quicken. The investment process is so complex that I don't have room to explain it all here. Refer to the Quicken User Manual to learn about complex investment transactions.

You can enter investment transactions by two methods: by using investment forms or by entering information directly into the investment account register. The investment forms are easier to use, especially if you're new to these sorts of transactions. After you become familiar with investment transactions, you may choose to use the other entry method, which is to simply enter the information into the investment account register.

Table 16.1

Investment actions	
ACTION	DESCRIPTION
Buy	Buy security with cash
Capital Gain Long	Receive cash from long-term capital gains distribution
Capital Gain Short	Receive cash from short-term capital gains distribution
Dividend	Receive cash from dividend
Interest Income	Receive cash from interest income
Miscellaneous Expense	Pay miscellaneous expense with cash
Miscellaneous Income	Receive cash from miscellaneous income
Move Shares In	Add shares to account
Move Shares Out	Remove shares from account
Reinvest Dividend	Reinvest in shares of the security with money from dividend or income distribution
Reinvest Interest	Reinvest in shares of the security with money from interest distribution
Reinvest Long	Reinvest in shares of the security with money from long-term capital gains distribution
Reinvest Short	Reinvest in shares of the security with money from short-term capital gains distribution
Return of Capital	Receive cash from return of capital
Sell	Sell security and receive cash
Stock Split	Change number of shares as result of stock split
Transfer Money	Transfer money into or out of this account

Managing Your Investments

Figure 16.11 Begin an investment transaction by clicking the Actions button in the toolbar.

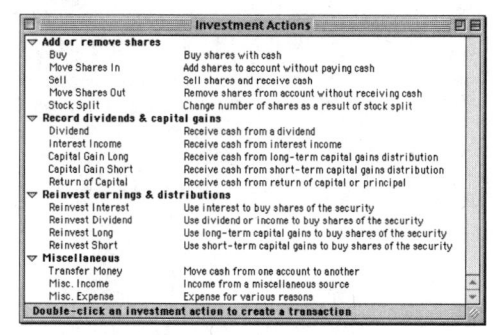

Figure 16.12 Choose the kind of investment transaction you want in the Investment Actions window.

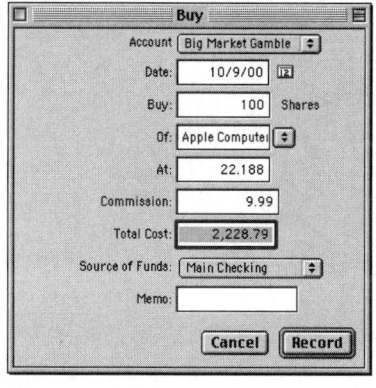

Figure 16.13 Fill out the investment detail window to complete your transaction.

To use investment forms for transactions:

1. Click the Portfolio button in the Investing section of the toolbar to open the Portfolio window.

2. Click a security to select it in the Portfolio window.

3. Click the Actions button in the Investing section of the toolbar (**Figure 16.11**).

    The Investment Actions window appears (**Figure 16.12**).

4. Find the transaction that you wish to perform in the Investment Actions window, and double-click it.

    The detail window for the transaction you choose opens (**Figure 16.13**). (In this case, Buy was chosen in the Investment Actions window.)

5. Fill out the information in the detail window, and then click the Record button.

✔ Tips

- If you're selling a security, you might want to choose which shares to sell, so that you get the most favorable capital gains treatment. In the detail window, click the Choose Lots button to pick a particular batch of shares to sell.

- If the Actions button isn't in your toolbar, you should add it. See "Customizing Your Workspace" in Chapter 1.

BUYING AND SELLING SECURITIES

155

Planning for the Future

One of the things I like about Quicken is its ability to shed light on the past, present, and future of my financial life. I can use it to look back to where I've been, to deal with my current finances, and to help me create my future financial scenario.

Sometimes I just want to look a little way into the future, so I use the Financial Calendar to see which payments are scheduled for next month. If my finances were a bit more predictable (that they aren't is a side effect of my life as a freelance writer), I might be interested in creating a yearly budget. However, I do plan to retire someday, so I use Quicken's retirement planners to see whether I'm on track with my savings and investment programs.

Quicken Deluxe 2001 includes two tools under the Financial Fitness banner that can help you now as well as in the future: the Emergency Records Organizer and the Tax Deduction Finder. In addition, Quicken Home Inventory is a small free-standing application that lets you go through your house room by room from the basement to the attic to make an exhaustive inventory of your possessions and their monetary values for insurance purposes.

Chapter 17

Through Quicken's connections to the Quicken.com Web site, you are a button's push away from the Retirement Planner and the Life Event Planner to help you make sure your resources will be sufficient when the time comes for your kids' college tuition, or the trip of your lifetime, or that wedding they'll be talking about for years. In a similar vein, Quicken.com gives access to your credit report and to a Debt Reduction Planner that will guide you through the process of paying down your debt as efficiently as possible, potentially saving you a lot of money that might otherwise go to the finance company as interest.

In this chapter you'll learn how to use the Financial Fitness planners and some of Quicken's other tools that can help you take control of your finances now and plan for your future financial well-being.

Using the Planning Tools

Quicken Deluxe 2001 includes two planning programs in the Activities menu that walk you through the process of collecting the relevant information. The Emergency Records Organizer tracks the locations of all your important documents, and Quicken Home Inventory helps you create an exhaustive list of your possessions and their values.

To make your work easier, these planners include audio and QuickTime movies that show examples and illustrate financial concepts. To hear the sounds and view the movies, the Quicken Deluxe CD must be in your CD-ROM drive. You can also run these programs without the CD (but you'll miss the multimedia treats).

Here's a rundown of Quicken's two built-in planning tools:

The **Emergency Records Organizer** helps you gather and track important financial and legal documents. It produces a variety of customized reports as well as a Comprehensive Report containing all the information you enter and an Emergency Report with important contact numbers, medical data, and health insurance information.

The **Quicken Home Inventory** program helps jog your memory about all the valuable things you own and even goes so far as to suggest replacement and resale values for these items. It includes information on your various insurance policies and helps you determine whether you have adequate coverage.

Web-Based Planners

You get to Quicken's Web-based planners by choosing them from the hierarchical menu that you see after you choose Online > To the Web. They can also be reached by clicking their buttons on the toolbar. These planners can help you go beyond the bookkeeping functions Quicken provides to take a more active role in the direction of your financial existence.

Each Web-based planner displays a menu on the left side of the screen that shows the topics covered by the planner. You can jump to any topic by clicking it, but it's usually best to work through the planner sequentially.

In the main part of the planner window, you'll see a worksheet, where you answer questions about your finances. At the end of the process, Quicken will show you an action plan—the actual steps you need to take to achieve your stated goal—that you can print out and use.

Because Intuit is adding and changing planners on a regular basis, I've only listed a representative sample of the planners available.

The **Retirement Planner** probes your savings and investment plans and tells you whether your current plan (if you have one) is adequate to meet your needs when you retire. If it's not, the planner will come up with a new plan to help you meet your goals.

The **College Planner** is similar to the Retirement Planner; it measures your projected earnings, investments, and savings against the major future expense of college for one or more of your children. If Quicken determines that you can't afford the expense(s), the planner offers some suggestions to help you create a successful financial plan that will enable you to meet expenses.

Planning for the Future

Many people are carrying too large a load of consumer debt, and the **Debt Reduction Planner** will show you how to get out of debt faster and save money while doing it. If you follow the recommendations in this planner, you can save hundreds or even thousands of dollars in interest payments.

The less tax you pay, the better your bottom line. By taking you through the survey step by step with a set of questions about each of a long list of possible deductions, the **Tax Deduction Finder** helps you determine whether you're eligible for certain tax deductions.

Besides the planners listed above, there are also choices in the To the Web menu that will take you to places on the Quicken.com Web site where you can get useful information. But they'll also give you a chance to buy some financial service, such as life insurance or a mortgage. This may be just fine with you; in fact, the insurance and mortgage quotes are often good deals.

The final Web tool I want to mention is a **Free Credit Report** that you can request from one of the major credit reporting agencies. The report will be delivered to your home address within four to six weeks. You can opt to pay a fee for faster delivery or pay a larger fee to get a consolidated report from all three of the major US credit bureaus.

Because each planner is used in a similar way, I'll go into only two of them in detail here: the Retirement Planner and the Debt Reduction Planner.

(continued)

WEB-BASED PLANNERS

161

✔ Tip

- It's a good idea to take advantage of the Free Credit Report or the more expensive, extra-value credit reports. It's an especially good idea to see your credit report before you purchase a major-ticket item like a house or a car. You want to have the same information that the mortgage or finance company will use when they decide how credit-worthy you are. Before I bought my first house, I paid for the consolidated bureau report, and it was interesting reading. It led me to contact one of the credit bureaus to remove inaccurate information; they had my occupation listed as "school bus driver," which was a job I had more than 20 years ago when I was a college student! What I learned was that once data gets into the credit bureau computers, it may never come out. It's best to get a report every few years just to check for inaccuracies. If you've been turned down for credit based on the information in a credit report, by federal law you are entitled to a free copy of your report from the credit bureau that supplied the negative report.

Planning for the Future

Chapter 17.1 The Retirement Planner button on the toolbar launches your browser and brings you to the Quicken.com Web site.

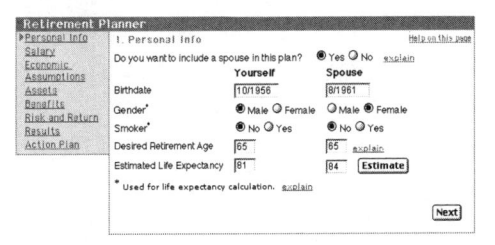

Chapter 17.2 Enter your personal information and click Next to go on.

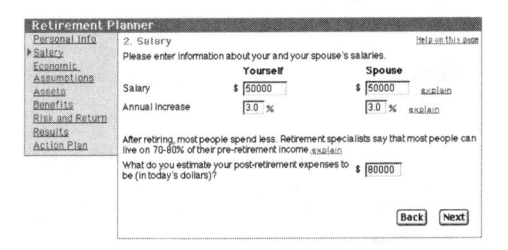

Chapter 17.3 Enter salary information in this window.

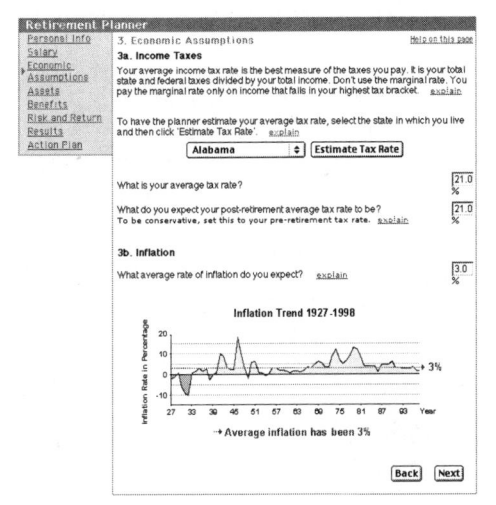

Chapter 17.4 The economic assumptions you make have a lot to do with the ultimate success of your plan.

The Retirement Planner

Careful planning can make your retirement years much more enjoyable and can significantly reduce anxiety levels in the years preceding them. Matching your earning levels to your investments and making realistic decisions about what kind of expenses you will have in the future are the keys to successful retirement planning. Quicken's Retirement Planner is one way of balancing your current needs against your future ones and optimizing the overall picture.

To set up a Retirement Plan:

1. Click the Retirement Planner button on the Planning section of the toolbar (**Figure 17.1**), or choose Online > To the Web > Retirement Planner.

   Quicken will open your default Web browser and go to the Retirement Planner on the Quicken.com Web site.

2. After reading over the introductory material on the Retirement Planner page, click the "Build your plan now" button to open the Personal Information worksheet (**Figure 17.2**). Fill in the required data and then click Next.

3. In the Salary worksheet (**Figure 17.3**), enter your salary and that of your spouse (if you are in this thing together). Guesstimate your annual increases and your future cost of living, and then click Next.

4. In the Economic Assumptions worksheet (**Figure 17.4**), you can let Quicken estimate your tax rate and project a rate of inflation or you can use your own, perhaps more conservative, figures. Then click Next.

(continued)

THE RETIREMENT PLANNER

163

Chapter 17

5. The Assets worksheet (**Figure 17.5**) asks about your current investments and how they are growing. Fill in the blanks and click Next.

6. The Retirement Benefits worksheet (**Figure 17.6**) sets up the assumptions about what your income will be after retirement. Fill it out where necessary and click Next.

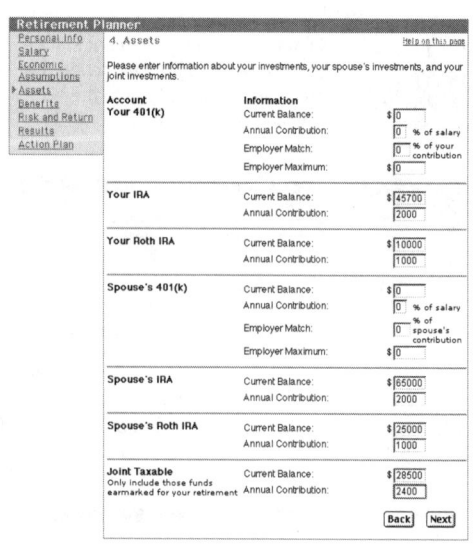

Chapter 17.5 Fill in information about your current and predicted assets.

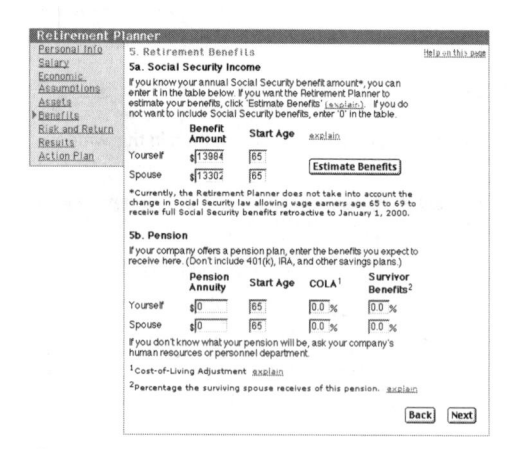

Chapter 17.6 Here is where you enter information about your Social Security and pension benefits.

Planning for the Future

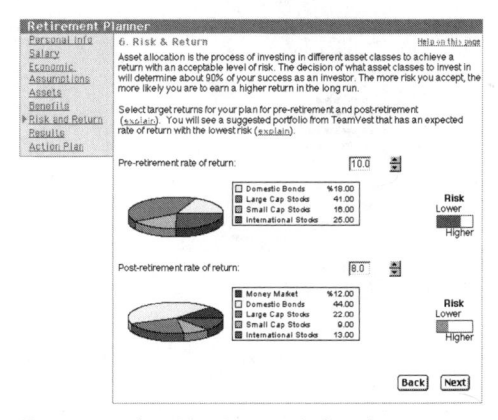

Chapter 17.7 The Risk & Return window shows a way of diversifying your portfolio to meet your goal.

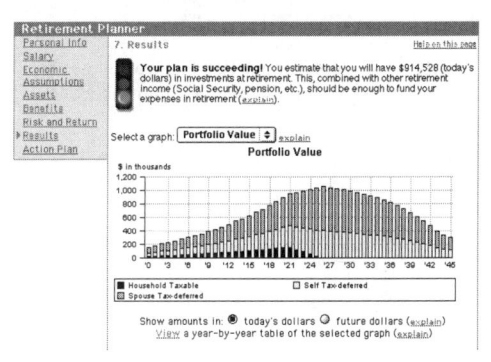

Chapter 17.8 The results are shown here in graphic fashion. If your plan succeeds, you'll get the green light. Otherwise, go back to make some changes.

Chapter 17.9 The What-If section allows you to play with the numbers.

7. In the Risk & Return (**Figure 17.7**) worksheet, you can set goals for the rate of return on your investments. Click Next.

8. The Results window (**Figure 17.8**) shows a graph of your portfolio value. Using the pop-up menu, you can also view income, savings, or expenses. If you plan is succeeding, you'll see a green light; if not, you'll see a red light; if you might be in trouble, you'll see a yellow light.

9. Scrolling down, you come to the What-If section (**Figure 17.9**) that makes the retirement planning process so useful. You can change the variables and see what happens, from wildly optimistic assumptions to financial Armageddon. Change a number and click the Recalculate button to get the new result. The Solve button next to each box asks Quicken to figure out what that number needs to be to make the plan work. Click Next to go to the final screen.

(continued)

THE RETIREMENT PLANNER

165

Chapter 17

10. The last window of the series (**Figure 17.10**) is the Action Plan.

    At the top of the window is the plan summary that contains all the information you entered as you went along. At the bottom are a Savings Schedule and a Suggested Investment Schedule that shows a way for you to allocate your investments. If you stick to the plan, you have reasonable assurance of achieving your goal. This is the proverbial bottom line.

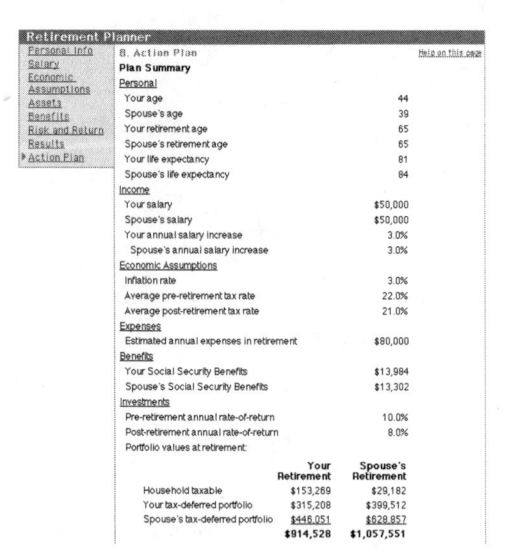

Chapter 17.10 Here is the Action Plan you'll need to follow to make your retirement a comfortable one.

Reducing Consumer Debt

Paying off your credit card and loan debts is an important step toward financial happiness. If you don't pay off your credit card and loan bills in full every month, you are charged interest to compensate the bank for your use of their money. Unfortunately, interest payments aren't a good deal for you; the money that you pay in interest is unproductive and could be spent in better ways.

Quicken's Debt Reduction Planner uses a simple philosophy. It analyzes your debt and pays off the highest interest rate cards first, which lets you get out of debt faster while paying less interest.

To use the Debt Reduction Planner:

1. Click the Debt Plan button on Assets & Debt section of the toolbar (**Figure 17.11**).

   Your Web browser connects to Quicken.com, and the Debt Reduction Planner Introduction window appears (**Figure 17.12**).

2. If you want to read one of the topics listed under "Overview," click it. Then click Next.

3. The Debts window appears (**Figure 17.13**). Enter the information for each debt and then click Save to add it to the "Your debts" list at the right. Click New to enter a new debt. When you're done, click Next to go on to the Summary window.

(continued)

Chapter 17.11 Click the Debt Plan button to go to the Debt Reduction Planner on the Web site.

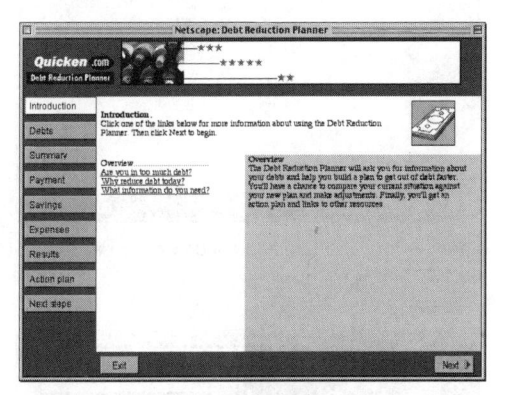

Chapter 17.12 You can ask questions about reducing your debt in the Introduction window.

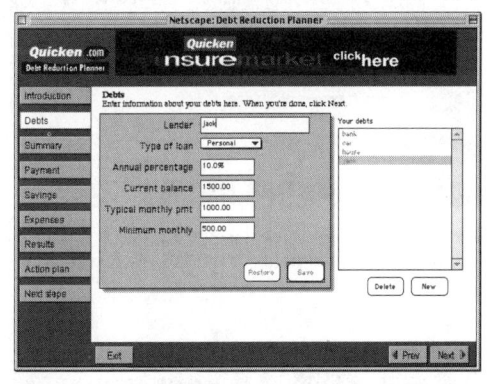

Chapter 17.13 The Debts window is where you begin the process by listing what you owe and to whom.

167

Chapter 17

4. The Summary window (**Figure 17.14**) shows what you owe, what your monthly payments are, when you'll be debt free, and what the total interest paid will be. When you're over the shock, click Next.

5. In the Payment window (**Figure 17.15**), Quicken begins to show how you can save some money and get out of debt sooner. Simply following the plan outlined on this page will help considerably. To do even better, click Next.

6. The Savings window (**Figure 17.16**) counsels you to apply some of your savings to pay down your debt immediately. Pick a figure you think you can afford and type it into the text field. Then click Save/Recalculate to see how much you can save and how soon you will be free of debt. When you have reached a figure you're comfortable with, click Next.

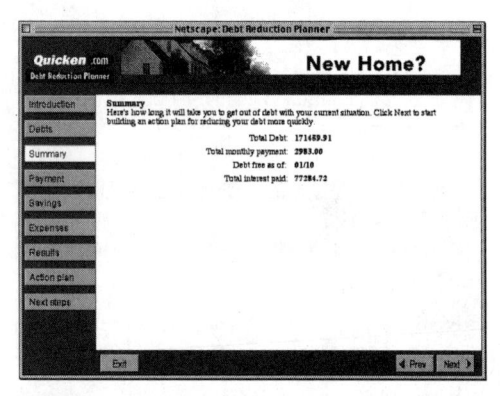

Chapter 17.14 The Summary window adds it all up and tells the sad story.

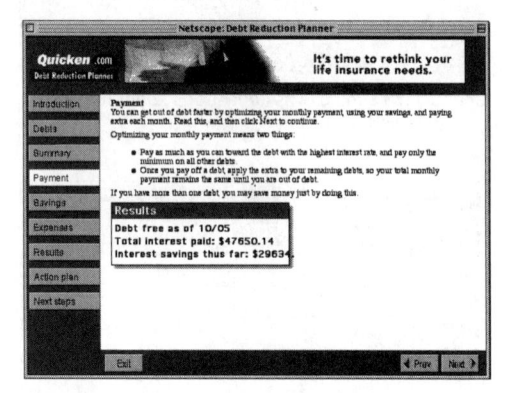

Chapter 17.15 The Payment window shows how you can improve your situation by simply restructuring your payments.

Chapter 17.16 If you can use some of your savings to pay off part of your debt, you may find your situation seems much rosier.

168

Planning for the Future

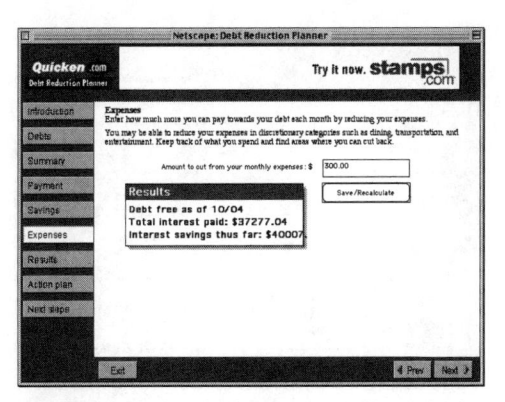

Chapter 17.17 Cutting back on your spending and using the money to pay off your creditors can help as well.

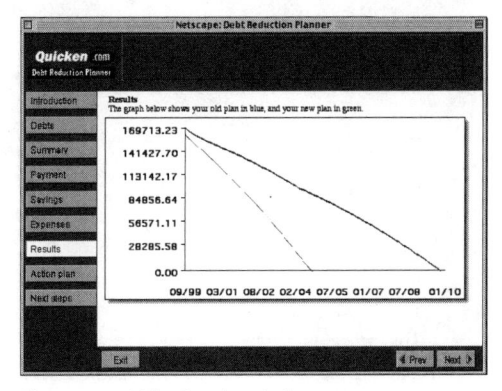

Chapter 17.18 The Results window presents a convincing argument for following the plan's recommendations.

7. In the Expenses window (**Figure 17.17**), you'll cut back on your expenditures and use the money to retire your debt. This window demonstrates immediately how this will benefit you. Set a figure, see how much it improves the results of your debt reduction plan, and click Next.

8. The Results window (**Figure 17.18**) is a very impressive argument for keeping to the plan you have developed in the previous steps. Meditate on it and then click Next.

(continued)

Spending Savings to Reduce Debt

If you already have some money saved, you might question the wisdom of taking money out of your savings or investment accounts to help pay off your consumer debt. Although it is a smart idea to have a financial cushion, you need to ask yourself if your money is working for you in the best way.

For example, assume that you have $2,000 in an investment that is earning 10 percent interest, but your credit cards are charging you 16 percent interest. At the end of the year, you'll have lost money by not paying off your credit cards. You're better off reducing your debt as quickly as possible.

Chapter 17

9. Across the top of the Action Plan window (**Figure 17.19**), you'll see the steps you need to take to follow the plan you have written. Below that is a schedule of your payments to your lenders (**Figure 17.20**) that optimizes your debt reduction.

10. The final window, Next Steps (**Figure 17.21**), refers you to other resources available to you that can help get you out of debt.

✔ Tip

- It's often more useful to leave your home and auto loans out of the Debt Reduction Planner, because these represent assets as well as liabilities. What you should focus on in debt reduction is expensive consumer debt such as credit cards.

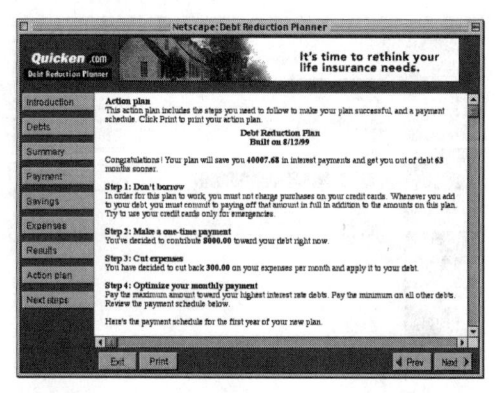

Chapter 17.19 The Action Plan makes it all very concrete.

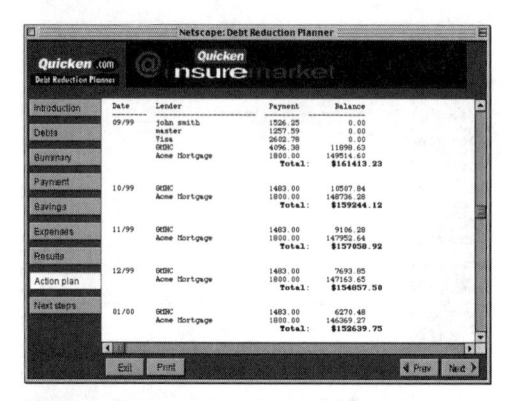

Chapter 17.20 Here's the schedule of payments you need to make.

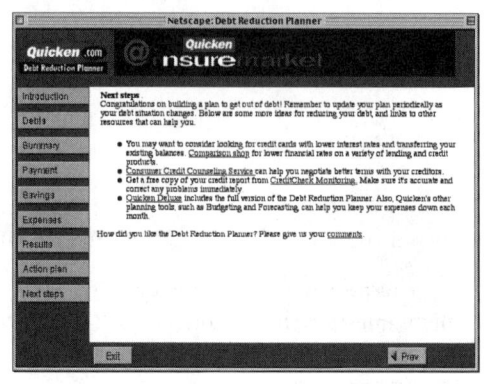

Chapter 17.21 This window offers other resources you may want to check into.

Planning for the Future

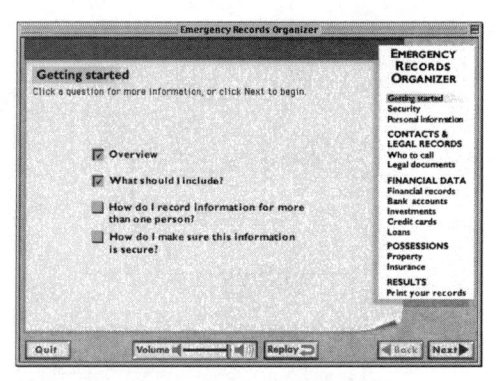

Chapter 17.22 You can ask Quicken these questions before you get started.

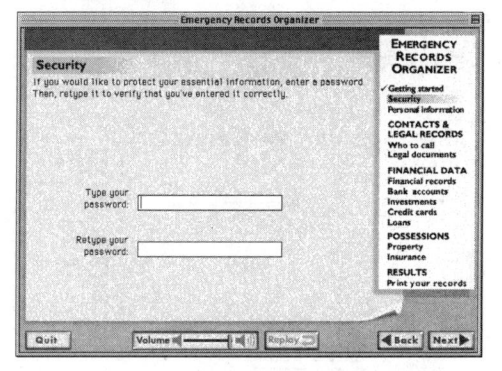

Chapter 17.23 To protect your essential information from others who may be using your computer, enter a password.

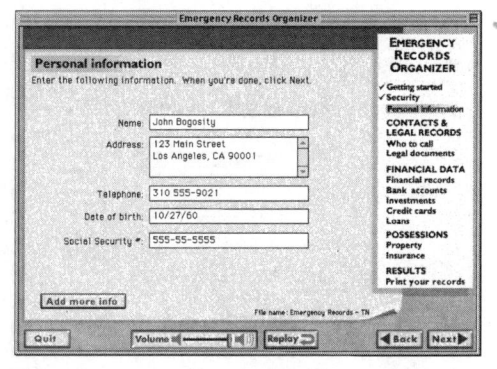

Chapter 17.24 Enter your name, address, telephone number, and other personal information here.

Getting Organized

So many documents in our lives are important, yet most of us don't bother to keep them in one place, ready for easy access in the event that a family member or we will need them.

The **Emergency Records Organizer** helps you bring together all of the information that you, your family, or your friends would need in an emergency, such as medical insurance information, medical contacts, bank accounts, and even wills and other legal documents.

Because each section in the Emergency Records Organizer works in a similar fashion, I'm going to discuss the planner's highlights rather than take you through every possible step.

To use the Emergency Records Organizer:

1. Choose Activities > Financial Fitness > Emergency Records Organizer. The Organizer's Getting Started window appears (**Figure 17.22**). Click Next to begin.

2. Click a question to view a QuickTime movie about that question. When you're done asking questions, click the Next button to open the Security window (**Figure 17.23**).

3. If you want to protect your emergency records file from prying eyes, enter a password and then enter it again for verification. Click Next to open the Personal Information window (**Figure 17.24**).

(continued)

171

Chapter 17

4. Fill in your name, address, telephone number, date of birth, and Social Security number. Then click the "Add more info" button.

   The More Personal Information window appears (**Figure 17.25**).

5. Fill in your driver's license number, your mother's maiden name, and other ID information, such as the license numbers of any professional licenses you hold. Also include any vital medical warnings, such as allergies. Click OK to return to the Personal Information window.

6. Click the Next button to enter the "Contracts & legal records" area. Read the information explaining what's in this section, and then click the Next button to open the Who to Call window (**Figure 17.26**).

7. Under the Contacts heading, choose one of the contact categories. An entry screen will appear in the middle of the window (**Figure 17.27**), where you can type in information about your contacts.

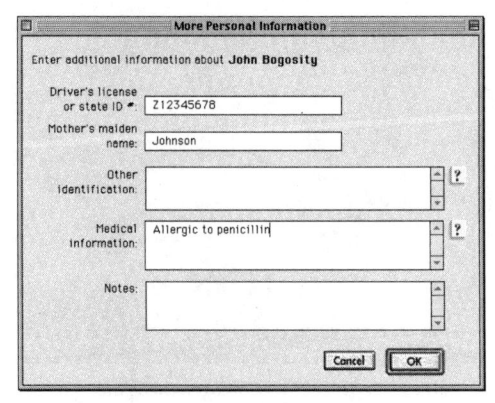

Chapter 17.25 Fill in additional personal information in this window.

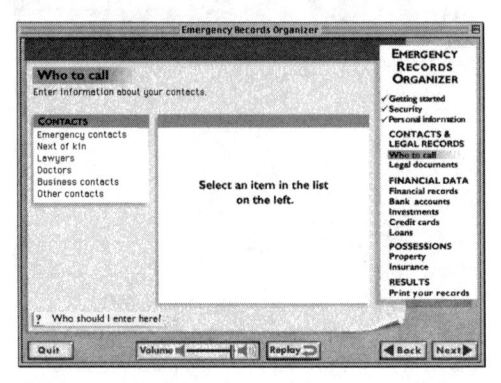

Chapter 17.26 Indicate the type of contacts you want to enter.

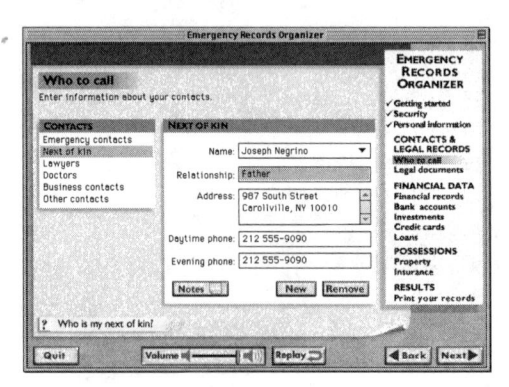

Chapter 17.27 After you indicate the contact category, enter each contact's name in this window.

172

Planning for the Future

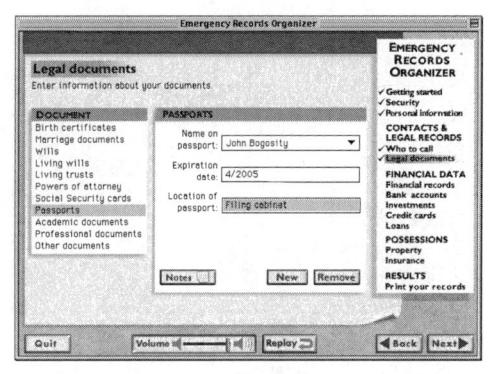

Chapter 17.28 Organize and keep track of all of your important documents in this window.

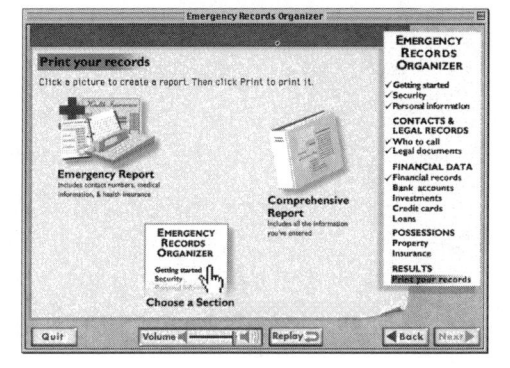

Chapter 17.29 You can print three kinds of reports.

8. Fill in the information in the entry screen, and then click the New button if you want to add more people in that category. Click another category of Contacts to add information to that category. When you're done adding contacts, click the Next button to get to the "Legal documents" area (**Figure 17.28**).

9. Choose one of the Document types to begin filling out a form describing that document. Repeat as necessary for all of the document types you wish to enter.

10. Repeat the entry steps above for all of the Financial Data and Possessions sections in which you want to enter data. When you're done, click "Print your records" from the checklist on the right side of the window.

    The Print Your Records window appears (**Figure 17.29**).

11. Click an icon to choose what type of report you want to print:

    ◆ The Emergency Report prints contact numbers, medical history, and insurance information.

    ◆ The Comprehensive Report prints all of the information you entered.

    ◆ Click Choose a Section to pick the sections of the Organizer that you want to print.

    A preview dialog box will open, showing you how the report will look when printed.

12. Click the Print button to print your report.

173

Using the Financial Calculators

Quicken Deluxe 2001 includes six financial planning calculators to let you try "what if?" scenarios. You can use these calculators to get quick answers when you're considering a financial move, such as taking on a new mortgage. Five of the financial planning calculators work in basically the same way—except that the information you enter and the calculations Quicken makes will be different. See Chapter 18 for information on using the sixth calculator, the Quicken Tax Planner.

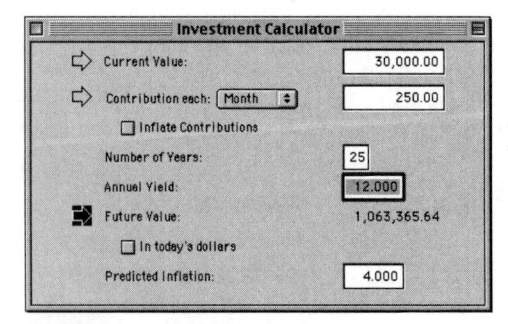

Chapter 17.30 Use the financial planning calculators for quick "what if?" analysis.

To use a financial calculator:

1. Choose Activities > Planning Calculators, and then choose the calculator that you want from the six on the menu.

    The calculator screen opens (**Figure 17.30**).

2. Click the arrow next to the type of calculation that you want Quicken to figure out.

3. Enter information into the calculator, and Quicken displays the results.

QUICKEN AT TAX TIME

18

Personally, I don't know anyone who enjoys paying taxes. I've heard that such people actually exist, but I've never met them. For the rest of us, preparing and paying taxes is a yearly ritual that we could easily live without.

Quicken can help to ease some of the pain (although if you end up writing a check instead of receiving a refund, Quicken can't do anything about the agony you'll feel). By categorizing your income and expenses, you'll be able to create reports that make filling out your tax forms much easier. Using these reports can also save you money if your taxes are prepared by someone else, because the preparer will have less digging to do to get a picture of your financial situation.

If you're the do-it-yourself type, you can export Quicken data to a tax preparation program called TurboTax for the Mac (previously called MacInTax), also made by Intuit. With federal and state tax forms built in, TurboTax for the Mac can do a complete job of tax preparation, from finding information to calculating and printing your final tax return.

When it comes to taxes, I hate surprises. I use the Quicken Tax Planner to get a ballpark figure for my taxes before I see my accountant.

In this chapter, you'll see how to do some tax planning, create these reports, and get your Quicken data ready for TurboTax for the Mac.

Chapter 18

Planning for Taxes

You can't avoid paying taxes altogether, but it's perfectly OK to work hard at finding and using every tax deduction that you can legally claim. Quicken has two tools that you can use to help reduce your tax load: the Tax Deduction Finder, one of the planners available from Quicken.com; and the Quicken Tax Planner, a financial calculator that lets you try out different tax scenarios.

To use the Tax Deduction Finder:

1. Choose Online > To the Web > Tax Deduction Finder, or click the Deduct button on the Planning section of the toolbar. Your Web browser opens, and the Tax Deduction Finder's Welcome screen appears. Click the link titled "Start the Deduction Finder now!"

   You may see another Welcome screen with an explanation of the Tax Deduction Finder (I say "may" because this screen has been on and off the site a few times, depending on changes Intuit's made to the site. If you see the screen, click the Continue link. The Introduction screen of the TurboTax Deduction Finder opens in a new window (**Figure 18.1**). If you don't see the Welcome screen, ignore this step.

2. Read the introductory text, and then click the Next button. The Main Categories screen appears (**Figure 18.2**).

3. Choose one or more of the General Categories of Deductions. Click the Next button, and the Deduction Types screen appears (**Figure 18.3**).

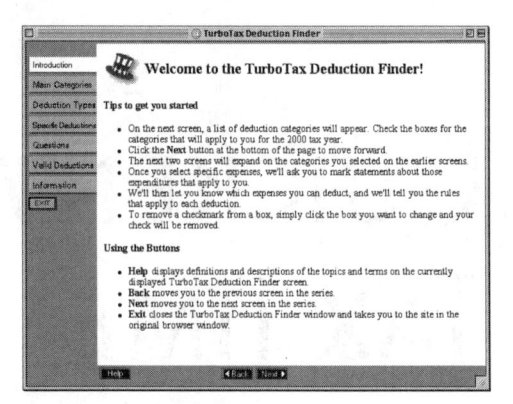

Figure 18.1 Read the introductory information, and then move on.

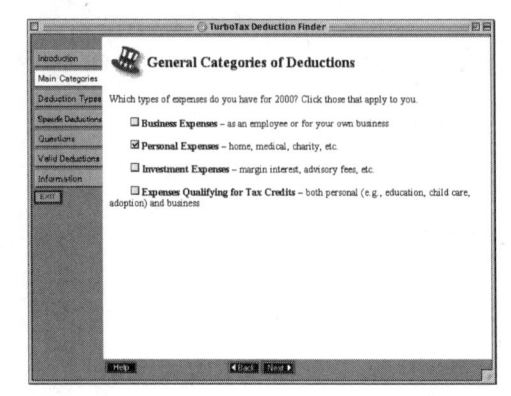

Figure 18.2 Choose one or more of the main deductions categories.

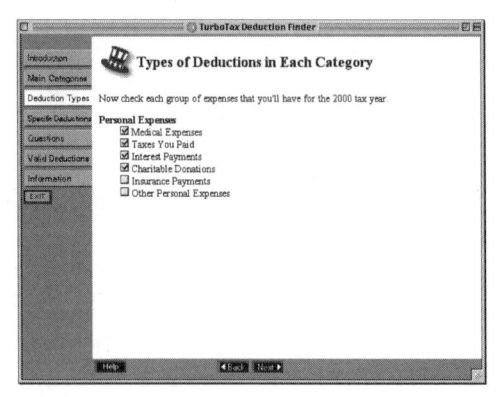

Figure 18.3 Narrow your deduction choices here.

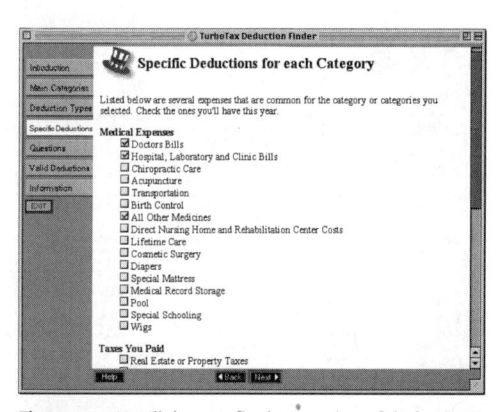

Figure 18.4 You'll do your final narrowing of deductions on this screen.

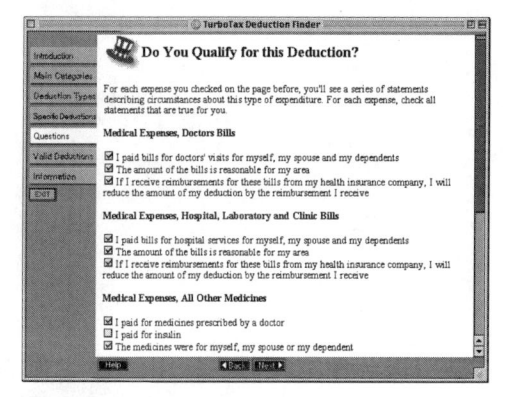

Figure 18.5 Before you find out what deductions you're eligible for, you'll need to answer some questions.

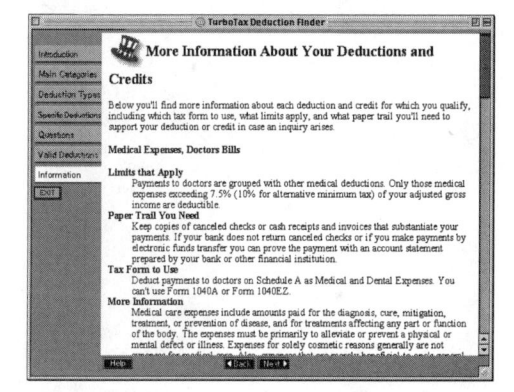

Figure 18.6 You'll find out what your valid deductions are here.

4. Depending on the Main Categories you chose in Step 3, you'll get a varying number of choices on this screen. Regardless of how many choices you have, make some deduction choices on this screen, and then click the Next button. The Specific Deductions screen appears (**Figure 18.4**).

5. Each of the choices you made on the Deduction Types screen gets expanded and detailed here. Continue checking the kinds of deductions for which you think you might be eligible. Click the Next button, and the Questions screen appears (**Figure 18.5**).

6. The planner will list questions for each of your previous specific deduction choices. Answer the questions, clicking the checkboxes next to the statements that are true for your situation. When you've worked your way through the list, click the next button, and the Valid Deductions screen appears (**Figure 18.6**).

(continued)

7. The planner lists the deductions for which it thinks you may qualify. Review these; if you're not happy with the list, you can click the Back button and revise your previous choices (but I do suggest you keep things truthful!). Click the next button to get to the Information screen (**Figure 18.7**).

8. The Information screen gives you all of the information you need to take advantage of the tax deductions you've found. For each deduction, you'll find the following:

    Limits that Apply: Tells you the maximum allowable deduction. For example, it tells you that you can only deduct medical expenses that exceed 7.5% of your adjusted gross income.

    Paper Trail You Need: Lists the paperwork you'll have to have to keep the IRS sharks from circling.

    Tax Form to Use: Which federal tax form you'll use to apply for the deduction.

    More Information: Any other useful information that applies to the deduction.

    IRS Publication(s) to Read: Lists the relevant IRS publications for the deduction. Under this item, you'll find a handy link to the online publication list.

9. If you want a copy of the Information screen to show to your tax preparer, choose File > Print in your Web browser.

10. When you're done, click the Exit button or close the Tax Deduction Finder window.

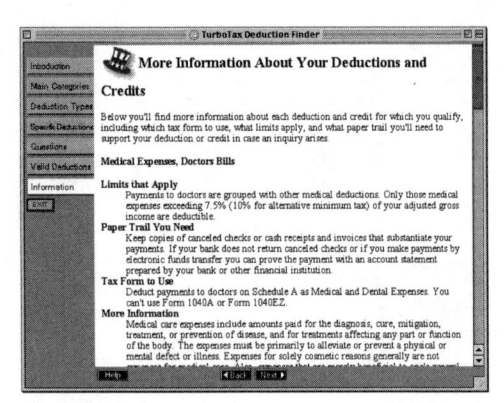

Figure 18.7 The Information screen gives you detailed information about deductions.

✔ **Tips**

- To use the Tax Deduction Finder, you'll have to have JavaScript enabled in your Web browser.

- You can call the Internal Revenue Service with general tax questions at (800) 829-1040.

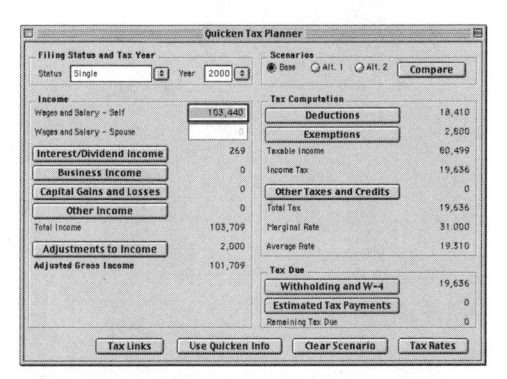

Figure 18.8 In the Quicken Tax Planner window, click the "Use Quicken Info" button and Quicken will draw on your data file to fill in the data.

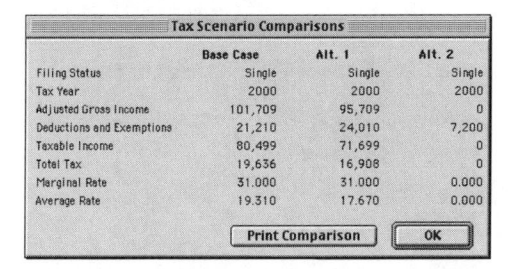

Figure 18.9 The Compare button gives you a quick side-by-side view of the tax scenarios.

To use the Tax Planner:

1. Choose Activities > Planning Calculators > Tax. The Quicken Tax Planner window appears (**Figure 18.8**).

2. Under "Filing Status and Tax Year" at the top of the window, choose your filing status and the tax year from the pop-up menus.

3. Click the "Use Quicken Info" button at the bottom of the window to have the planner import your financial data from the data file.

4. Click the "Tax Links" button at the bottom of the window to open the Assign Tax Links window, where you can assign Quicken categories to specific line items on federal tax forms.

   For more information about Tax Links, see Chapter 3. (In general, the more Tax Links you assign the better, in terms of the Quicken Tax Planner's accuracy.)

5. You can click any of the buttons in the Income or Tax Computation areas to enter detailed information.

6. After you have entered all your tax information, the tax planner calculates your total tax, which shows you the amount you owe the IRS or the amount of your refund.

✔ Tip

- If you want to see the tax implications of decisions such as buying a home or filing taxes jointly or separately, you can try out three different tax scenarios and Quicken will give you the results. Click the Scenarios radio buttons, fill in the alternate information, and then click the Compare button to see the difference between the scenarios (**Figure 18.9**). If you want a hard copy, click the Print Comparison button.

Creating Tax Reports

Your accountant will probably be interested in four kinds of Quicken reports while preparing your tax return:

- A **Category Summary** report shows the totals for all of your income and expense categories.

- A **Tax Summary** report shows your tax-related income and expenses, subtotaled by category.

- The **Tax Schedule** report groups information from all accounts in your data file that have tax lines assigned to them. The report lists information grouped by tax form.

- A **Capital Gains** report shows the realized capital gains from your investment accounts.

You create and print each of these reports in almost exactly the same way. (For more information about creating reports, see Chapter 12.)

Quicken at Tax Time

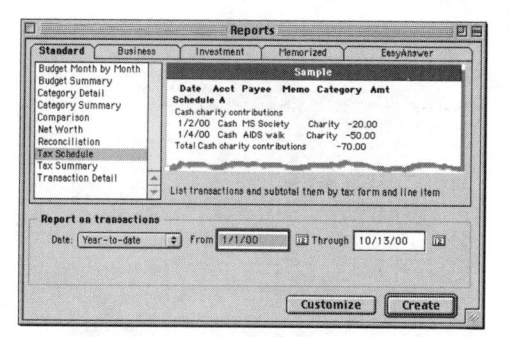

Figure 18.10 You can obtain specific tax reports from this window.

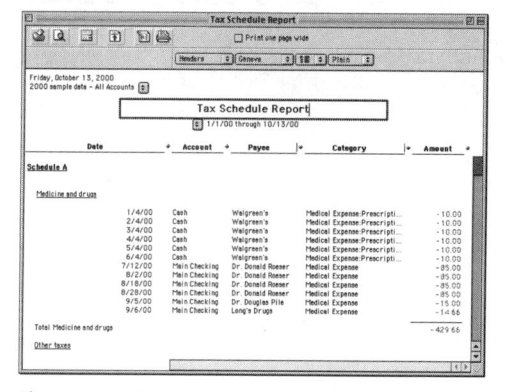

Figure 18.11 This Tax Schedule report shows you the results of your Tax Links, organized by the federal forms to which they pertain.

To create a tax report:

1. Click the Reports button in the Reporting section of the toolbar or choose Activities > Reports & Graphs > Reports to open the Reports window (**Figure 18.10**).

2. Click the Standard tab in the Reports window, and then click Category Summary, Tax Schedule, or Tax Summary in the scrolling list on the left side of the window.

   or

   Click the Investment tab in the Reports window, and then click Capital Gains in the scrolling list on the left side of the window.

3. Change the date range in the bottom of the window to print reports for particular dates, as needed.

4. Click the Create button. Quicken creates and displays the report (**Figure 18.11**).

CREATING TAX REPORTS

181

Exporting Quicken Data to TurboTax

Quicken can save data from a tax schedule report or a capital gains report in a format that's compatible with TurboTax for the Mac. This format is called Tax Exchange Format (TXF). TurboTax for the Mac can then read in the TXF file, saving you from having to do a lot of repetitive data entry.

To export Quicken data:

1. Create the tax report you want to export, and leave it open on your screen.

2. Choose File > Export Report. The standard Save dialog box will appear (**Figure 18.12**).

3. Enter a name for the report file in the "Export to File" box.

4. Click the MacInTax (TXF) button.

5. Click the Save button.

✔ Tips

- If the MacInTax (TXF) button is not visible in the Save dialog box, it is probably because you have created a report that isn't a tax schedule or capital gains report and therefore isn't appropriate to send to TurboTax for the Mac.

- The reason that the Save dialog box still refers to MacInTax, instead of TurboTax for the Mac, is that Intuit changed the name of the program after Quicken 2001 was completed.

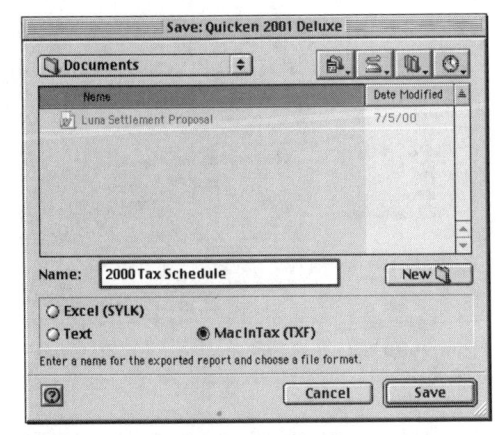

Figure 18.12 For the report to format correctly for TurboTax for the Mac, you must select the MacInTax (TXF) radio button in the Save dialog box.

Using Quicken.com

19

Quicken is a terrific tool for helping you manage your money, but these days, an incredible amount of financial options are available to you. To make smart financial decisions, you're going to need the most up-to-date financial and investment information. That's where Quicken.com, Intuit's huge Web site at http://www.quicken.com, comes in.

Quicken.com offers up-to-the-minute news, price quotes, and information about the securities markets; tips from financial experts; access to online stock brokerages; retirement planning tools; and current tax information, including explanations of wacky changes Congress makes in the tax code.

The Web site tries to cover every aspect of your financial life by organizing its content into six sections: Investing, Mortgage, Insurance, Taxes, Banking, and Retirement. Besides these six, the front page of the site is a portal page that you can customize with your investment portfolio, breaking financial news, and an overview of the markets. In this chapter, you'll see how to use some of Quicken.com's financial tools. Alas, I barely have room to scratch the surface. But do spend some time browsing the site; it will be time well spent.

Getting Around on Quicken.com

Before you start browsing the site, you should know what equipment and software you need to view Quicken.com. At a minimum, you'll need the following:

- A modem or another connection device. If you're using a modem, its speed should be at least 33.6 kilobits per second (Kbps). These days, most modems sold are 56 Kbps. If you're lucky enough to have a faster connection to the Internet, such as a cable modem, a DSL or ISDN line, or a local area network, so much the better.

- An account with an Internet Service Provider (ISP). An ISP sells access to the Internet. When you sign up with an ISP, you usually get an e-mail account and the ability to create your own Web site, as well as access to the various Internet services. Many people use America Online as their ISP, and the America Online 5.0 software comes on the Quicken Deluxe 2001 CD-ROM.

- Web browsing software. Microsoft Internet Explorer 5.0 is included on the Quicken Deluxe 2001 CD-ROM.

The process of getting an account with an ISP and signing onto the Internet for the first time is beyond the scope of this book, so I will assume you've taken care of that part.

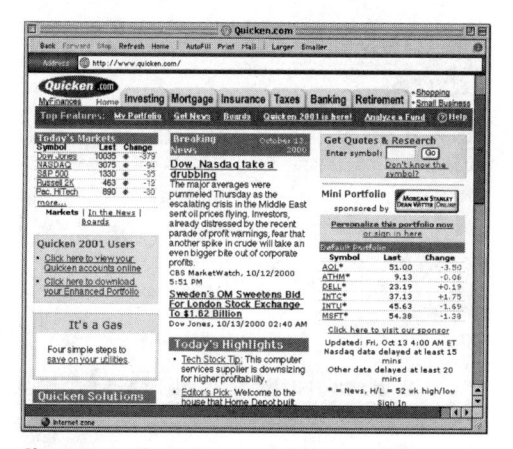

Chapter 19.1 The Quicken.com front page is a financial portal with news and market information.

To log on to Quicken.com:

1. Choose Online > To the Web > Quicken.com.

    You should see a screen like the one shown in **Figure 19.1**. If you get to Quicken.com and the screen looks different, chances are Intuit has redesigned the site since I wrote this book in the summer and fall of 2000. Don't panic; companies are forever changing their Web sites. Just poke around until you find what you're looking for. Believe me, there is enough stuff here—if you were to follow all the links—to keep you entertained for days.

2. Along the top of the screen, in the navigation bar, you can click one of Quicken.com's department names to go to that section of the site.

    To the left you'll see a capsule of the market close, financial news takes up the middle of the window, and a Mini Portfolio table appears on the right.

✔ Tips

- If you need to return to a previous page, use the Back button at the top of the browser window.

- You can click the Quicken.com logo at the top of most pages on the site to return to the Quicken.com home page.

Finding Investment Information

The Quicken.com department people use most often is Investments. It's impossible to discuss everything you could do in the Investments department in the amount of space that I have here, so I'll focus on just a few common tasks.

To find a security quote:

1. If you're interested in a quote on a particular security, and you know the security's ticker symbol, type the symbol in the "Get Quotes and Research" area in the "Enter symbol" box.

2. Click the Go button, and a detailed quote page for the security appears (**Figure 19.2**).

3. If you're interested in finding out other information about the same security, choose an option from among the links that run down the left side of the page, under the security's name.

   (For example, after you click the Chart link, you'll see a page that looks like **Figure 19.3**.)

4. Continue your research on the stock by clicking other links from the left column or by modifying the type of chart or the period it covers from the pull-down menus that appear above it.

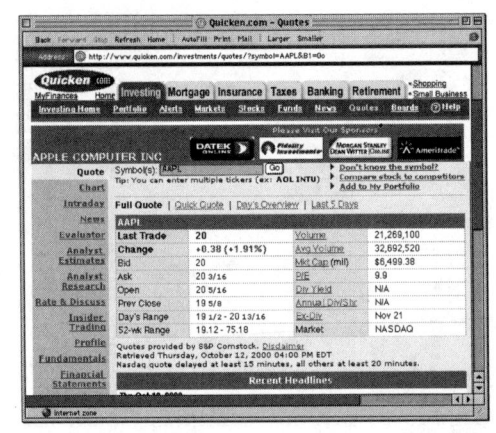

Chapter 19.2 This is the kind of detailed security information you can find on Quicken.com.

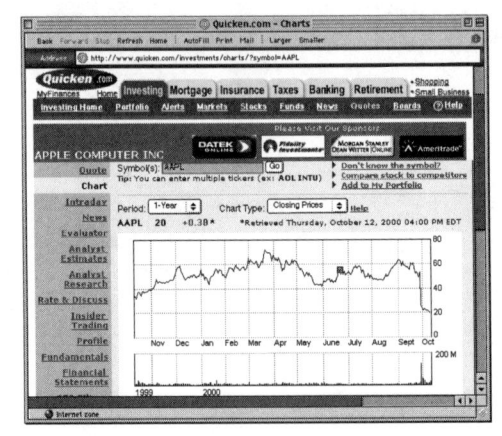

Chapter 19.3 Click the Chart link on the quotes page to see a chart showing information about the security.

✔ Tip

- You can add another stock to the chart by typing its symbol into the Symbols box at the top of the page. Quicken will even help you find the stock's competitors with the "Stock Comparison" lookup feature that appears next to the box.

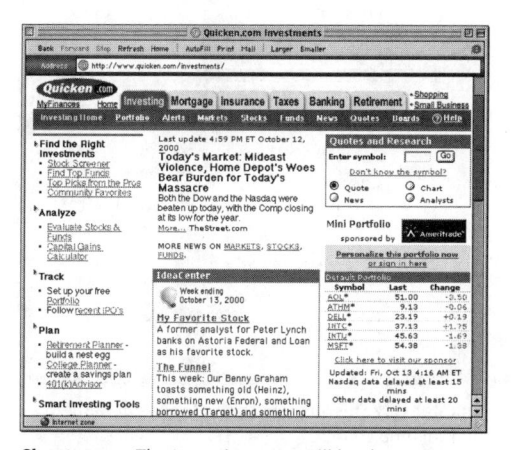

Choosing a Mutual Fund

Thousands of mutual funds are available, and each fund has its own investment objectives. Selecting a mutual fund that meets your criteria for investment is fairly easy using Quicken.com, because it contains detailed information on almost all funds.

To find a mutual fund:

1. Click the Investing tab in the navigation bar across the top of the screen. The Investing page appears (**Figure 19.4**).

2. Click "Pick Top Funds" from the "Find the Right Investments" section at the upper left. The Mutual Fund Finder page (**Figure 19.5**) appears.

3. Click the "Popular Searches" link.

   A list of canned (but still useful) searches appears (**Figure 19.6**).

   (continued)

Chapter 19.4 The Investing page will be the springboard for your investing activities.

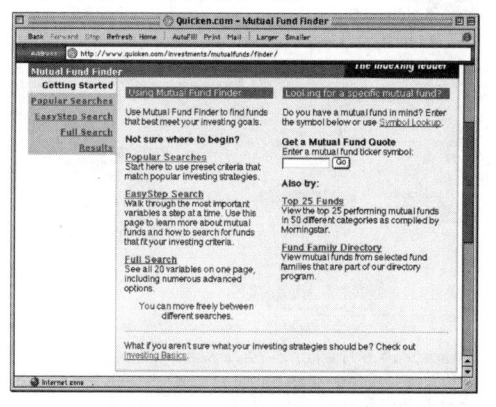

Chapter 19.5 The Mutual Fund Finder page help you research different mutual funds.

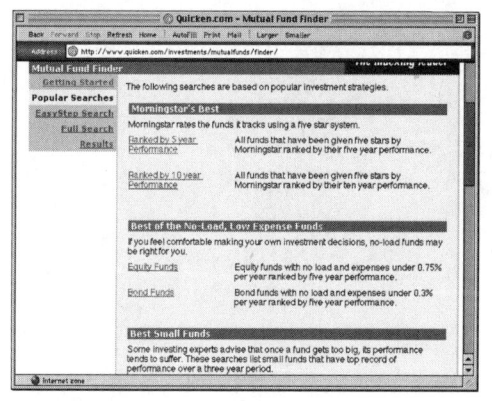

Chapter 19.6 The easiest way to get started is to choose one of the standard searches.

Chapter 19

4. Click a type of search that interests you. The Mutual Fund Finder will show the results of your search (**Figure 19.7**). (For example, clicking "Ranked by 5 year Performance" will show you a ranking of the mutual fund against other funds.)

5. To refine your search, change the variables listed above the chart in the Display and Sort pull-down menus, or click the EasyStep Search wizard link to go step by step through a more customized process. Or you can make a more sophisticated search by clicking the Full Search link on the left.

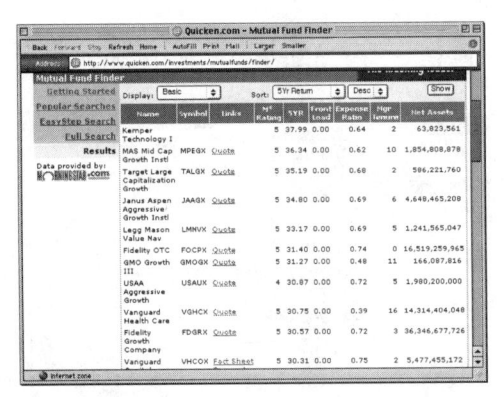

Chapter 19.7 This window shows the result of the mutual fund search.

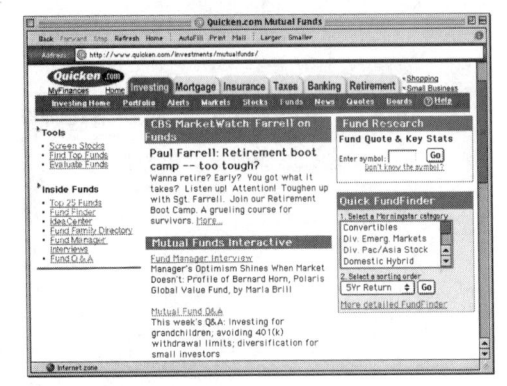

✔ Tip

■ You can find more information on mutual funds by clicking Funds on the navigation bar across the top of any of the screens in the Investing section to open the Mutual Funds page (**Figure 19.8**).

Chapter 19.8 The Funds Page has additional information and tools to help you choose a fund that's right for you.

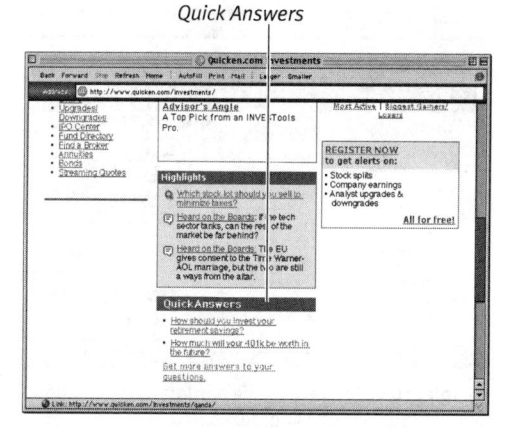

Insights on Investing

Investing can be confusing. The terminology is often complex, with arcane concepts, weird acronyms, and convoluted explanations. Do you know what an index fund is? Why is Morningstar important? What does it mean to sell a stock short? Are DRIPs good for you? Thankfully, Quicken.com has a place where you can find answers to your questions.

To get answers to basic investing questions:

1. From the Investments page, scroll down and click one of the questions under the Quick Answers category (**Figure 19.9**). One of the Quick Answers pages will open with the information you requested.

2. Return to the Investments page by clicking your browser's back button. Click the "Get more answers to your questions" link to open the QuickAnswers page (**Figure 19.10**).

3. Find the question that you want answered in the QuickAnswers list, and then click the question to jump to its answer page. If you can't find the question that you want answered in the list, look through the Quick Answer Categories list on the left side of the page for a section of the site that might help you.

Chapter 19.9 Choose one of the topics under QuickAnswers to learn more about investments.

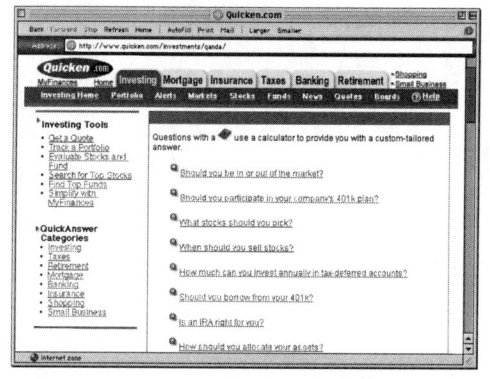

Chapter 19.10 Find the question that you want answered in the QuickAnswers list.

Chapter 19

Getting Tax Information

The more information you have about taxes, the more likely you are to make intelligent decisions when tax time comes. The Taxes section of Quicken.com has a lot of general tax information and a tax estimating tool—and you can even download federal and state tax forms from the site.

To find tax tips and advice:

1. From the main Quicken.com page (shown in **Figure 19.1**), click Taxes in the top navigation bar.

   The main Taxes page appears (**Figure 19.11**).

2. At the top of the page, under the navigation bar, click the "Tax Filing" link to get step-by-step information about filing, and the Expert Answers section gives you tips on avoiding the tax man's outstretched hand.

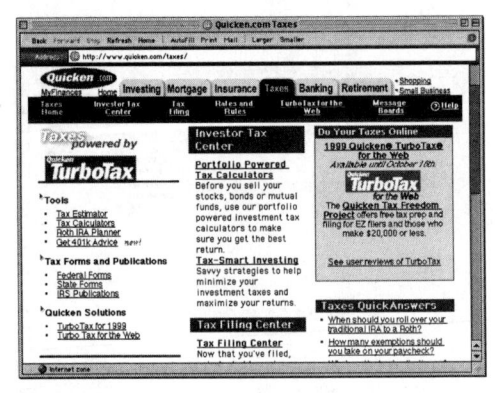

Chapter 19.11 The Taxes page has lots of information to help you minimize your taxes.

Using Quicken.com

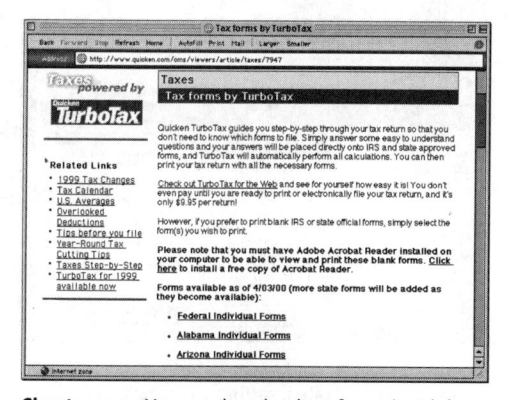

Chapter 19.12 You can download tax forms in Adobe Acrobat format right from the TurboTax Web site.

Downloading tax forms

Quicken.com lets you download federal and state tax forms from the TurboTax Web site. You can then print these forms and use them to file your taxes. The files are in the Adobe Acrobat format (sometimes called PDF files, for Portable Document Format). To read Acrobat files, you need to install the free Acrobat Reader program. It comes on the Quicken Deluxe 2001 CD-ROM, it's available on the Quicken.com Web site, or you can download it from Adobe's Web site at http://www.adobe.com.

To download tax forms:

1. In the Tax Forms and Publications section on the left side of the main Taxes page (shown in **Figure 19.11**), click the link "Federal Forms."

   The Retrieve Forms and Instructions page on the Internal Revenue Service site appears (**Figure 19.12**).

2. Scroll down the list until you find the tax form or forms that you want to download. Click the title of a form to download it to your hard disk.

GETTING TAX INFORMATION

191

Finding Low-Rate Credit Cards

Credit cards are handy to use, but they can be a major source of financial frivolity. If you don't pay off your credit card balance in full every month, you rack up interest charges. If you can't avoid carrying a balance, you can at least try to minimize the amount of interest you're paying by finding a credit card with a low interest rate.

Quicken.com's Banking area offers a list of credit card providers with the lowest rates as well as other useful information, such as mortgage interest rates, savings account interest yields, and general banking information.

To find low-rate credit cards:

1. From the main Quicken.com page, choose Banking from the top navigation bar.

    The main Banking page appears (**Figure 19.13**).

2. Click Credit from the navigation bar. The Credit Card page appears (**Figure 19.14**).

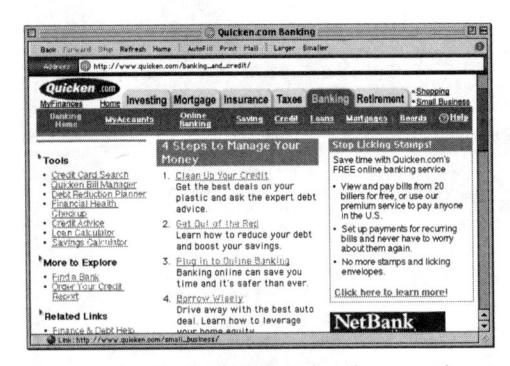

Chapter 19.13 The Banking page has tips on getting better credit card rates, setting up online banking, and a variety of useful financial calculators.

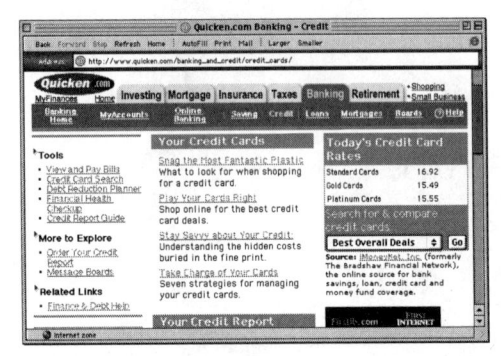

Chapter 19.14 In the navigation bar at the top of this page, click "Credit" under the Banking tab to get useful credit card information.

Using Quicken.com

Chapter 19.15 Choose the credit card criteria that's right for you.

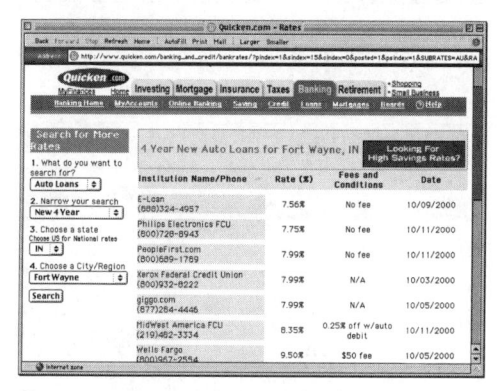

3. Under the Search for & Compare Credit Cards heading on the right side of the page, choose the card criterion you wish to search on from the pop-up menu (**Figure 19.15**), and then click the Go button.

   The results screen appears, showing credit card companies ranked by the parameter you chose.

✔ Tip

- From the results screen, you can change your search criteria using the pull-down menus next to the list. You can even make quick searches for other interest rates, choosing from the options in the pull-down menus that appear for the rate type you have selected. For example, **Figure 19.16** shows how you can get rates for four-year automobile loans in Fort Wayne, Indiana.

Chapter 19.16 You can find other interest-rate information by choosing options from the pop-up menus.

FINDING LOW-RATE CREDIT CARDS

193

Other Areas of Interest

Each of the six departments on the Quicken.com site has its own wealth of information. (It also has, as you have probably noticed, quite a bit of advertising.)

The Insurance department (**Figure 19.17**) explains the different types of insurance and even lets you shop for good rates on life, auto, and health insurance.

The Retirement department (**Figure 19.18**) is an important section for you to check out. It provides tons of good economic advice on your 401(k), Individual Retirement Accounts, Pension plans, Keogh plans, and much more.

The Message Boards area (**Figure 19.19**) is a collection of wide-ranging forums on stocks, insurance, and other issues; from here you can read what other people have to say about these issues and add comments of your own.

In general, you will find that Quicken.com and all the links it provides are about as rich a resource for economic advice and research as you are likely to find without paying for it.

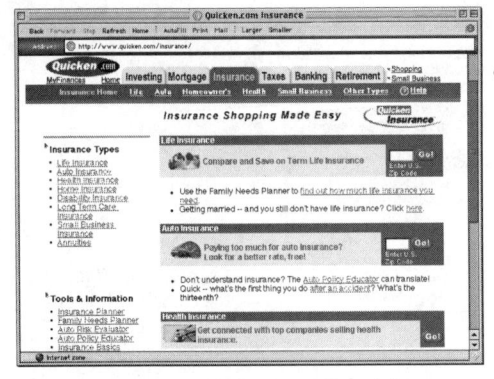

Chapter 19.17 The Insurance area will explain—or sell—a variety of insurance choices.

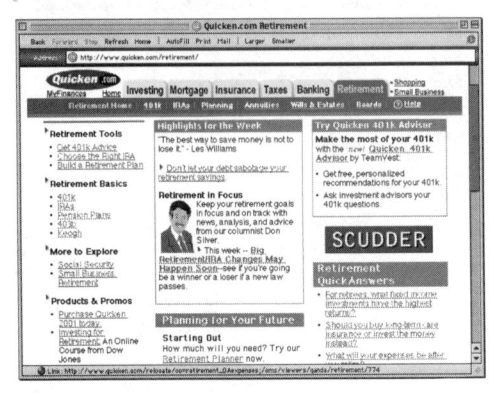

Chapter 19.18 You can make sure your retirement plan is on track in the Retirement area.

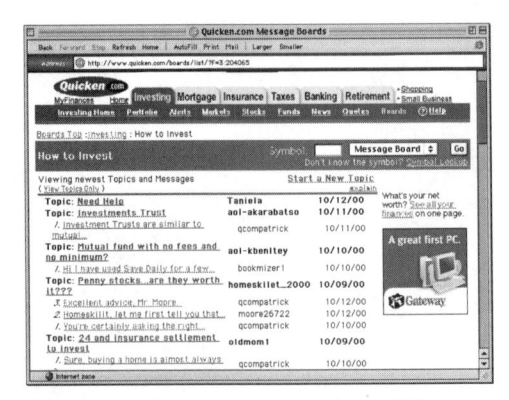

Chapter 19.19 In the Message Boards, you'll find a free-flowing exchange of information, misinformation, and gossip for you to sort through.

INDEX

Symbols
/ (slash), 29
[ ] (square brackets), 42

A
account buttons
   illustrated, 7
   minimizing space for, 9
account register mode button (Enter Transaction window), 68
account registers, 33–50
   about transactions and, 33
   check editing in, 60
   deleting transactions in, 45, 72
   depositing paychecks, 40
   editing transactions in, 45, 60
   entering checking account transactions, 34–36
   entering credit card charges, 41, 98
   finding and replacing transactions in, 46–48
   illustrated, 34
   for mutual funds, 148
   printing, 125
   QuickEntry with, 50
   QuickMath for, 49
   sorting, 37
   splitting transactions, 38–39
   transferring money between accounts, 42–44
   voiding transactions on, 45
   zooming from reports to, 117
   See also accounts; reconciling accounts

accounts
   adding mutual fund, 148
   adjusting balance during reconciliation, 94
   automatically creating liability, 135
   choosing checking, 34
   creating, 20–22
   deleting, 22
   editing or hiding, 21, 22
   enabling for online use, 105
   entering opening balances in, 21
   loan, 136–137, 139
   number of allowable, 17
   problems with beginning, 91
   setting up Portfolio, 144–145
   transferring money between, 42–44
   types of, 20
   See also account registers; reconciling accounts; *specific accounts by name*
Accounts list, 99
Accounts window, 20
Action Plan window (Debt Reduction Planner), 170
Action Plan window (Retirement Planner), 166
Action Type dialog box, 147
Actions, 79, 80, 81
Actions button, 155
activity areas, 5, 7
Add Security dialog box, 147
Adjust Ending Balance window, 94
Adjust Total button, 39

Adobe Acrobat, 15, 191
amortization, 135
Asset account
   about, 20
   entering opening balances in, 21
   using for investments, 142, 143
Assets & Debt area, 5, 7
Assets worksheet (Retirement Planner), 164
Assign Tax Links window, 28
ATM withdrawals, 36

B
backdrop
   about, 6
   changing or removing, 8
backing up files
   automatically, 11
   before converting, 4
   creating strategy for, 13
balances
   adjusting reconciliation, 94
   entering opening, 21
balancing accounts, 89–94
   about, 89
   adjusting balance, 94
   for checking, savings, and money market, 90–91
   for credit card, 92
   finding and correcting differences, 93
balloon help, 14
Bank accounts
   about, 20
   entering opening balances in, 21

195

Index

Bank accounts *(continued)*
    setting up online banking, 104–105
    using for investments, 142, 143
    See also online banking and bill payment
Banking area, 5, 7
Beginning Balance box (Reconcile Startup window), 90
Bill Candidates window, 73
Billminder, 77
bills
    allowing time for electronic payment processing, 111
    paying using Calendar, 75
    scheduling payment on Calendar, 73–74
    setting preferences for suggesting, 75
    setting up online payment for, 110–111
    See also online banking and bill payment; payments
browser software, 184
Budget Monitoring window, 102
Budget Setup window, 101
budgets
    setting up, 100–101
    tracking expenditures with Budget Monitor, 102
    using graphs to develop, 127
Buy dialog box, 155
Buy window, 148

C

calculators, 174
Calendar, 67–77
    about, 67
    adding transaction to, 68–70
    creating notes on, 76
    deleting transactions on, 72
    displaying, 68
    editing transaction, 71
    paying bills using, 75
    scheduling bills on, 73–74
    using Billminder with, 77
    viewing scheduled transactions, 71
Calendar button (Write Checks window), 58
Calendar icon, 35
Capital Gains report, 180

Cash account
    about, 20
    entering opening balances in, 21
categories, 23–31
    adding, 31
    assigning and creating, 24–25
    creating subcategories, 26
    deleting subcategories and, 27
    demoting to subcategory, 31
    editing subcategories and, 26–27
    linking to tax forms, 28, 179
    overview, 23
    renaming, 31
    sorting in Categories & Transfers window, 27
    See also classes
Categories & Transfers window, 25, 26
Category Summary report, 180
CD-ROM
    Acrobat Installer on, 15
    America Online software on, 184
    Microsoft Internet Explorer on, 184
certificate of deposits (CDs), 142, 143
changing dates, 35
Chart link (Quicken.com Web site), 186
charts. *See* graphs
checking accounts
    balancing, 90–91
    choosing and opening, 34–35
    creating data file and, 18–19
    entering post-dated checks, 36
    entering transactions in, 34–36
    See also checks
checks, 57–65
    about, 57
    deleting, 61
    editing, 60
    memo and note lines on, 60
    memorizing transactions for, 40
    ordering, 61, 62
    positioning in printer, 65
    post-dated, 36
    preparing to print, 63
    printing, 64–65
    source for computer checks, 61

checks *(continued)*
    voiding, 61
    write checks mode for Enter Transaction window, 69
    writing, 58–60
Checks button, 58
Chooser window, selecting printer in, 63
classes
    about, 29, 31
    creating, 30
    editing or deleting, 31
    renaming, 31
    See also categories
Classes window, 30
Collapse header icon, 120
College Planner, 160
command buttons, 7
Configure Toolbar window, 9
Confirm Scheduled Transaction window, 75
Content tab (Customize Category Summary Report), 121
controlling credit card debt
    about, 95
    by budgeting, 100–101
    setting credit limits, 99
    tracking expenditures with Budget Monitor, 102
    See also Credit Card accounts; debt
converting old files, 4
Create Budget window, 100
Create QuickReport dialog box, 116
Credit Card account button, 97
Credit Card accounts, 95–102
    about, 20, 95
    balancing, 92
    charges for, 41
    credit limits for, 99
    entering transactions in, 97–98
    opening balances in, 21
    setting up budget, 100
    setting up for online banking, 41
    tracking credit card transactions, 96
    See also controlling credit card debt
Credit Card page (Quicken.com), 192–193

Index

credit limits for credit cards, 99
credit reports, free, 16, 161, 162
custom reports, 121
Customize Category Summary
  Report window, 121
Customize Expense Comparison
  Graph window, 85
Customize Graph window, 132
Customize Insights dialog box, 82
customizing
  graphs, 132
  Insights page, 82
  layout of reports, 119–120
  toolbar, 8–9

D

data files
  backing up, 11, 13
  creating checking account
    and, 18–19
  exporting to TurboTax, 182
  having multiple, 19
  protecting with password, 12
  using preset category lists
    for, 24
Date field
  keyboard shortcuts for, 35
  sorting account registers by, 37
dates
  changing, 35
  quick entry of, 36
debt
  controlling credit card, 95,
    99, 101–102
  finding low-rate credit cards,
    192–193
  planning reduction of, 167–170
  spending savings to reduce,
    169
Debt Plan button, 167
Debt Reduction Planner, 16, 88,
  161, 167–170
Debts window (Debt Reduction
  Planner), 167
Deduct button, 176
deleting
  accounts, 22
  categories and subcategories,
    27
  checks, 61
  classes or subclasses, 31
  memorized graphs, 133
  QuickFill transactions, 56

deleting *(continued)*
  transactions in account
    registers, 45, 72
  transactions on Calendar, 72
deposits, 34–36, 40
Difference this Statement field
  (Reconcile window), 93
displaying
  Calendar, 68, 69
  current net worth value on
    Net Worth graph, 131
  detail on EasyAnswer graphs,
    129
Download button, 106
Download Historical Prices
  dialog box, 153
Download Summary window, 152
Download Transactions window,
  106
downloading
  historical prices from
    Quicken.com, 153
  prices for stocks, 152
  tax forms, 191
  transactions, 106–108

E

Easy Install option, 2
EasyAnswer graphs, 128–129
EasyAnswer reports, 115
EasyAnswer tab (Reports
  window), 115
Edit Account window, 21, 99
Edit columns icon, 120
Edit Columns window, 120
Edit Command Key dialog box,
  10
Edit menu, 10
editing
  account register transactions,
    45
  accounts, 21
  categories and subcategories,
    26–27
  checks, 60
  classes or subclasses, 31
  QuickFill transactions, 55
  transactions on Calendar, 71
EFT (Electronic Funds Transfer),
  108
Emergency Records Organizer
  about, 16, 159
  using, 171–173

Enable Online Banking window,
  105
encryption, 108
Enter Online Payment, 110
Enter Transaction window, 68, 69
EPay button, 110
expenses
  categories for, 24
  tracking with classes, 31
Expenses window (Debt
  Reduction Planner), 169
exporting Quicken data to
  TurboTax, 182

F

fields
  Date, 35, 37
  defined, 34
  moving between, 36
  Number, 36, 37
  scrolling entries in QuickFill,
    36
files
  backing up, 11, 13
  converting old, 4
finance charges, 41
financial analysis, 79–88
  customizing Insights page
    for, 82
  drilling deeper into
    accounting data, 85–86
  Insight features for
    customizing, 83–84
  retrieving information from
    Internet for, 87–88
financial calculators, 174
Financial Calendar.
  See Calendar
financial institutions downloading transactions from,
  106–108
  list of online, 104
financial planning. *See* planning
Find and Replace dialog box
  finding transactions in, 46
  replacing transactions in, 48
finding
  differences during reconcilia-
    tion, 93
  low-rate credit cards,
    192–193
  mutual funds, 187–188
  search criteria for, 47

197

Index

finding *(continued)*
    security quotes on Quicken.com, 186
    tax tips and advice on Quicken.com, 190
finding and replacing
    categories, 27
    transactions, 46–48
fonts and style options for reports, 118
forgotten passwords, 12
free credit report, 16, 161, 162
Funds page (Quicken.com), 188

G

graphs, 127–134
    about, 127
    customizing, 132
    deleting memorized, 133
    EasyAnswer, 128–129
    memorizing, 133
    Net Worth, 131
    printing, 134
    Standard, 130
    using QuickZoom on Easy-Answer graphs, 129
Graphs button, 128
Graphs window, 128, 130, 133

H

handwritten checks, 65
headers for reports, 120
help
    balloon, 14
    for Quicken, 14
    in user's guide, 15
hiding accounts, 21, 22
Historical Price button, 153

I

icons
    Calendar, 35
    Collapse header, 120
    Edit columns, 120
    Install Quicken 2001, 2
    Page break, 120
    Quicken 2001 Deluxe, 3
income categories, 24
Income vs. Expenses graph, 83
Insights button, 82
Insights page, 79–88
    about, 79–81

Insights page *(continued)*
    customizing, 82
    features for customizing financial analysis, 83–84
    investigating deeper into accounting data on, 85–86
    retrieving information from Internet for, 87–88
Install Quicken 2001 window, 2
installing Quicken, 2
Insurance department (Quicken.com Web site), 194
interest. *See* loans and mortgages
Internal Revenue Service, 178
Internet
    connecting to Quicken.com Web site, 184
    retrieving information for Insights page, 87–88
    setting up online banking, 104–105
    See also online banking and bill payment; Quicken.com Web site
Internet Service Provider (ISP), 184
Investing area, 5, 7, 52
investment accounts, 141–148
    about, 141
    adding Mutual Fund account, 148
    adding securities to portfolio, 146–148
    creating Portfolio account, 145
    downloading price quotes, 152
    setting up portfolio, 144–145
    types of, 142–143
    updating portfolio prices, 150, 152
    updating security prices, 151
    See also investments
Investment Actions window, 155
Investment Calculator window, 174
investments, 149–155
    basic questions about, 189
    buying and selling securities, 154–155
    downloading historical prices, 153
    downloading price quotes for, 152

investments *(continued)*
    searching Quicken.com for information on, 87
    transactions available in Quicken for, 154
    updating prices in portfolio, 150, 152
    updating security prices, 151
    See also investment accounts
ISP (Internet Service Provider), 184

J

JavaScript enabled for Tax Deduction Finder, 178

K

keyboard shortcuts
    for commands, 10
    for Date field, 35
    for Number fields, 36

L

launching Quicken, 3
Layout tab (Customize Category Summary Report), 121
Liability accounts
    about, 20
    creating automatically, 135
    entering opening balances in, 21
lists
    entering transactions from QuickFill, 54
    printing, 125
Lists menu, 34
Loan Interview window, 136
Loan Payment window, 140
loans and mortgages, 135–140
    about, 135
    creating loan as borrower, 136–137
    creating loan as lender, 139
    making payments on, 140
    researching on Quicken.com, 183
    viewing loan payment schedule, 138
Loans window, 136
locked transactions, 53, 55
logging on to Quicken.com, 185

Index

M

MacInTax. *See* TurboTax for the Mac
MacInTax (TXF) radio button (Save dialog box), 182
memo and note lines on checks, 60
Memorize Graph Template dialog box, 133
Memorize Report Template window, 122
Memorized tab (Graphs window), 133
Memorized tab (Reports window), 122
memorizing
   graphs, 133
   paychecks, 40
   QuickFill transactions, 53
   reports, 122
   transactions for check writing, 60
menu bar, 6
Message Boards (Quicken.com Web site), 194
minimizing account buttons, 9
Missed Bills options (Preferences window), 75
mistakes
   common, 94
   finding and correcting, 93
modem, 184
money market accounts
   balancing, 90–91
   selecting account type for tracking, 142, 143
More Personal Information window (Emergency Records Organizer), 172
Mortgage page (Quicken.com Web site), 88
mortgages. *See* loans and mortgages
mouse
   displaying detail on Easy-Answer graphs with, 129
   displaying detail on Net Worth graph, 131
multiple data files, 19
Mutual Fund account
   about, 20
   adding, 148

Mutual Fund account *(continued)*
   entering opening balances in, 21
   for mutual fund investments, 142, 143
Mutual Fund Finder page (Quicken.com), 187
mutual funds
   account registers for, 148
   online updates of, 152
   researching, 187–188

N

navigating on Quicken.com, 184
Net Worth Analysis, 16
Net Worth graph, 84, 131
New File dialog box, 18
New Price dialog box, 151
Next Steps window (Debt Reduction Planner), 170
notes on Calendar, 76
Number field
   keyboard shortcuts for, 36
   sorting account registers by, 37

O

Observations, 80, 81
online banking and bill payment, 103–111
   about, 103
   applying for online banking, 104–105
   balancing accounts with, 94
   creating and sending online payments, 110–111
   downloading transactions, 106–108
   enabling Quicken account for, 105
   security and, 108
   setting up Credit Card accounts for, 41
   setting up payees for, 109
   switching to online payment mode, 69
online payment mode, 69
online payments button (Enter Transaction window), 68
Online Transmissions Summary window, 107
Open File dialog box, 4
Open split button, 34

opening
   account register, 34
   Write Checks window for selected accounts, 59
opening balances, 21
ordering checks, 61, 62
Organization tab (Customize Category Summary Report), 121
organizing emergency records, 16, 159, 171–173
Out Box window, 110
Outbox button, 110

P

page breaks for reports, 120
parallel transactions for transfers, 43
passwords, 12
Pay button (Pay Credit Card Bill window), 92
Pay Credit Card Bill window, 92
paychecks. *See* checks
payees. *See* payments
Payees window, 109
Payment Schedule window, 130
Payment window (Debt Reduction Planner), 168
payments
   allowing time for electronic processing of, 111
   creating and sending online, 110–111
   making on loans and mortgages, 140
   previewing loan, 137
   scheduling on Calendar, 73–74
   scheduling payees for online, 109
   viewing schedule of loan, 138
   See also bills; online banking and bill payment
PIN number, 105, 107
planning, 157–174
   about, 157–158
   with Debt Reduction Planner, 167–170
   for insurance and retirement decisions, 194
   investigating tax implications of financial decisions, 179

Index

planning *(continued)*
    organizing emergency records, 16, 159, 171–173
    with Retirement Planner, 163–166
    for tax deductions, 176–179
    using financial calculators, 174
    using Quicken Home Inventory, 16, 159
    using Web-based planners, 160–162
    See also debt; taxes
Planning area, 5, 7
Portfolio accounts
    about, 20
    adding securities to, 146–148
    creating, 145
    entering opening balances in, 21
    setting up, 144–145
    using for investments, 142, 143
Portfolio window, 150
positioning checks in printer, 65
post-dated checks, 36
Preferences dialog box, 8, 50
preventing QuickFill entries, 36, 52
Preview Payment window, 137
prices
    downloading historical, 153
    downloading stock, 152
    updating in portfolio, 150
    updating security, 151
principal. *See* loans and mortgages
Print Checks Preferences window, 63
Print Checks window, 64
printer
    positioning checks in, 65
    selecting, 63
printing
    account register or list, 125
    checks, 64–65
    customizing report layout, 119–120
    emergency information reports, 173
    graphs, 134
    preparing to print checks, 63

printing *(continued)*
    reports, 118, 124
    selecting printer, 63
    stopping check, 65
programs and services of Quicken, 16

Q

QuickAnswers page (Quicken.com), 189
QuickBudget window, 100
Quicken 2001 Deluxe, 1–16
    activity areas in, 5
    backdrop in, 6
    backing up data files, 11, 13
    changing or removing backdrop, 8
    converting old files, 4
    customizing toolbar, 8–9
    enabling account for online use, 105
    exporting data to TurboTax, 182
    help for, 14
    how to use reports in, 114
    icon for, 3
    installing, 2
    keyboard shortcuts for commands, 10
    launching first time, 3
    menu bar, 6
    number of allowable accounts, 17
    programs and services, 16
    protecting data with password, 12
    quitting, 4
    toolbar in, 7
    transactions available for investments in, 154
    user's guide for, 15
Quicken.com Web site, 87, 183–194
    about, 183
    additional features of, 194
    downloading tax forms, 191
    finding tax tips and advice, 190
    getting answers to basic investing questions, 189
    getting security quotes on, 186

Quicken.com Web site *(continued)*
    logging on to, 185
    low-rate credit card information on, 192–193
    navigating on, 184
    planning with Retirement Planner, 163–166
    researching mutual funds, 187–188
    using Web-based planners, 160–162
Quicken Home Inventory, 16, 159
Quicken Quotes server, 87
Quicken Quotes window, 152
Quicken Tax Planner window, 179
QuickEntry, 16, 50
QuickFill, 51–56
    about, 52
    deleting transactions, 56
    disabling in split transactions, 39
    editing transactions for, 55
    entering transactions from list, 54
    locking or unlocking transactions, 55
    memorizing transactions, 53
    preventing or turning off, 36, 52
QuickMath, 49
QuickReport, 116
QuickZoom
    displaying graph details with, 129
    showing report details with, 117
quitting Quicken, 4
Quotes button, 152

R

real estate, 142, 143
recalculating
    Portfolio window, 150
    split transactions, 39
Reconcile button, 90
Reconcile Complete window, 91
Reconcile Startup window, 90
Reconcile window, 91

Index

reconciling accounts, 89–94
   about, 89
   adjusting balance, 94
   for checking, savings, and money market accounts, 90–91
   for credit card, 92
   finding and correcting differences, 93
Record button, 19, 34
Register section (Preferences dialog box), 60
registers. *See* account registers
renaming classes and categories, 31
Reporting area, 5, 7
reports, 113–125
   about, 113
   account register or list, 125
   custom, 121
   customizing layout, 119–120
   displaying details with QuickZoom, 117
   EasyAnswer, 115
   effect of deleting accounts on, 22
   emergency information, 173
   free credit, 16, 161, 162
   how to use, 114
   memorizing, 122
   printing, 118, 124
   searching for multiple transactions in, 47
   setting up QuickReport, 116
   shortcut, 123
   standard, 118
   tax, 180–181
   See also specific reports by name
Reports button, 115
Reports window, 115, 118, 122
Research Security dialog box, 87
Restore button, 34
Results window (Debt Reduction Planner), 168
Results window (Retirement Planner), 165
Retirement Benefits worksheet (Retirement Planner), 164
Retirement department (Quicken.com Web site), 194

Retirement Planner
   about, 16, 160
   setting up plans, 160, 163–166
Retirement Planner button, 163
Review Payee Info. window, 109
Risk & Return window (Retirement Planner), 165

S

Save dialog box, 18, 182
savings
   balancing account, 90–91
   spending to reduce debt, 169
Savings window (Debt Reduction Planner), 168
Scan for Bills button (Upcoming Bills and Scheduled Transactions window), 73
Scenarios radio button (Quicken Tax Planner), 179
scheduling
   bill payment, 73–74
   recurring transactions, 70
   transactions as recurring bill, 74
   viewing scheduled transactions, 71
Scheduling pop-up menu, 70
securities
   account types to use for, 142, 143
   adding to portfolio, 146–148
   downloading historical prices for, 153
   finding quotes on Quicken.com, 186
   selling, 155
   updating prices of, 151
security
   passwords, 12
   PIN numbers and, 108
Security Detail window, 151
Security Name dialog box, 146
Select Account to Enable window, 105
Select Checks to Print dialog box, 64
service charges for ATM and EFT, 108
Services area, 5, 7
Set Up Account window, 18, 145

Set Up Category dialog box, 25, 26
Set Up Class dialog box, 30
Set Up Loan window, 136
Set Up Monitoring window, 102
Set Up Payee window, 109
Set Up Security dialog box, 146
setting up accounts, 17–22
   creating data file and checking account, 18–19
   creating new accounts, 20–22
   overview, 17
   types of accounts, 20
   See also accounts
shortcut reports, 123
Shortcuts pop-up menu, 123
showing accounts, 22
slash (/), adding class to transaction with, 29
sorting
   account registers, 37
   transactions in Bill Candidates window, 74
split transactions
   loan payments as, 140
   recalculating, 39
   using, 38–39
square brackets ([ ]), around transfer categories, 42
standard checks, 62
Standard graphs, 130
Standard reports, 118
Standard tab (Reports window), 118
starting Quicken, 3
stock prices, 152
stock symbols, 152, 186
subcategories
   creating, 26
   deleting, 27
   editing, 26–27
   promoting to categories, 31
subclasses
   creating, 30
   deleting, 31
   editing, 31
Summary window (Debt Reduction Planner), 168
switching between data files, 19

Index

T

Tax Deduction Finder
  about, 16, 161
  enabling JavaScript for, 178
  using, 176–179
Tax Planner, 179
Tax Scenario Comparisons window, 179
Tax Schedule report, 180, 181
Tax Summary report, 180
taxes, 175–182
  about, 175
  assigning tax links to categories, 28, 179
  creating tax reports, 180–181
  downloading tax forms, 191
  exporting Quicken data to TurboTax, 182
  finding tax tips and advice on Quicken.com, 190
  using Tax Deduction Finder, 176–179
  using Tax Planner, 179
Taxes page (Quicken.com), 190
tip window, 7
toolbar
  adding Actions button to, 155
  customizing, 8–9
  illustrated, 7
tracking
  credit card transactions, 96–98
  expenditures with Budget Monitor, 102
expenses with classes, 31
transaction detail report, 116
Transaction Detail Shortcut Report, 123
transactions
  in account registers, 33
  adding to Calendar, 68–70
  choosing type of, 35
  classes added to, 29
  deleting accounts and effect on, 22
  deleting on Calendar, 72
  disabling QuickFill for split, 39
  downloading, 106–108
  editing on Calendar, 71
  effect of deleting categories on, 27

transactions *(continued)*
  finding and replacing, 46–48
  locked or unlocked, 53, 55
  memorizing check writing, 60
  memorizing for deposits, 40
  monitoring pending and overdue, 77
  QuickFill, 53–56
  replacing, 48
  scheduling recurring, 70, 74
  searching reports for multiple, 47
  splitting, 38–39
  tracking credit card, 96–98
  using investment forms for securities, 154–155
  using QuickZoom to see, 117
  viewing on Calendar, 71
transfer category, 24, 42
Transfer Money command, 44
transferring money between accounts, 42–44
TurboTax for the Mac
  about, 175
  exporting Quicken data to, 182
  using TurboTax Deduction Finder, 176–179
turning off QuickFill, 36, 52

U

U.S. federal taxes
  creating tax links between categories and tax form, 28
  IRS 800 number, 178
unlocked transactions, 53, 55
Upcoming Bills and Scheduled Transactions window, 73, 74
updating
  investment prices in portfolio, 150, 152
  security prices, 151
user's guide for Quicken, 15

V

viewing
  history of loan, 140
  loan payment schedule, 138
  scheduled transactions, 71

voiding
  checks, 61
  transactions on registers, 45
voucher checks, 62

W

wallet checks, 62
Watch List, 84
Web site. *See* Quicken.com Web site
Web-based planners, 160–162
What-If section (Retirement Planner), 165
windows. *See specific window by name*
write checks button (Enter Transaction window), 68
write checks mode, 69
Write Checks window
  opening for selected accounts, 59
  paying credit card bills from, 92
  writing checks in, 58–59
writing checks, 58–60

Z

Zip disks, 13
zooming
  displaying EasyAnswer graph details, 129
  in on report details, 117

New from Peachpit Press

VISUAL QUICKSTART ONLINE LIBRARY!

FREE TRIAL OFFER

25 top Web and Graphics QuickStarts, just $49.95 a year!

25 Books! a $450 value for $49.95

Our new **Visual QuickStart Online Library** offers you

- Easy access to the most current information on Web design and graphics via the Web—wherever you are, 24 hours a day, 7 days a week
- Powerful, advanced search features that enable you to find just the topics you want across multiple books, ranked by relevance
- Updates to new editions of the books as they become available
- Easy ways to bookmark, make notes, and send email alerts to colleagues
- Complete access to 25 bestselling books for only $49.95 (that's more than $450 worth of books for less than the price of three *Visual QuickStart Guides*!)

You'll find all your favorite *Visual QuickStart Guides,* as well as those you want to read next, including:

HTML 4 for the World Wide Web
Photoshop for Macintosh and Windows
Illustrator for Windows and Macintosh
Perl and CGI for the World Wide Web
Flash for Windows and Macintosh

Free Trial Offer!

Check it out! We invite you to sample a FREE trial subscription to Peachpit's new Visual QuickStart Online Library for one week. Just go to www.quickstartonline.com and sign up for your free trial today! You'll have complete access to the Library for one week, absolutely free.

www.quickstartonline.com

Quick search... Quick find... QuickStart!

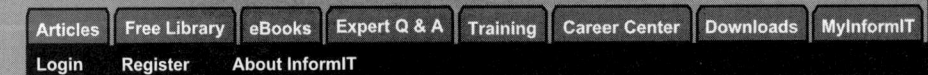

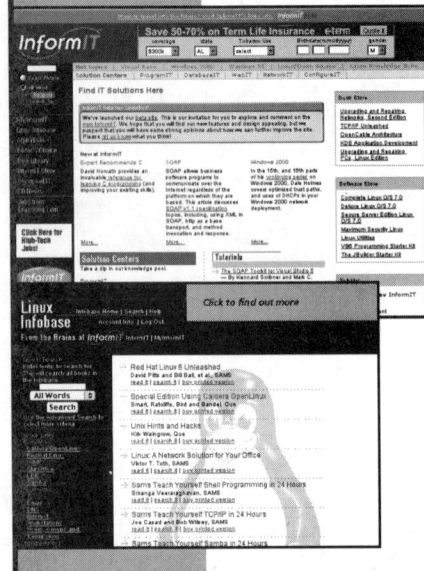